I0818826

ALEXANDRA FULLERTON

THE ULTIMATE GUIDE TO DIOR BAGS

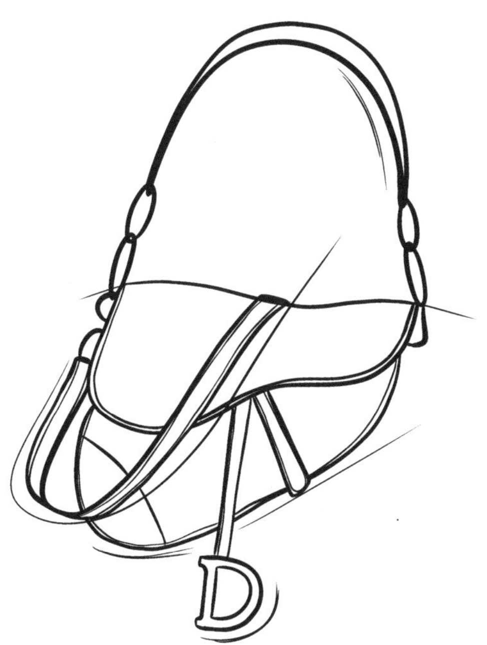

teNeues

Next page: A model showcases bags from Dior's Spring/Summer 2022 collection during Paris Men's Fashion Week, 2021

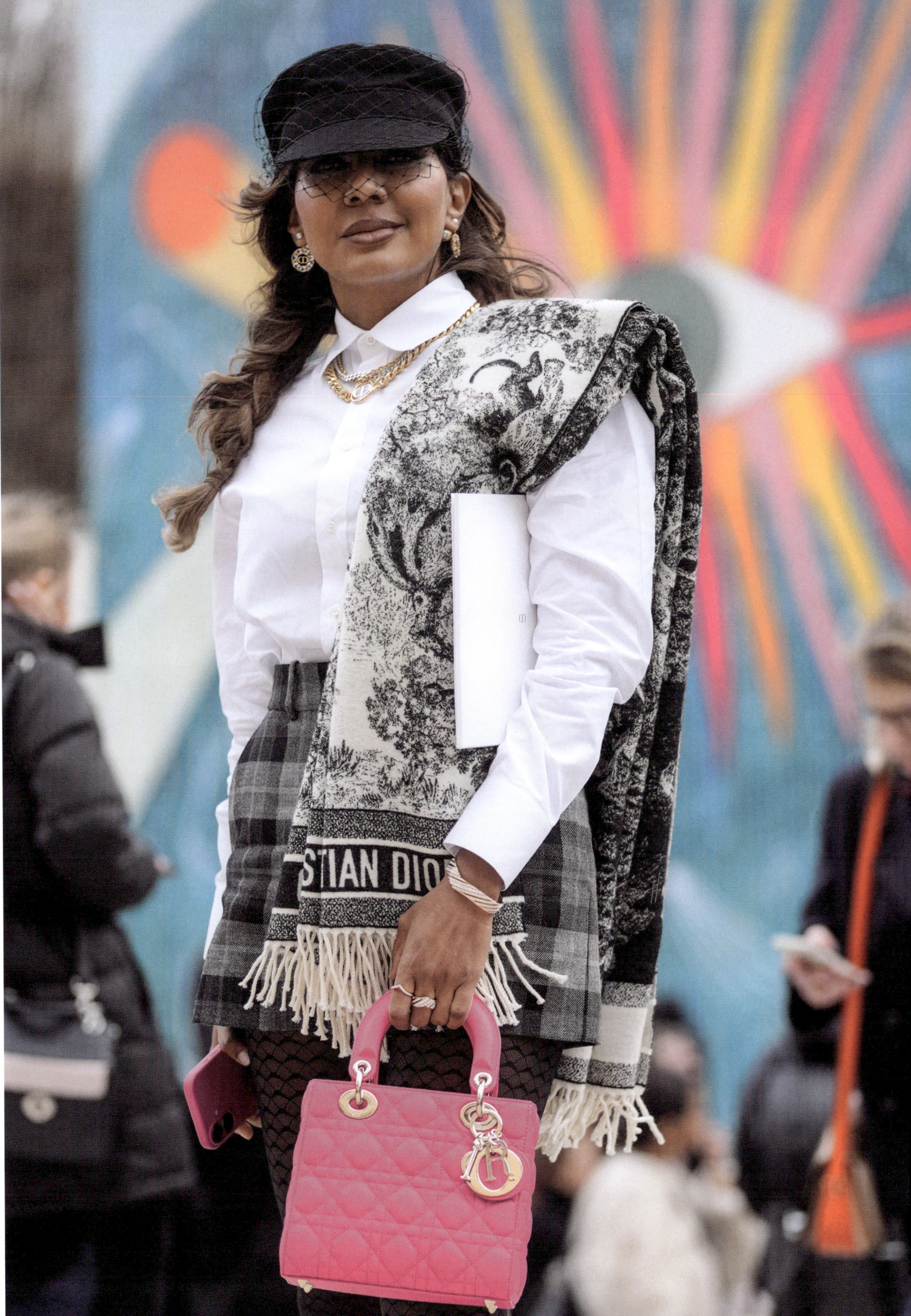
STIAN DIO

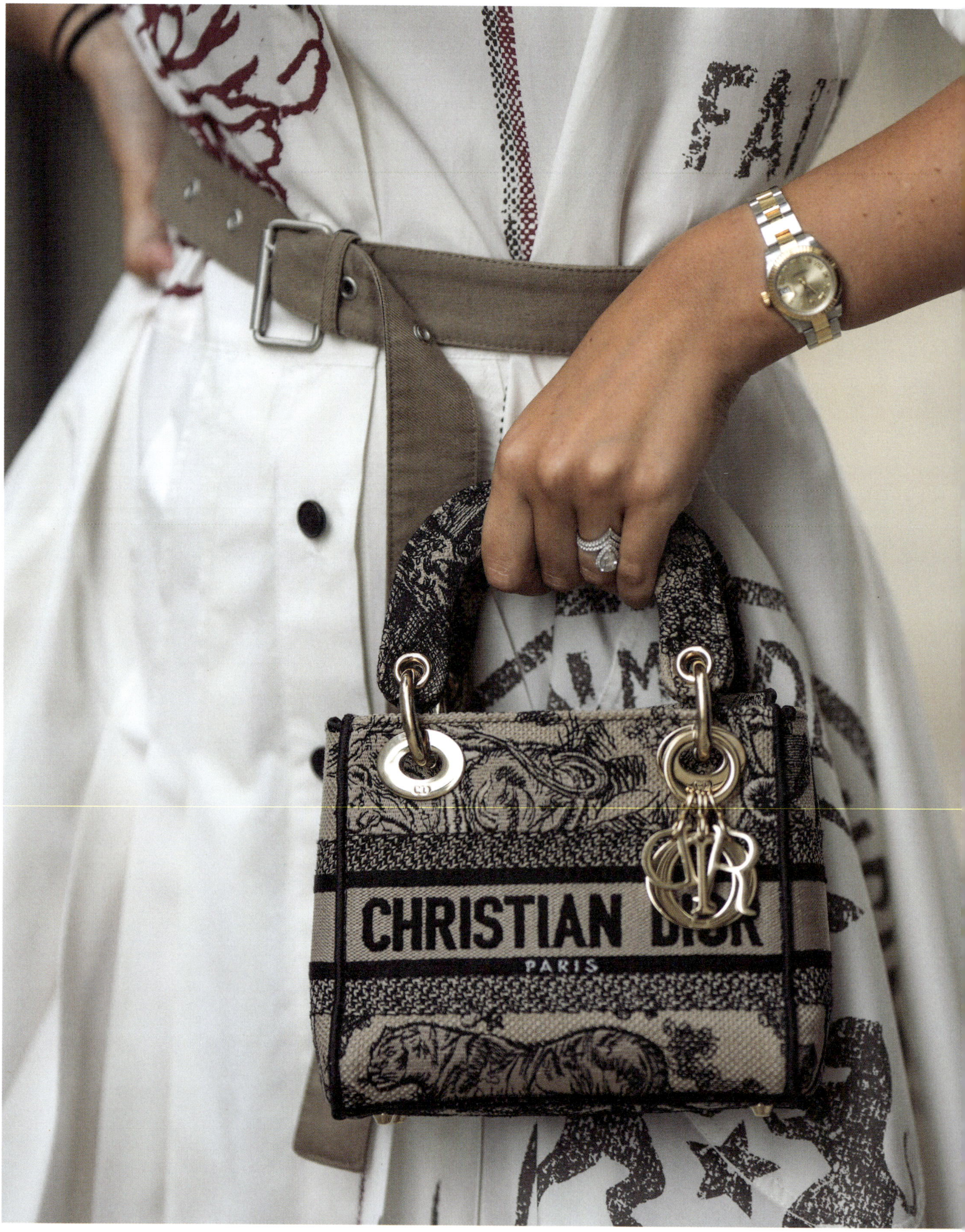

Page 42: Phoebe Price is seen pushing her red Lady Dior (and her dog) in a stroller in Los Angeles, 2024

Page 43: A guest at the Christian Dior Spring/Summer 2025 Haute Couture show carries a pink Lady Dior in Paris, 2025

Pages 44/45: Gabriella Berdugo showcases a beige and blue Lady D-Lite during a street style fashion photo session in Paris, 2022

Page 46: Rosalia attends the Christian Dior Fall/Winter 2024 show with a small black Lady Dior in Paris, 2024

Page 47: Sonam Kapoor is photographed at the Christian Dior Spring/Summer 2025 show in Paris, 2024

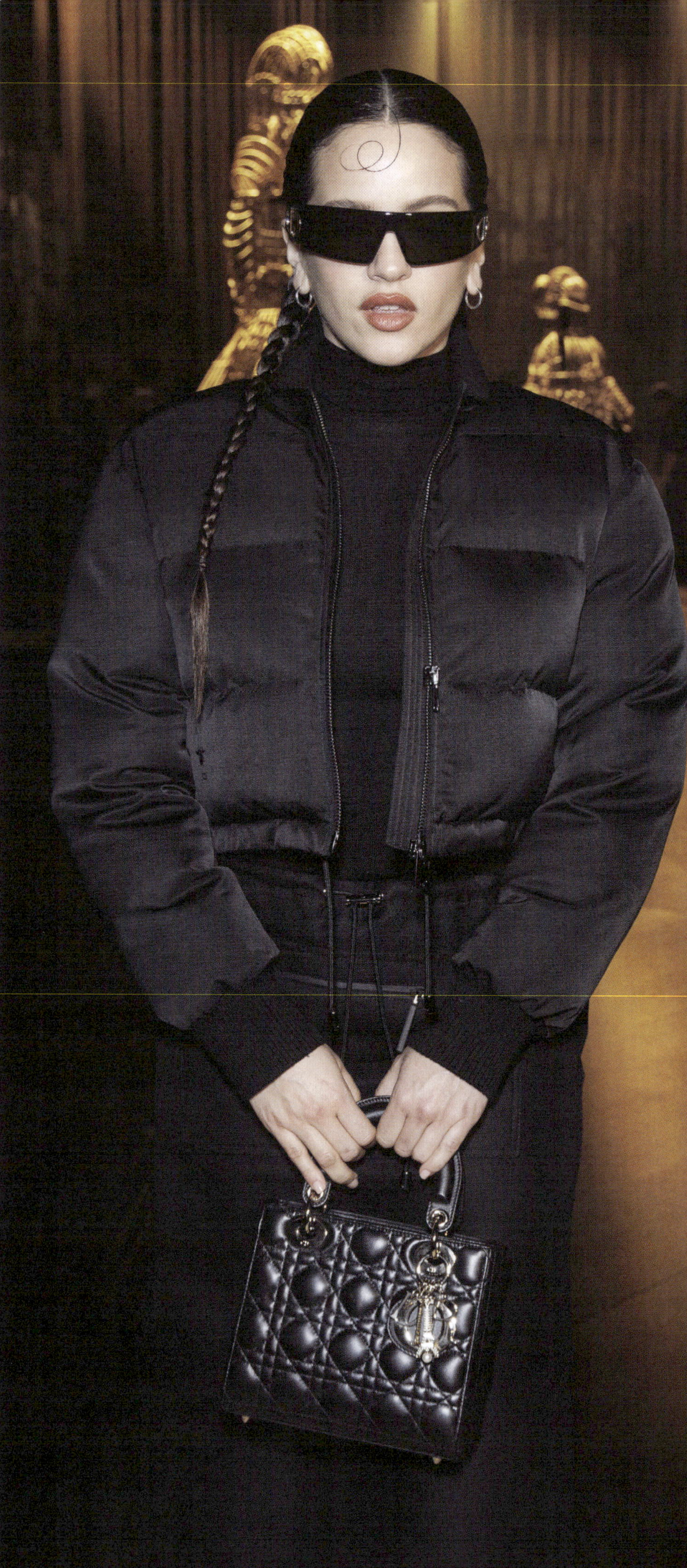

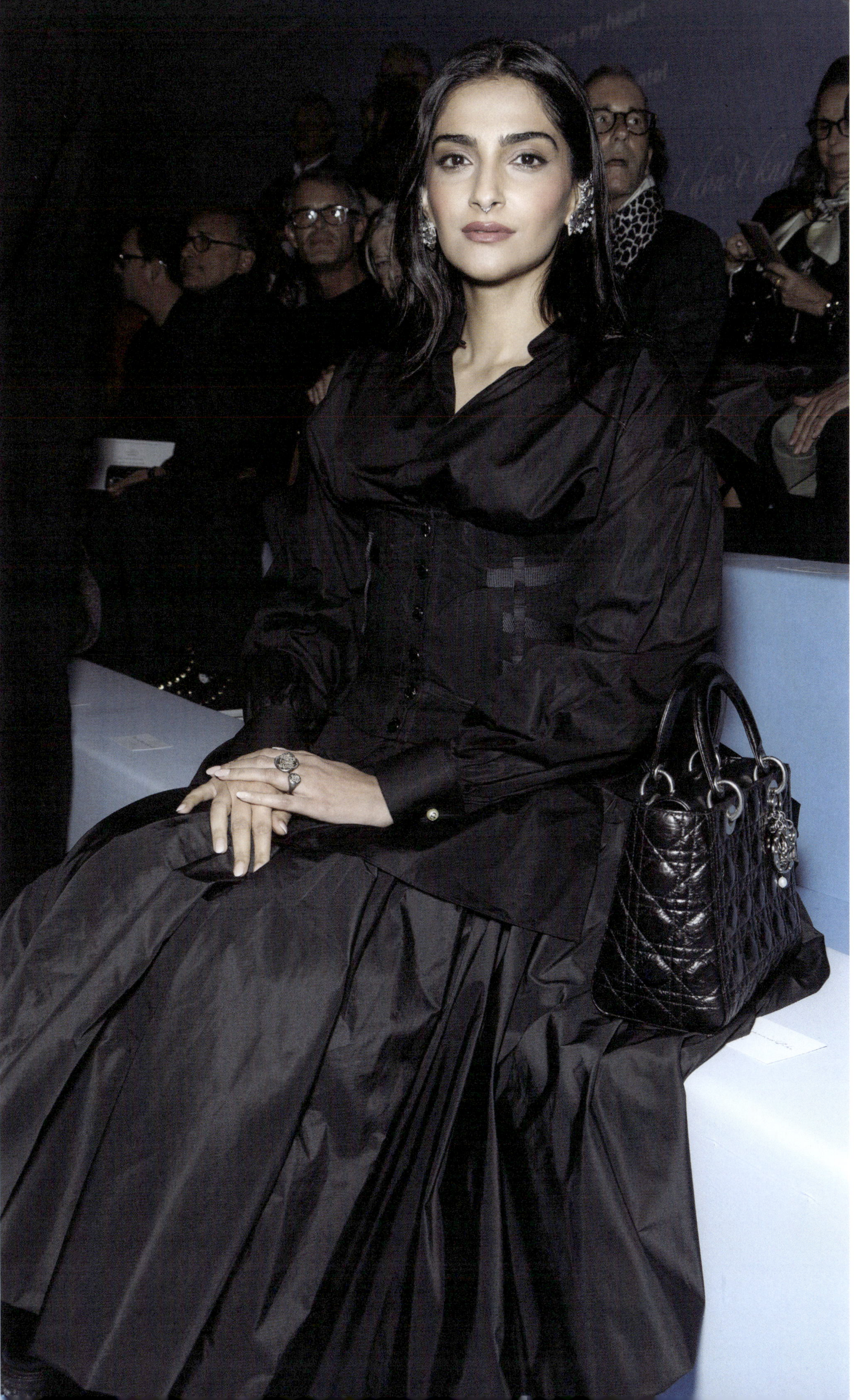

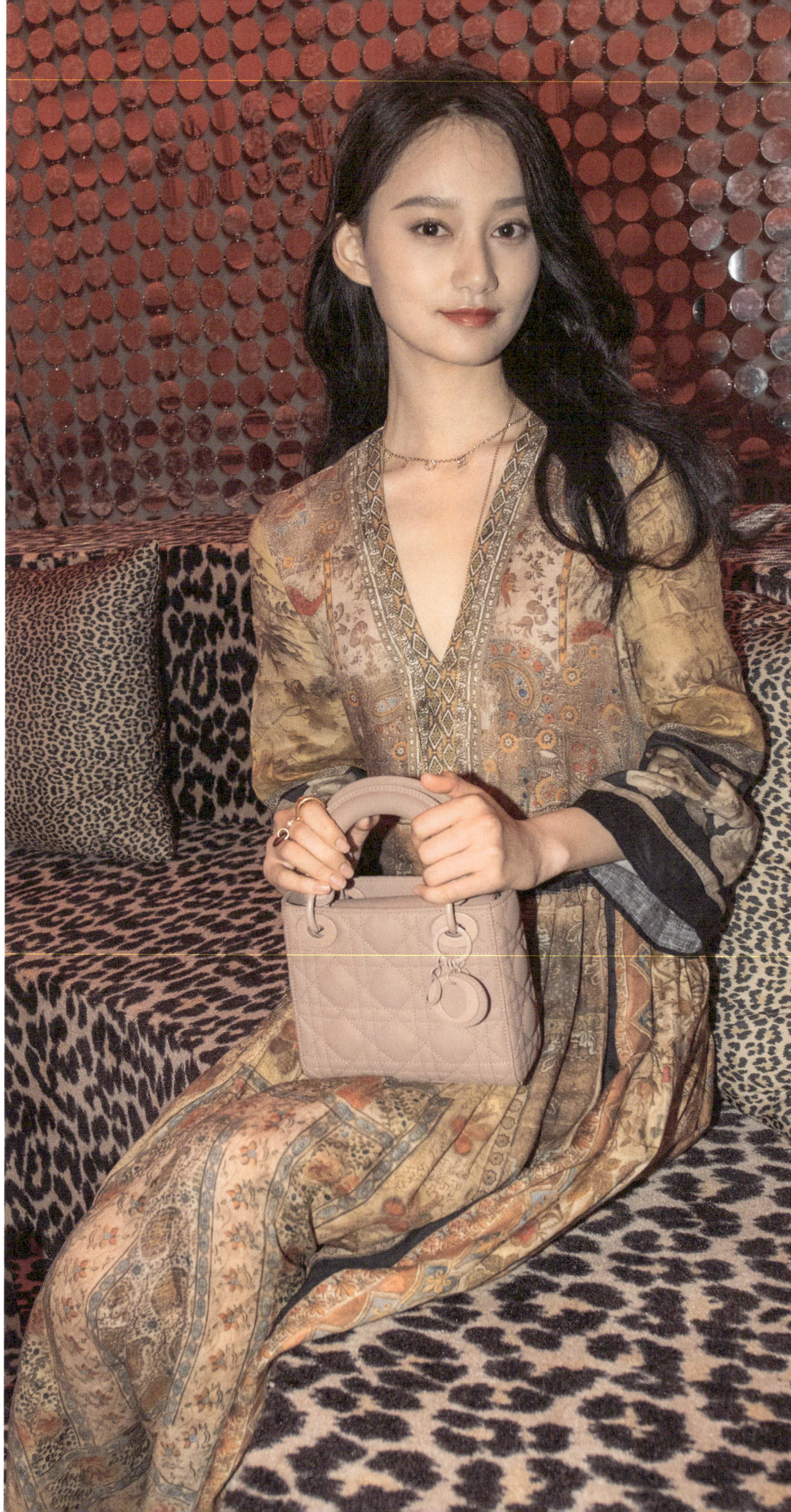

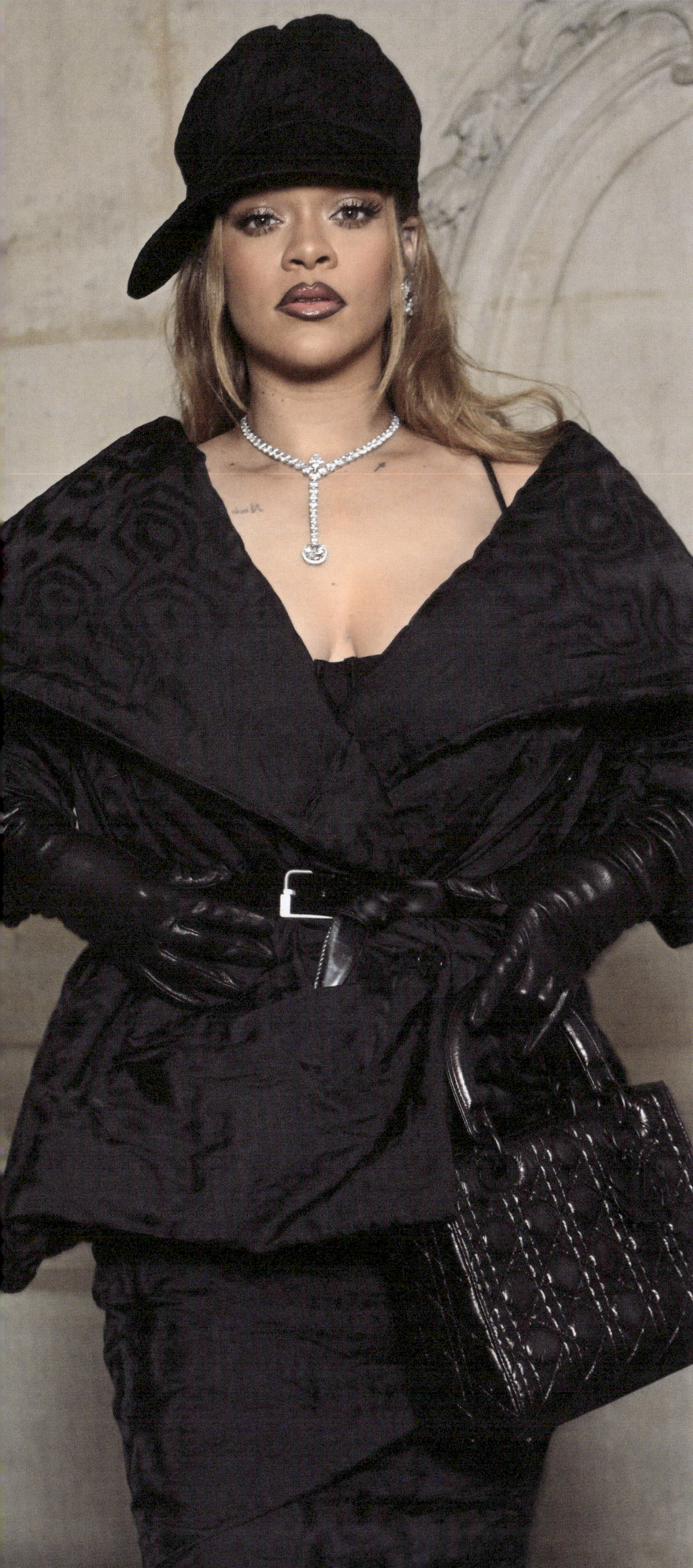

Previous page: Xia Meng flaunts a tan-colored mini Lady Dior bag at the Dior runway show in Shanghai, 2021

This page: Rihanna attends the Christian Dior Haute Couture Spring/Summer 2024 show featuring a medium black Lady Dior in Paris, 2024

Pages 50/51: Rosamund Pike (with a white medium-sized Lady Dior) and Mickalene Thomas appear at Dior's Pre-Fall 2024 show held at the Brooklyn Museum on April 15, 2024, in New York

Page 52: Street style close-up: A green crocodile leather Lady Dior, 2024

Page 53: A model walks the runway during the Christian Dior ready-to-wear Spring/Summer 2018 fashion show showcasing a checkered Lady Dior in Paris, 2017

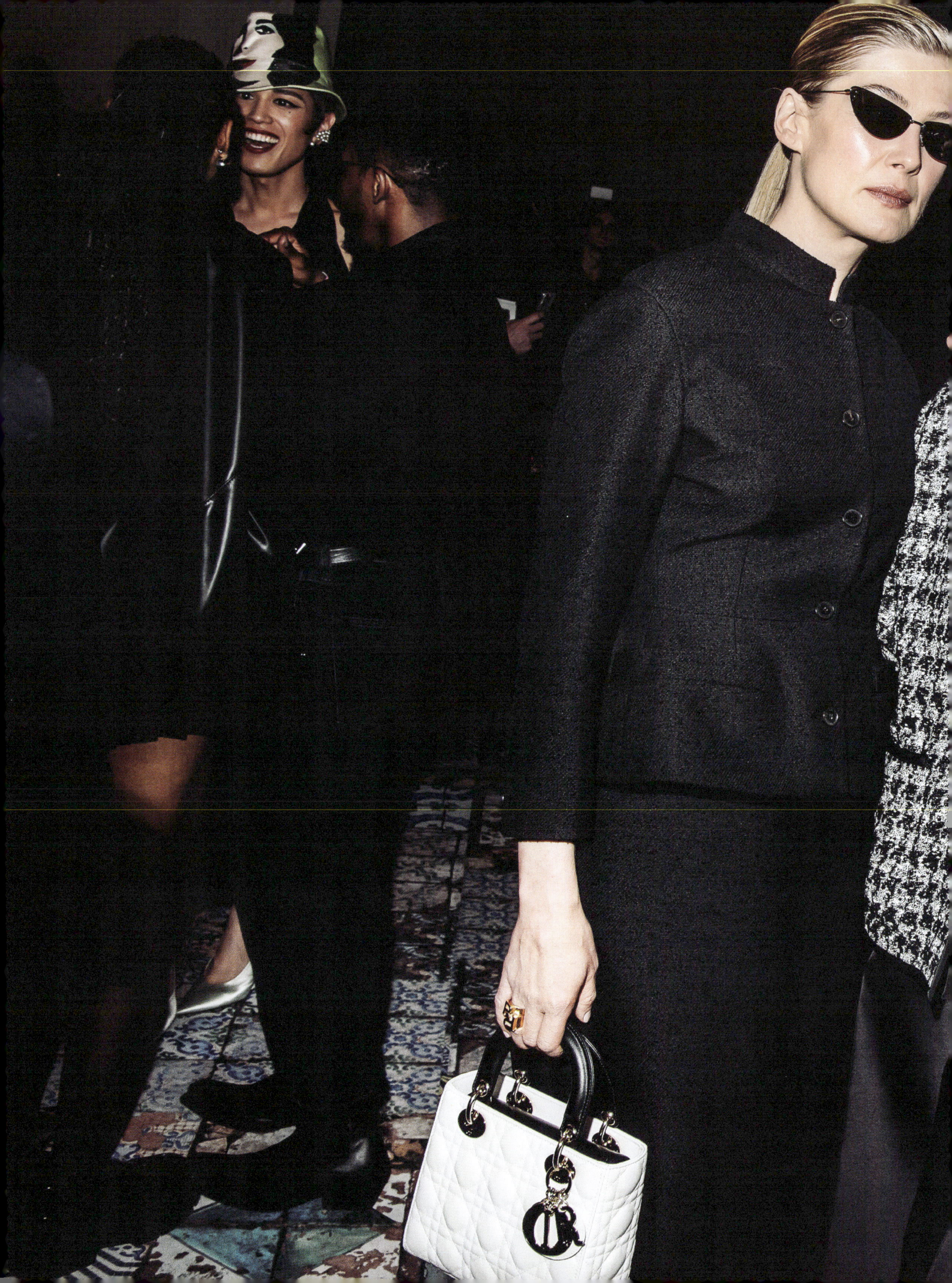

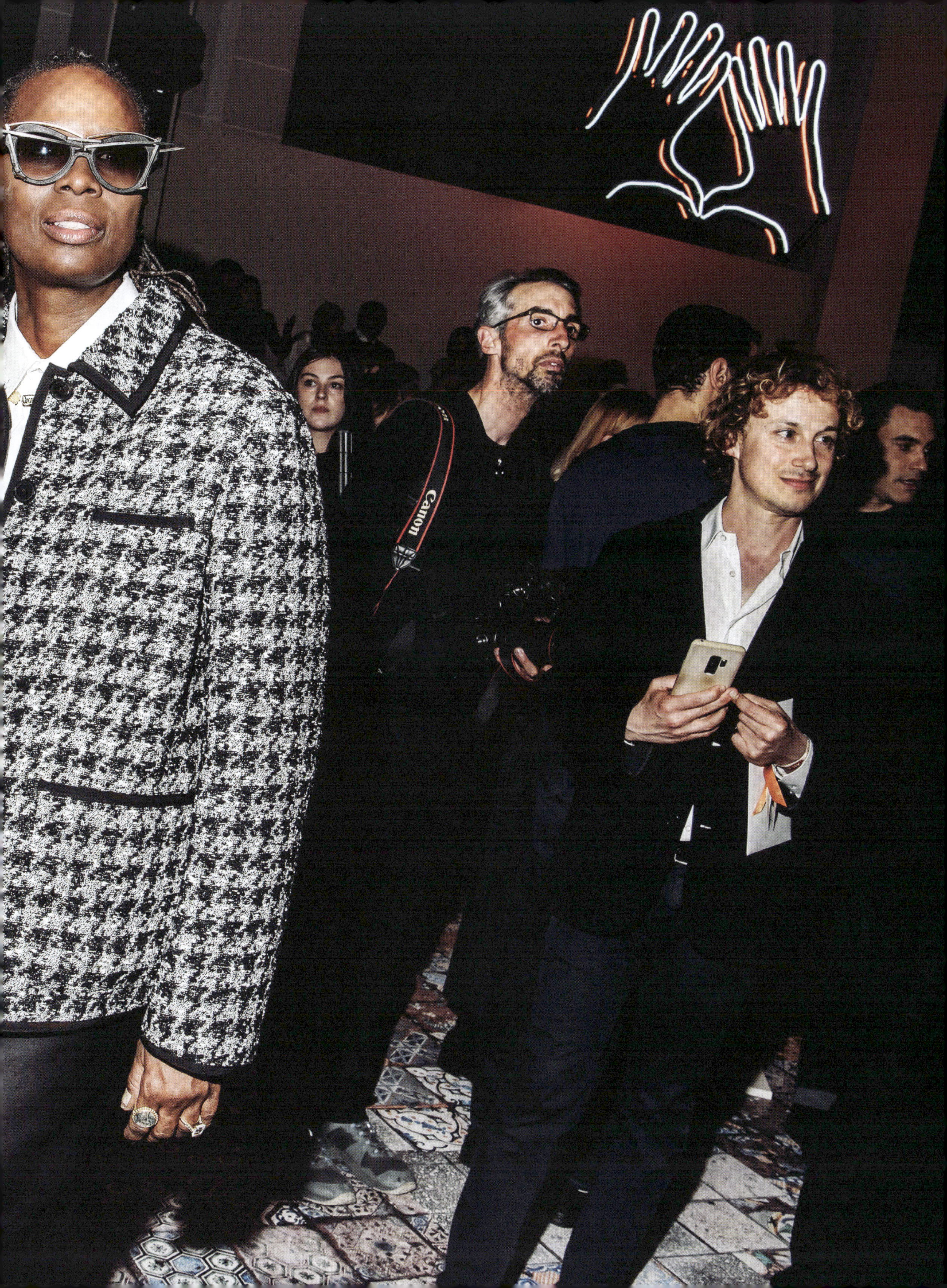
Canon

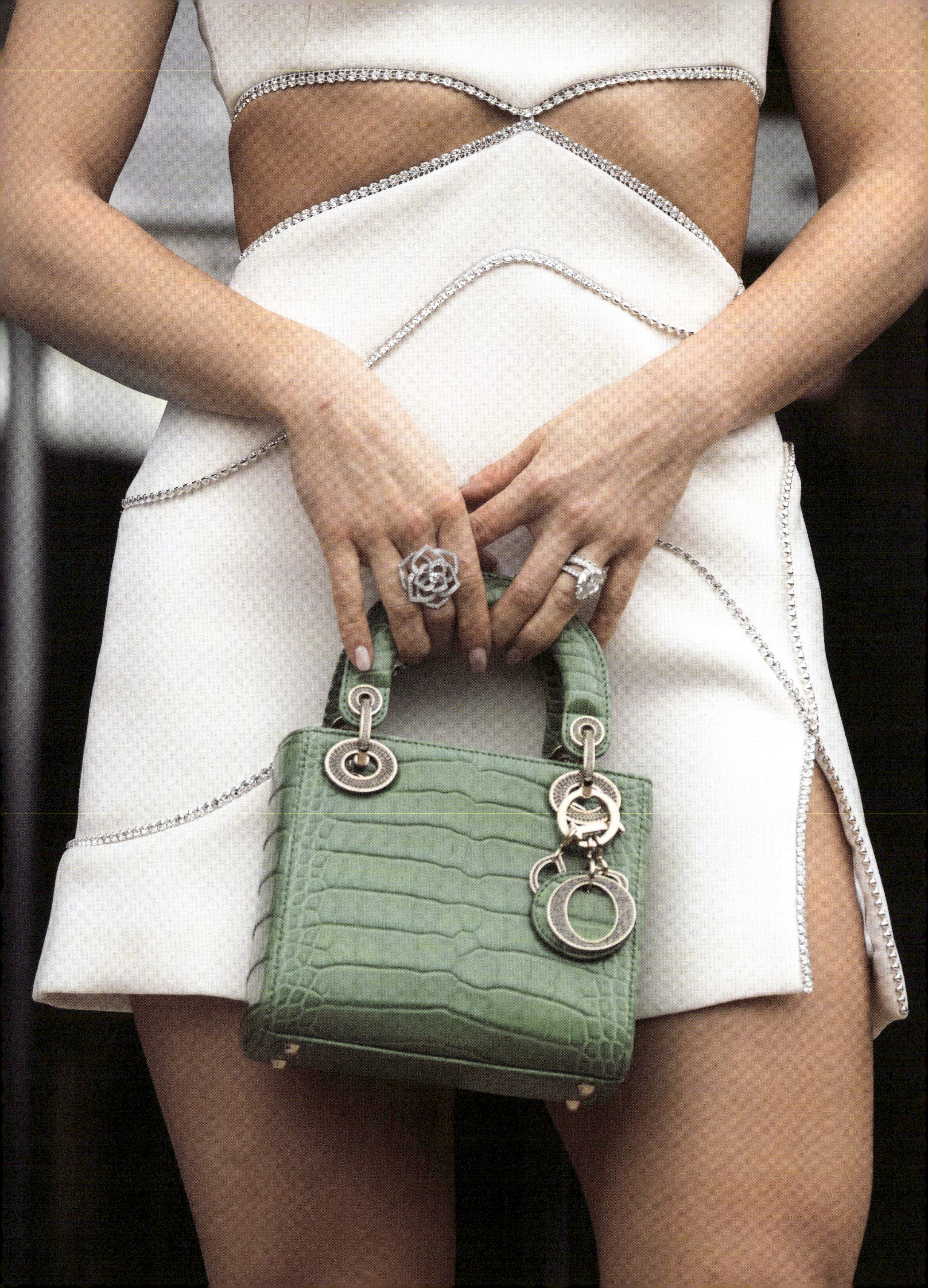

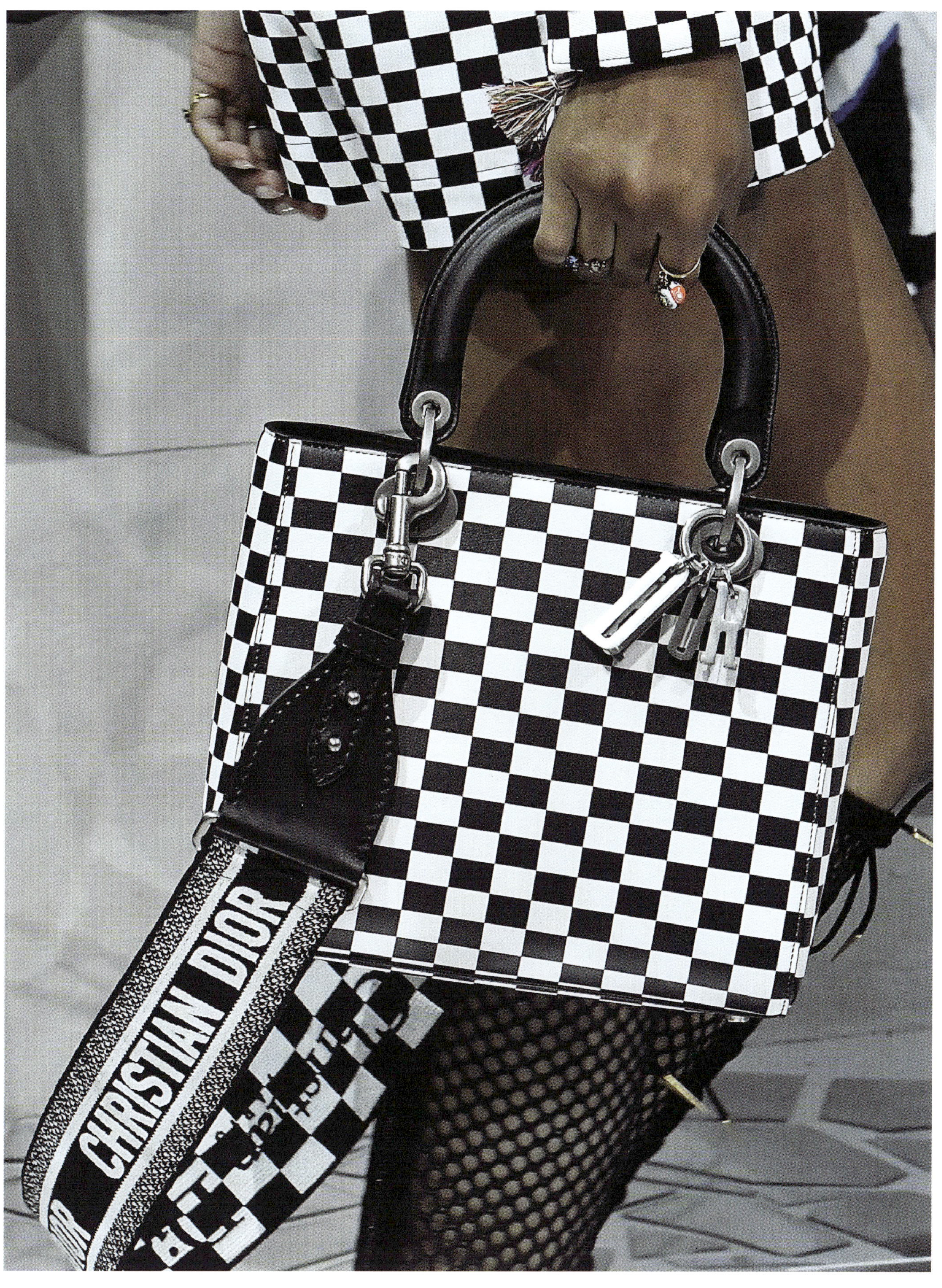
CHRISTIAN DIOR
DIOR

This page: A guest presents a white Lady Dior My ABCDior bag outside Dior Homme during the Menswear Fall/Winter 2025 show in Paris, 2025

Next page: A visitor to Haute Couture Spring/Summer 2025 Fashion Week is spotted outside the Dior venue with a micro Lady Dior in Paris, 2025

Page 56: Close-up of a limited edition beaded Lady Dior from Milan Fashion Week

Page 57: Another form of embellishment includes wrapping a scarf around the handle of a Lady Dior, as observed during Paris Fashion Week 2018

Page 58: Maria Bernad showcases a limited edition Lady Dior featuring a beaded cat motif in Paris, 2022

Page 59: Alison Toby wears an embroidered D-Joy bag in Paris, 2025

Pages 60/61: Caroline Daur carries a Saddle bag during Fall/Winter 2019 Paris Fashion Week, 2019

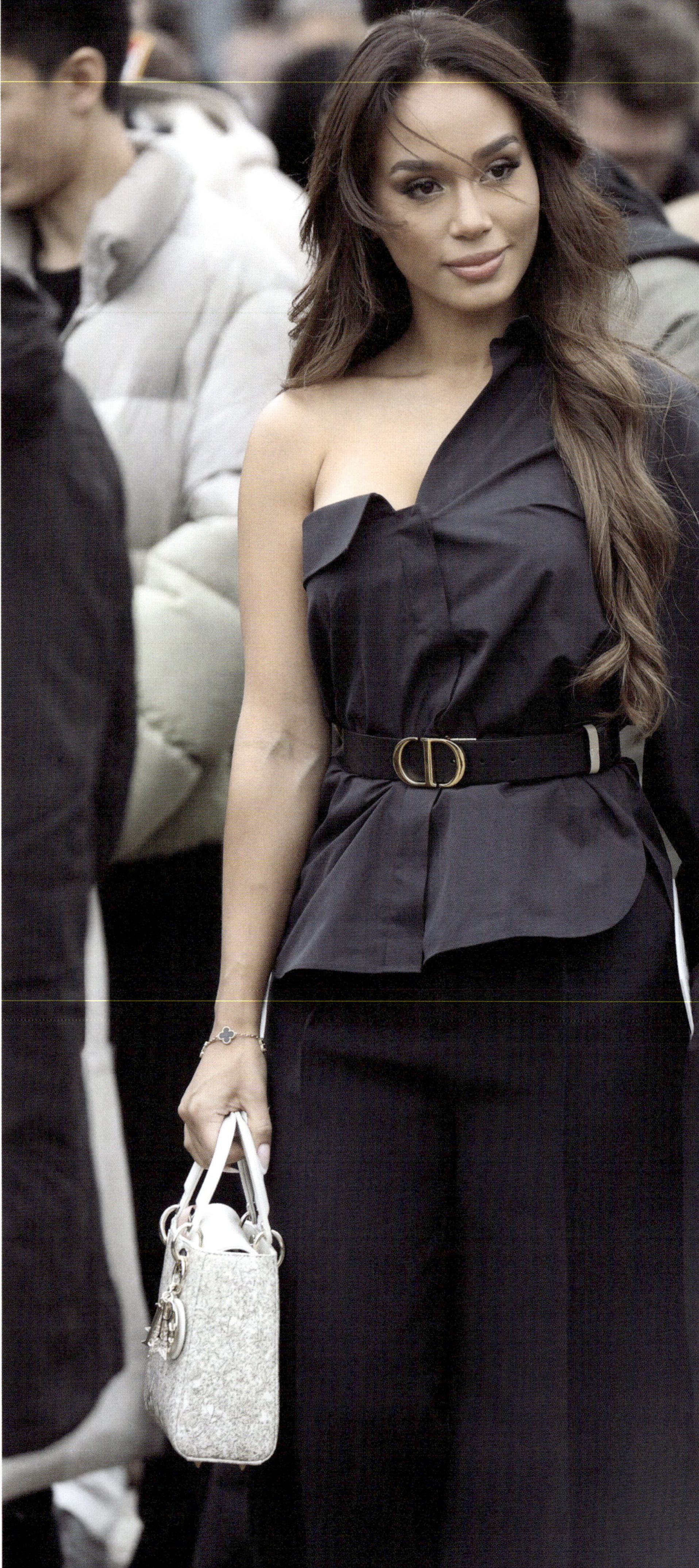

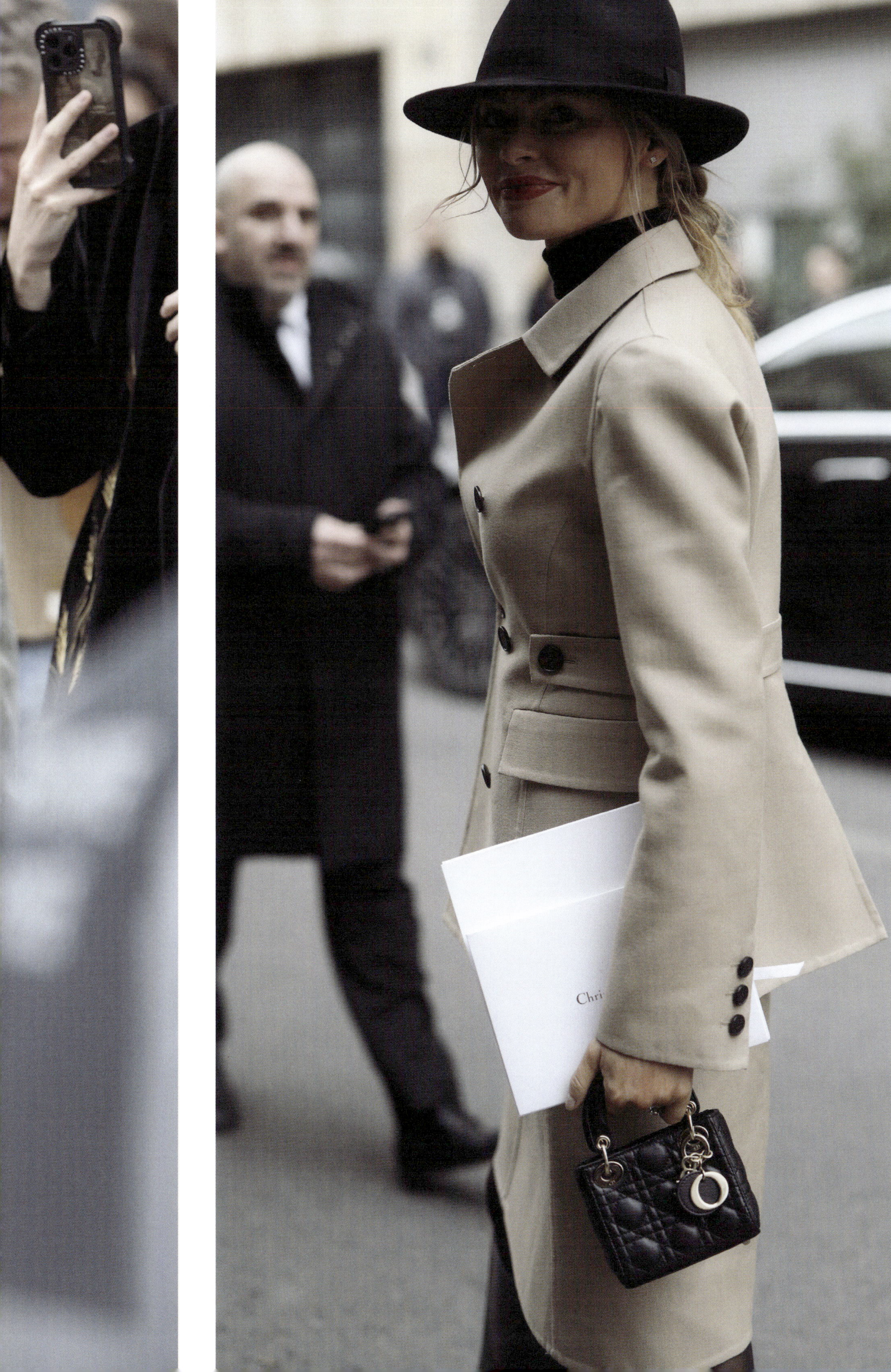

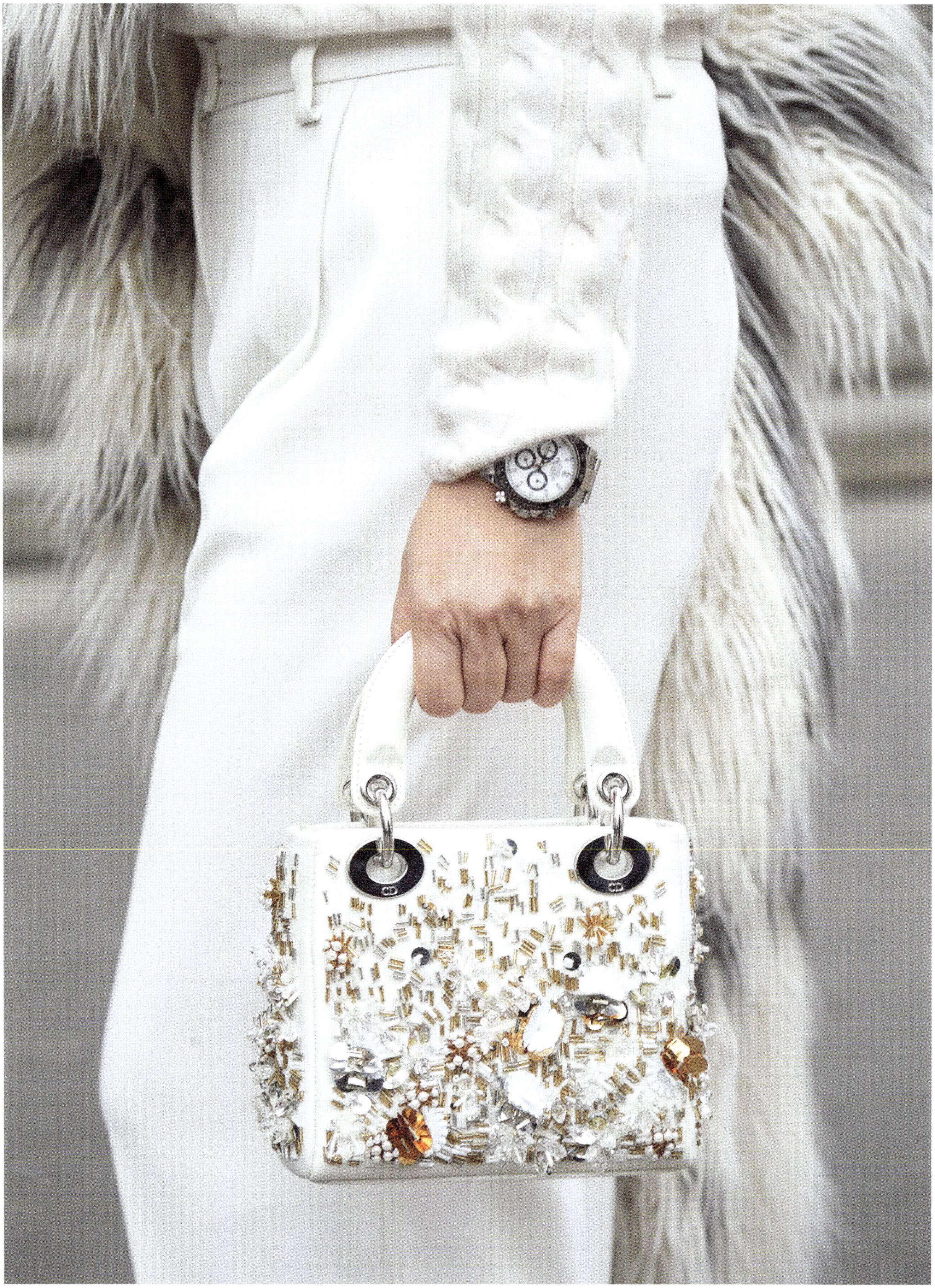

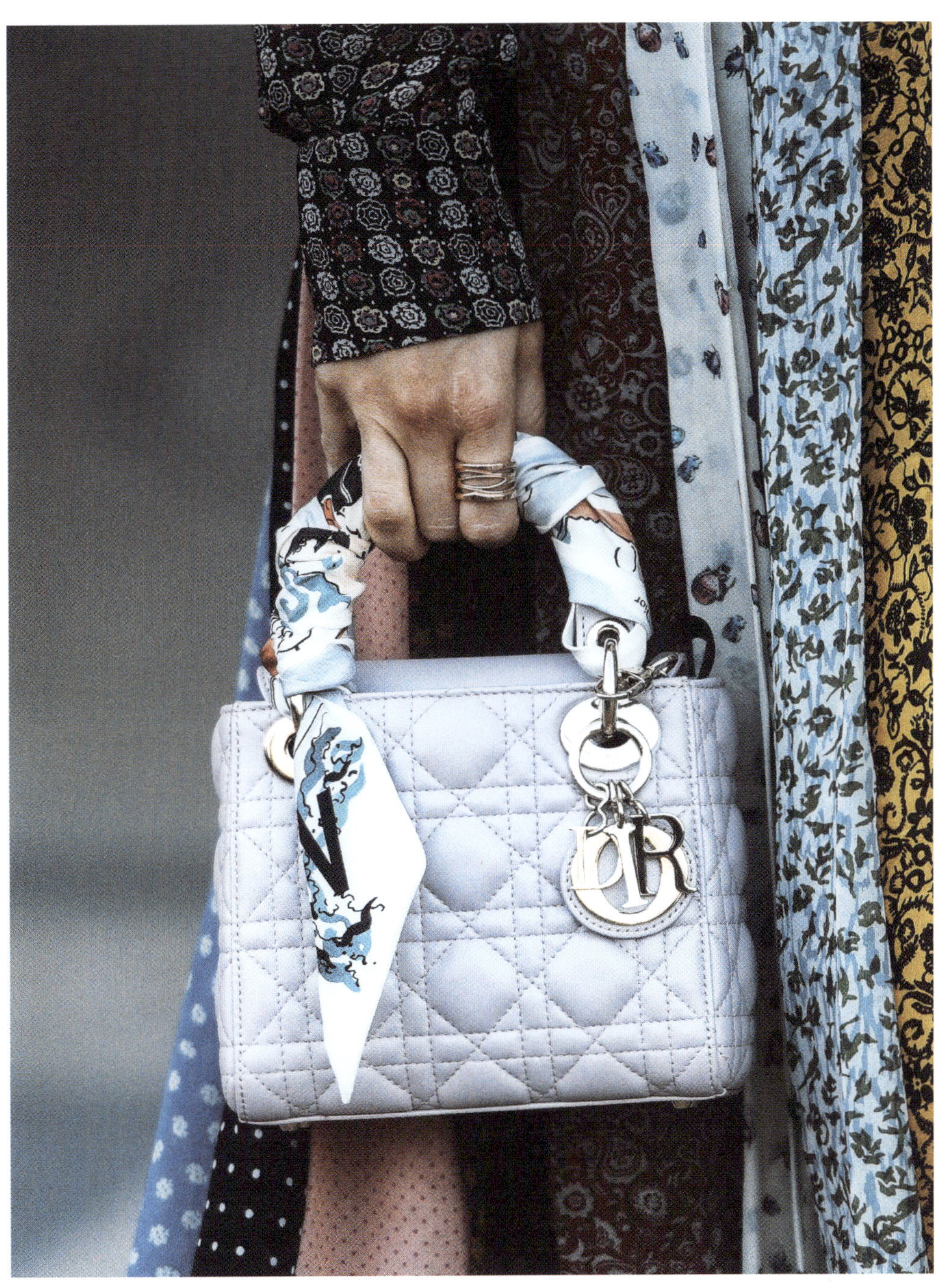
DIOR

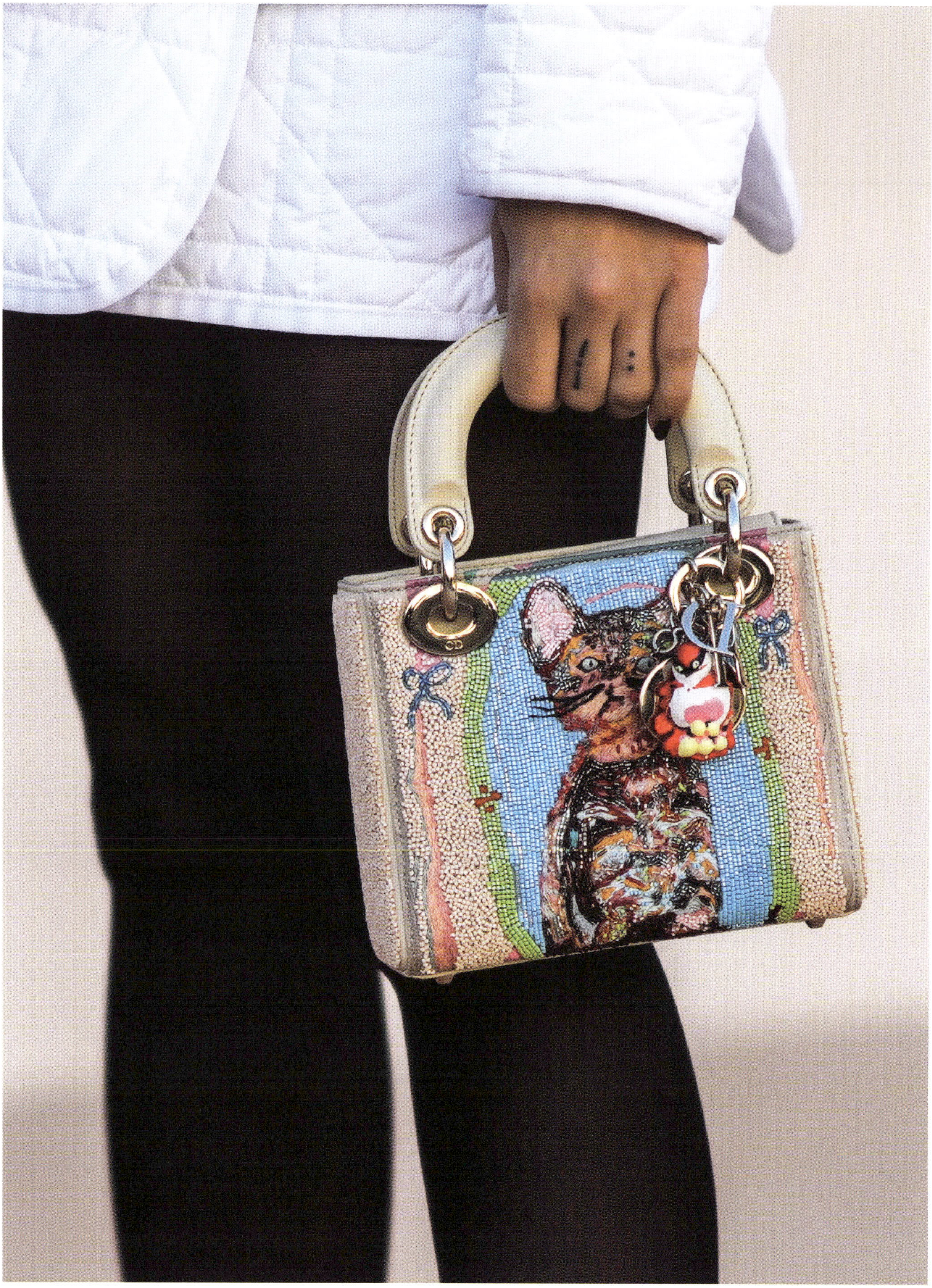

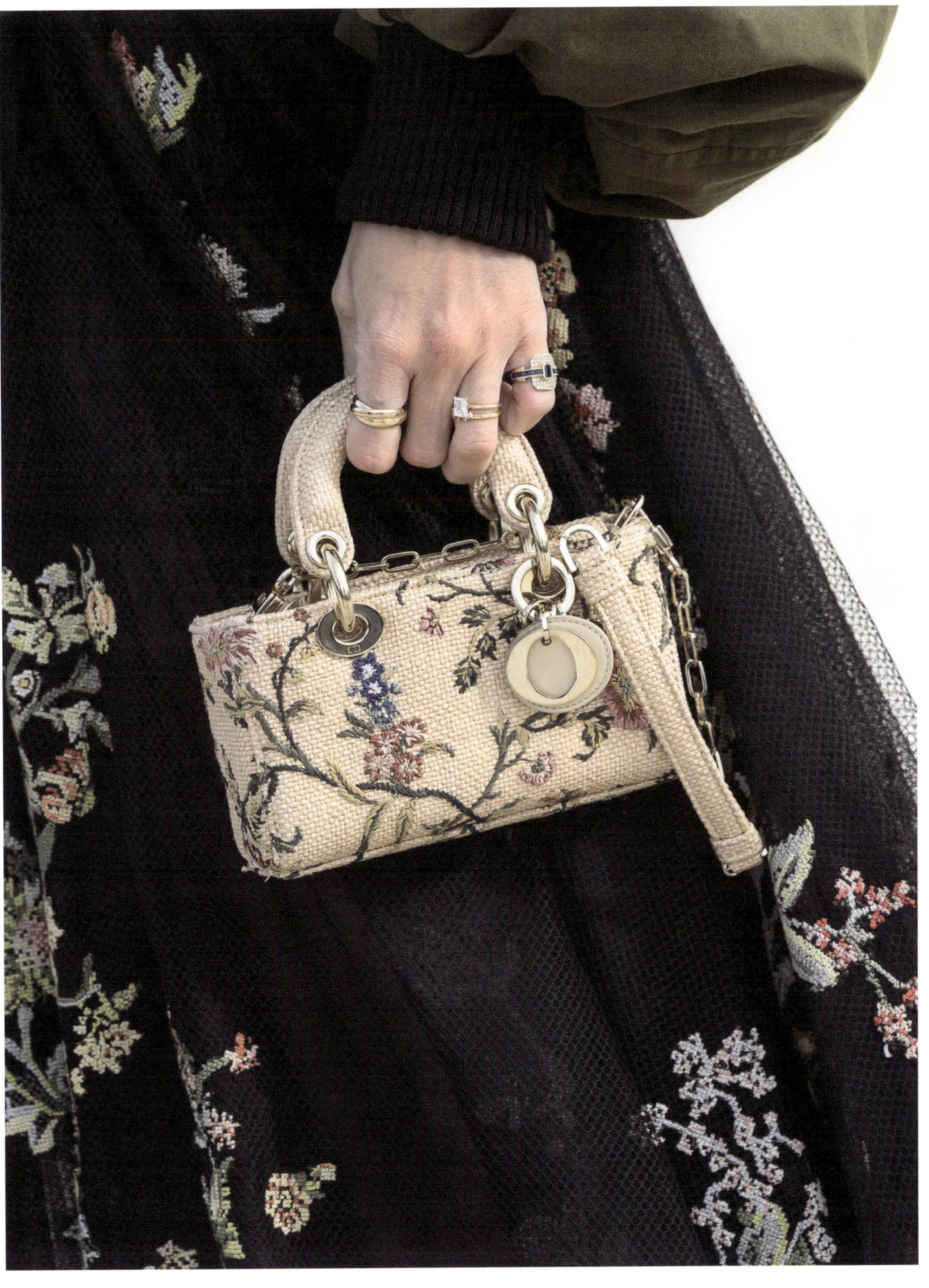

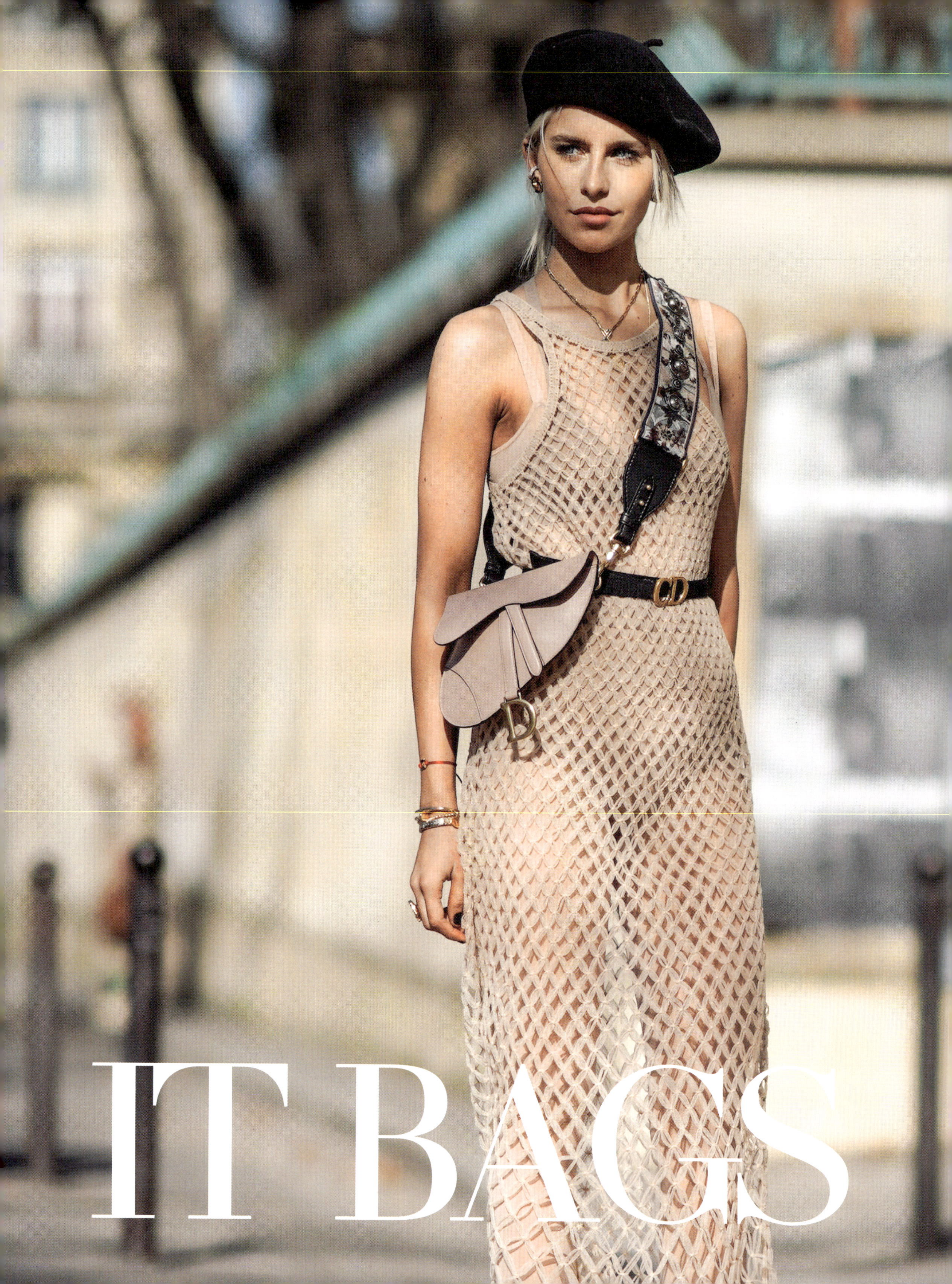

IT BAGS

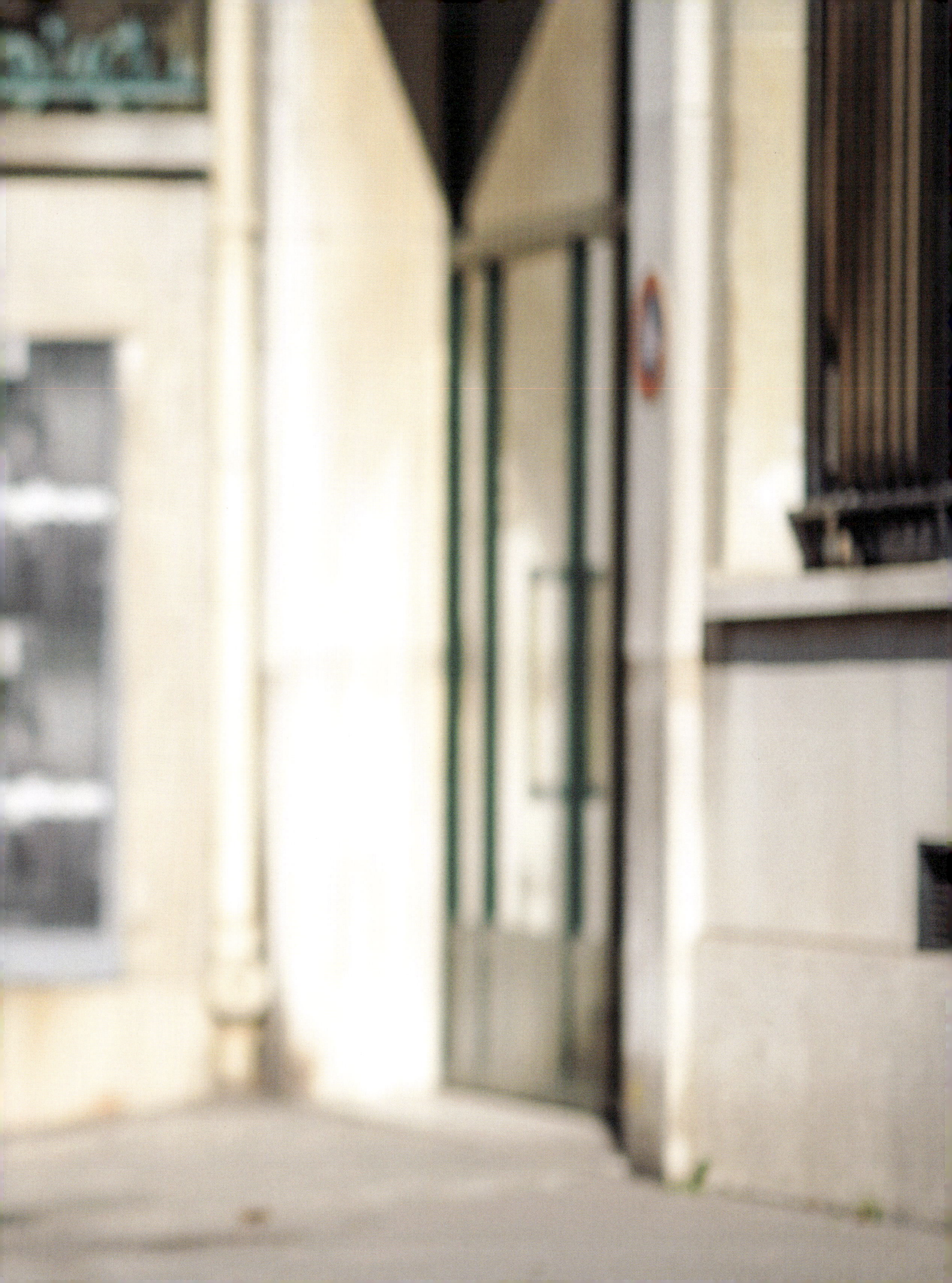

SADDLE BAG

Tracking the development of the Saddle Bag's status offers fascinating insights into a zeitgeist-y trend, combined with this century's unique brand of celebrity influence. Created by John Galliano in 1999, the Saddle Bag's first appearance on the catwalk was as part of the Spring/Summer 2000 collection. The show was full of reworked equestrian motifs: bourgeois silk scarves worn as tops, giant horse bits turned into belts, plenty of sexy denim, 1970s silhouettes—and a hefty dose of cultural appropriation, as Galliano was heavily influenced by hip-hop culture.

The bags—brand new, shrunken shapes that tucked under the model's arms—were an instant hit. Sales figures confirmed the Saddle Bag's popularity. Fashion trade publication WWD reported that Dior's accessory sales had risen by 60% in 2001. Alongside a stellar PR and advertising campaign, the bag's desirability leapt into the public consciousness. That was undoubtedly due in part to the incredible influence of TV series *Sex and the City*. Carrie Bradshaw, portrayed by Sarah Jessica Parker, was a Dior devotee. In season three, episode five of the show, which aired in July 2000, Bradshaw carried a pink, white and gold printed Saddle Bag. Costume designer Patricia Field had a knack for picking It items that clicked perfectly with her fashion-obsessed character's style—as well as that of society beyond the screen. From that seasonal starting point, the Saddle Bag was reimagined in Dior's house 'Oblique' logo, leopard print, floral Girly print, a green, gold and red toned 'Rasta' colorway and newspaper print. Recently, a vintage newsprint saddle bag was listed on FarFetch with a price tag of over £21,000.

In the early 2000s, every It girl from LA to Tokyo was carrying a Saddle Bag. In 2006, Galliano created a collection of limited edition Saddle Bags, each dedicated to one of 12 countries that inspired him. The designer told the New York Times, "It was the first bag I created here at the house of Dior, and she's still with us. She's become a classic."

But with any item that is suddenly elevated to It status, a wild decline in popularity sometimes follows. Fashion is fickle, and by the middle of the decade, the world economy was faltering. The sexy flashy mood of Y2K and its accompanying logomania was on the wane, soon to be replaced by a more minimal mood. Sales of the Saddle Bag were reportedly dropping, fast, and by fall 2006, Saddle Bags were absent from the Spring/Summer 2007 show. Instead, elegant ladylike bags appeared on the runway, and Saddle Bags started to be spotted on resale sites like eBay for as little as £100. The speed at which the bag rose and then fell from grace was astounding.

Next page: Emili Sindlev (with a denim Saddle bag) and Thora Valdimars attend the Mykke Hofmann presentation during Copenhagen Fashion Week, 2018

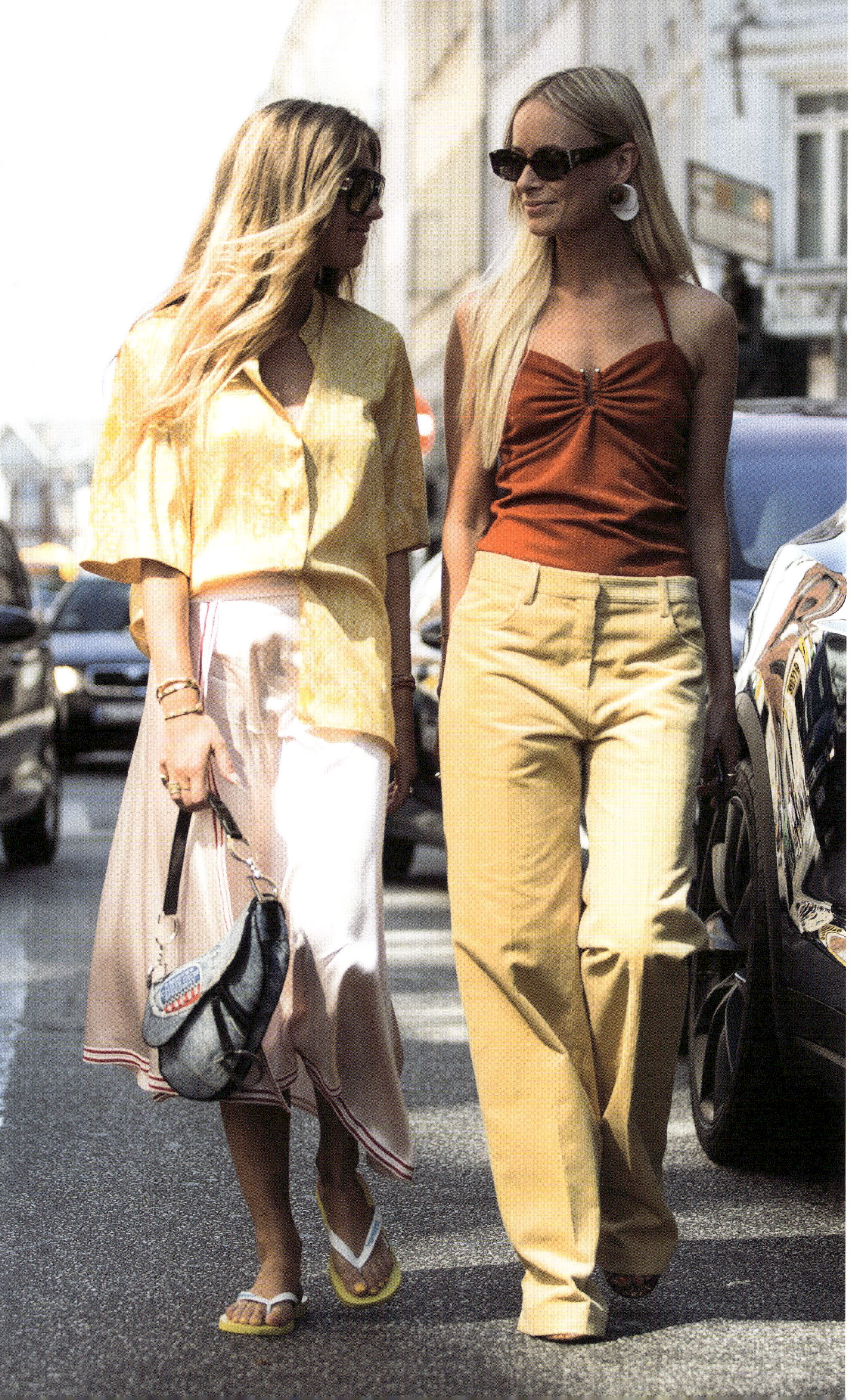

IN THE EARLY 2000s, EVERY IT GIRL FROM LA TO TOKYO WAS CARRYING A SADDLE BAG

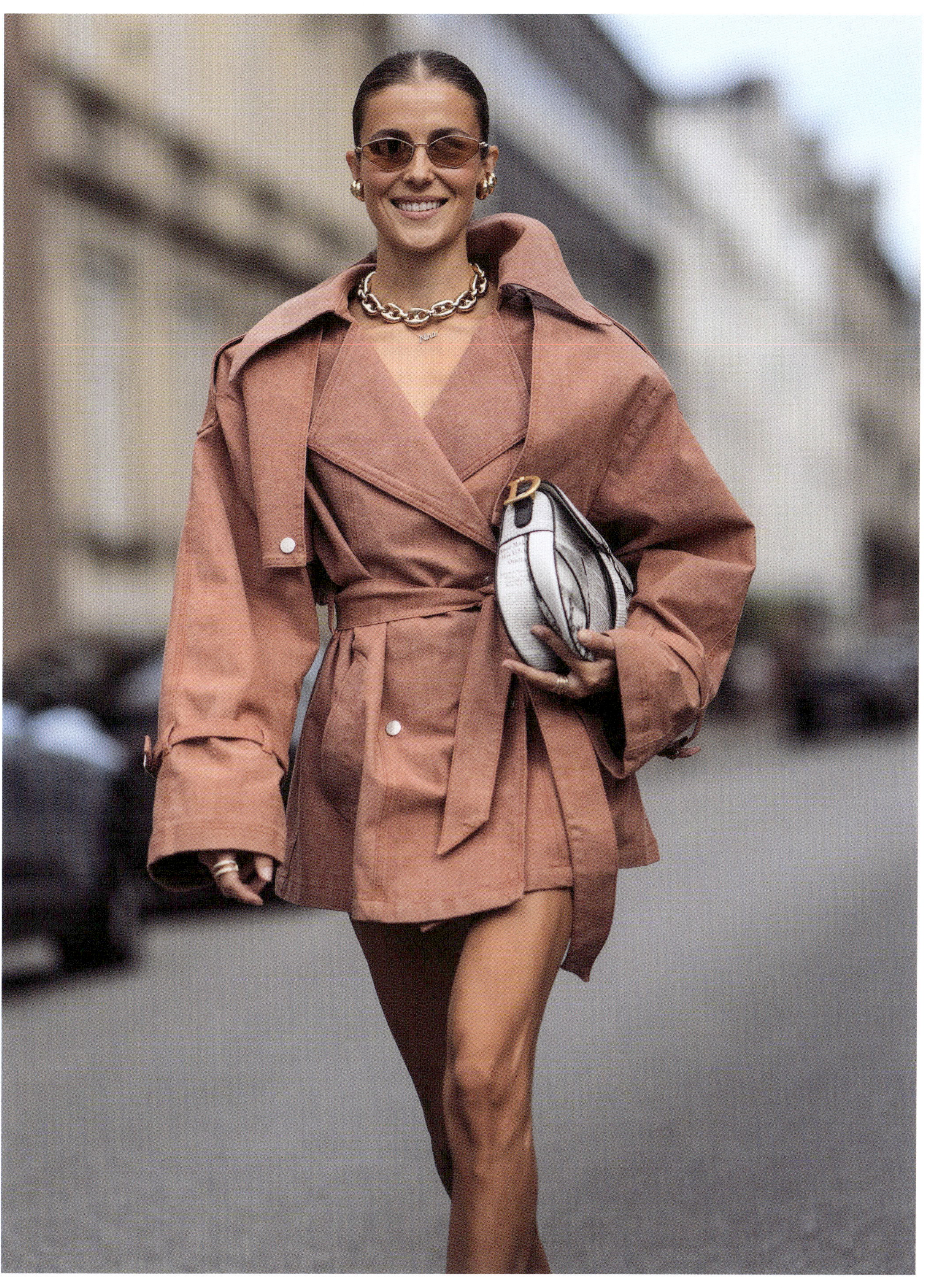

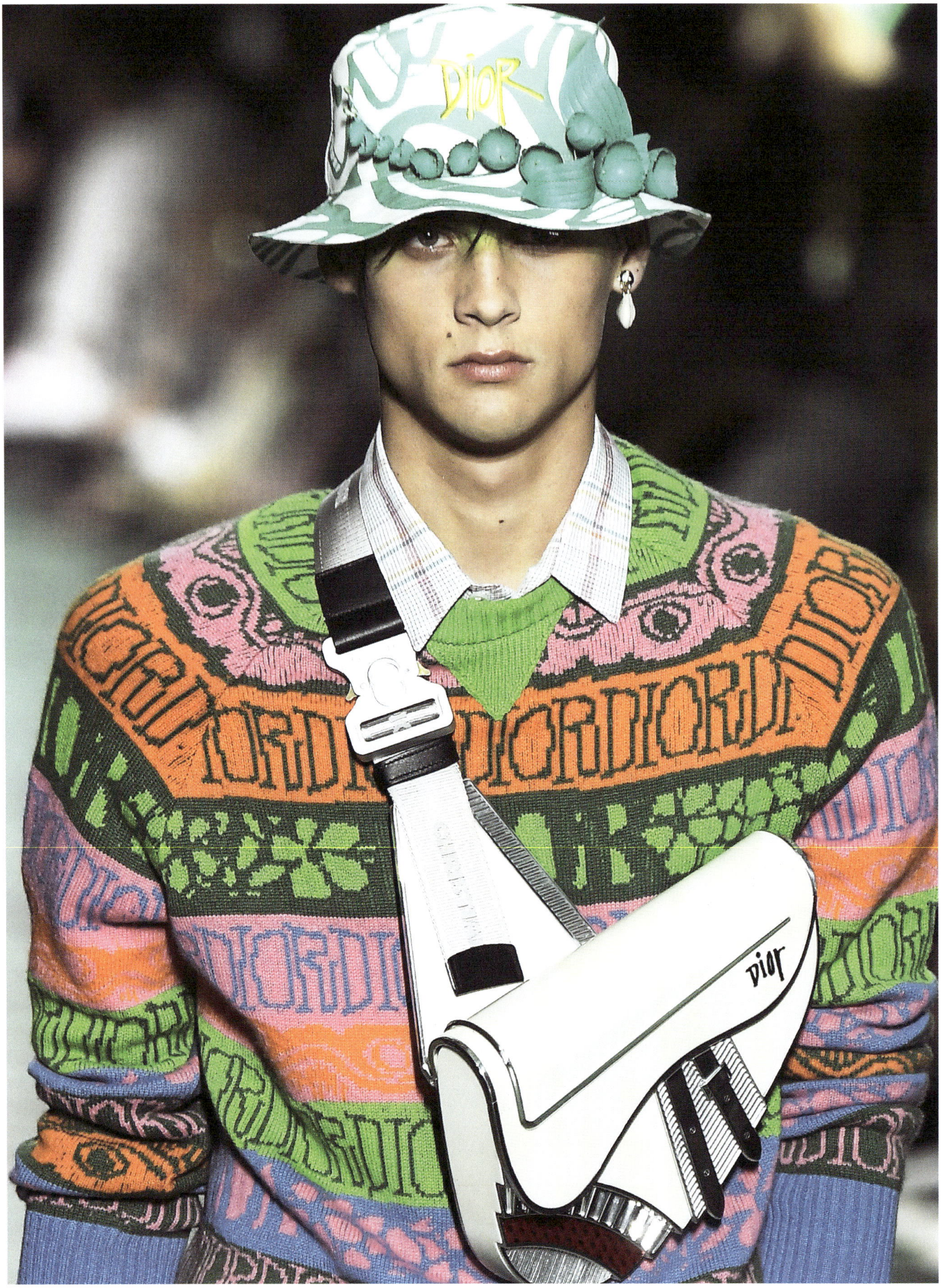

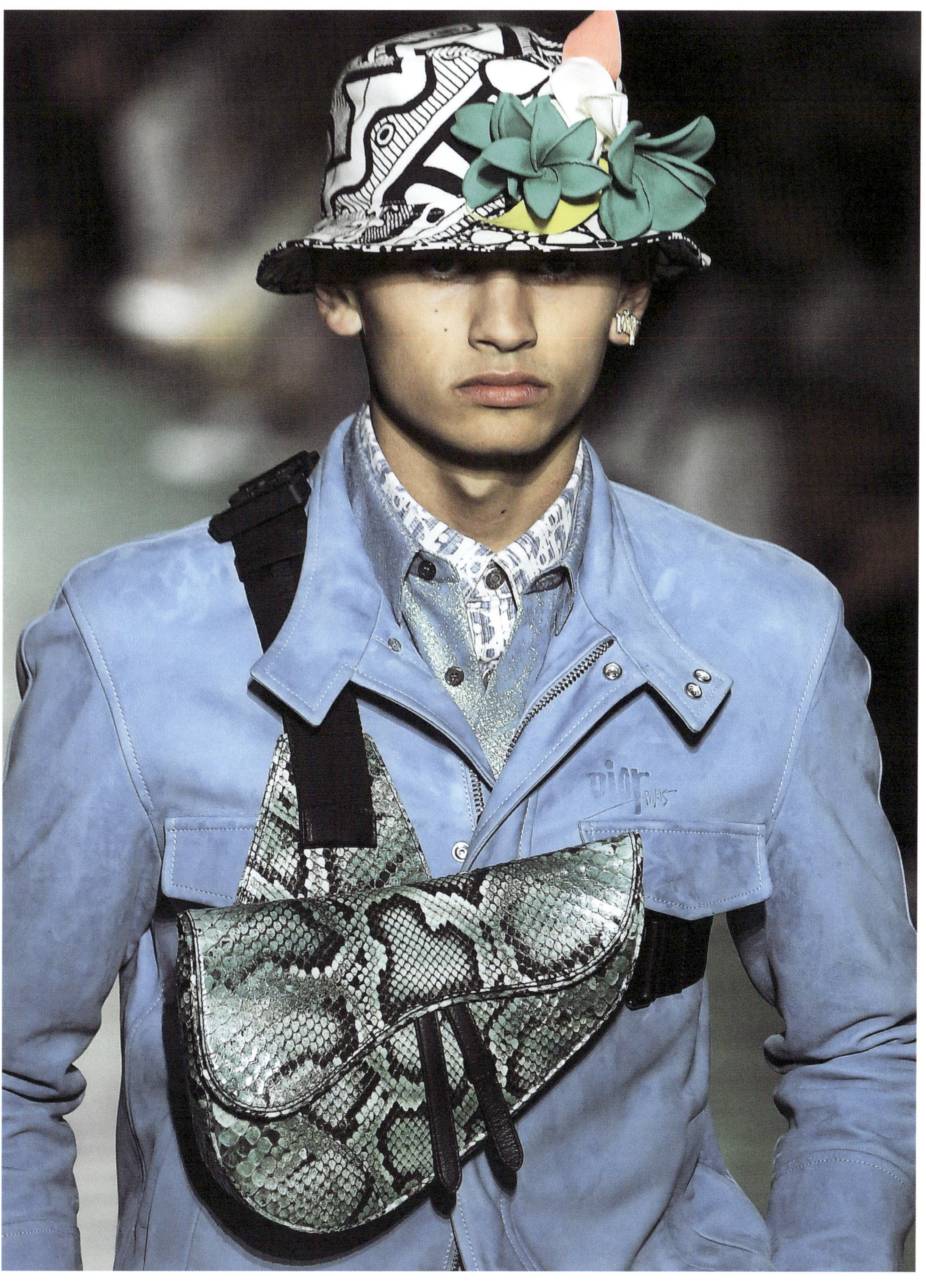

But time is a great healer of It bags, and the Saddle Bag has risen again to prove its enduring relevance. Beyoncé was the first to kick off the redux. She was spotted in 2014 with a tie-dyed Saddle Bag. K-pop superstar CL shared her rare Adiorable Saddle Bag in 2016 and the buzz only grew from there. Anyone who bought a pre-loved bag for a bargain between 2007-2014 must have felt rather smug. Demand meant resale shops were selling out of Saddle Bags, and the desire for vintage versions continues to this day. Limited editions of the first iteration of the style are now some of the most expensive Dior pieces at resale. Prices can range from £1000-£12,000; as always, the price depends on the bag's condition, material, print and scarcity. Although coveted, Dior bags don't reach the excruciating prices that bags from other *maisons* do, so shopping for a Saddle Bag as an investment is unlikely to make you a fortune. However, research from American retailer NYCleatherjackets.com showed that the Saddle Bag had the biggest increase in online searches from 2005-2025, with a jump of 7400% online search interest, beating Hermès Kelly and Birkin bags *and* the Chanel 2.55.

In 2018 a reissued version of the Saddle Bag was back on the Dior catwalk for Fall/Winter 2018, this time from creative director Maria Grazia Chiuri. The stirrup-style D charm was preserved, along with the distinctive saddle silhouette with a CD logo on either side of the top handle. For its relaunched appearance, the Saddle Bag was presented in patchwork denim, textured leather, fringing and beadwork. The redesigned bag came with a practical longer strap and was also available in a larger size to accommodate a cell phone. Global fashion search platform Lyst revealed that pre-owned Saddle Bag searches started to peak as soon as the show was streamed, from fans eager to get their hands on an original, before the reissued bags were released into stores.

Dior capitalized on the buzz with a clever social media campaign featuring 100 influencers and fashion insiders, all of whom posted #DiorSaddle, resulting in a 957% search spike online. Mixing nostalgia for the Y2K original with a futuristic Instagram campaign that showcased the new bag was a way to unite the two camps of potential Saddle Bag fans chomping at the bit to carry the iconic bag. In 2025, Saddle Bags are available in classic size, medium or mini, and the universe of the Saddle Bag has stretched beyond the classic shoulder bag. Collectors can also buy a belt pouch, phone case, and a men's version of the Saddle Bag with a larger capacity and a messenger silhouette.

Kim Jones, the former artistic director of Dior Homme, even created a metal version of the Saddle Bag for the pre-fall 2019 menswear show. Only ten of these futuristic bags were made and priced at $35,000 each. Jones collaborated on the design with artist Hajime Sorayama, who is best known for his airbrushed depictions of highly sexualized female robots. With its high-gloss finish and incorporation of headphone jacks as tassels, the bag echoes Sorayama's design style. It caught the eye of Kim Kardashian. The reality star was spotted wearing one of the bags with an oversized t-shirt and trainers in Malibu, adding the metal version to her existing collection of Saddle Bags, which also appear to include classic black, white, taupe and python versions.

While the dip in the Saddle Bag's popularity may read as a cautionary tale of the danger of piling onto over-saturated trends, the future of the style now seems secure, and it's It status has been confirmed once and for all.

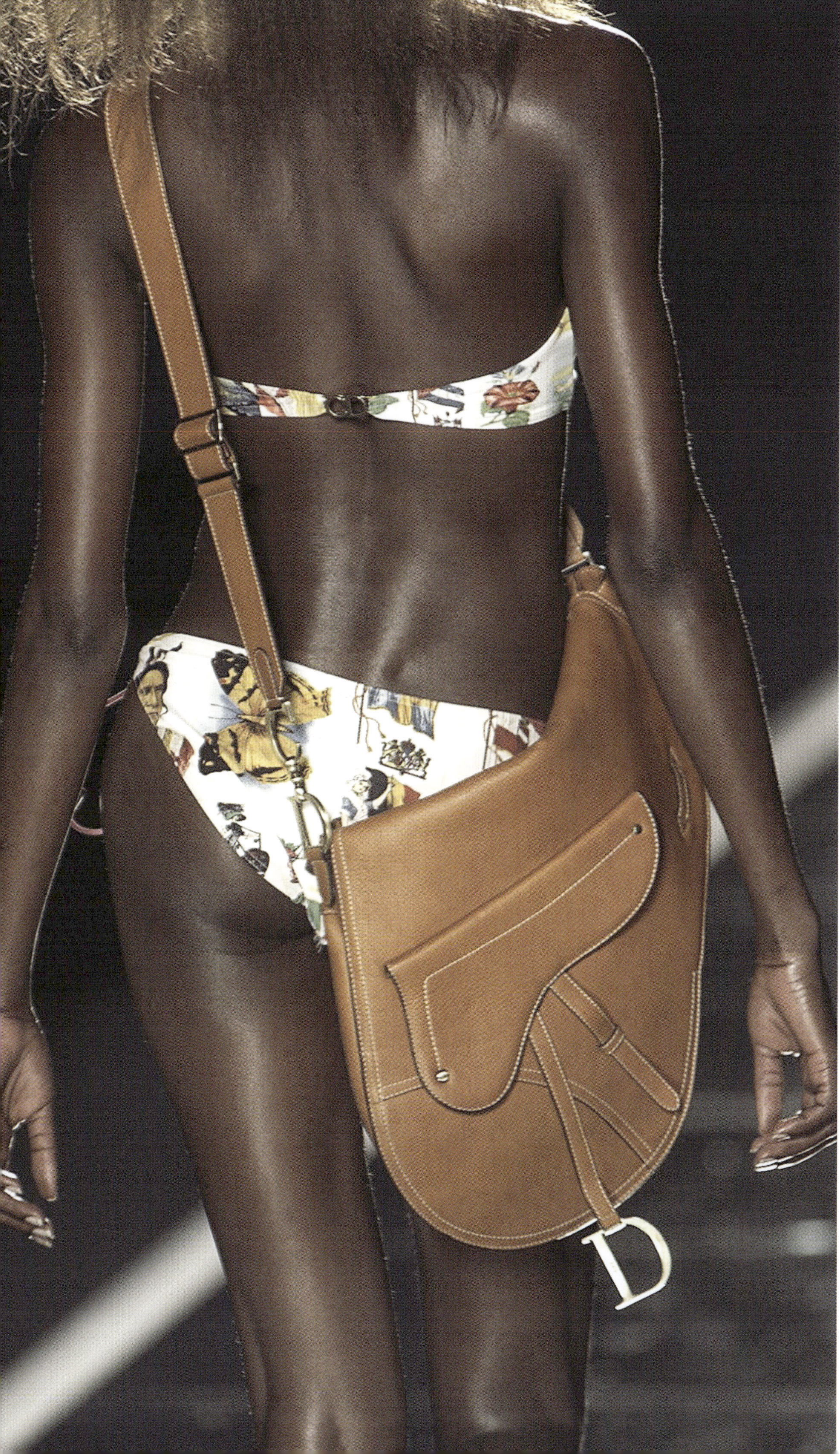

Page 65: Nina Sandbech holds her Saddle bag under her arm at Copenhagen Fashion Week, 2024

Pages 66/67: Male models cross the runway with Saddle bags slung cross-body during Dior's Men's Pre-Fall 2020 show in Miami, 2019

Page 69: A model walks the runway at the Christian Dior ready-to-wear Spring/Summer 2002 fashion show wearing a Baudrier Saddle bag and minimal attire in Paris, 2001

Page 70: Dariia Prokopovych dazzles in YSL sunglasses, gold earrings, a TTSWTRS beige floral bodysuit, and a pinstriped blazer and skirt combo, complemented by a Dior burgundy Saddle bag in Berlin, 2024

Page 71: Riccardo Simonetti sports a Y Project denim jacket adorned with rhinestone star brooches, Levi's straight-leg jeans, and an oblique-print Dior Saddle bag in Berlin, 2024

Pages 72/73: Debra J. Quinn's unique outfits are enhanced by Saddle bags in various sizes in Melbourne, 2024

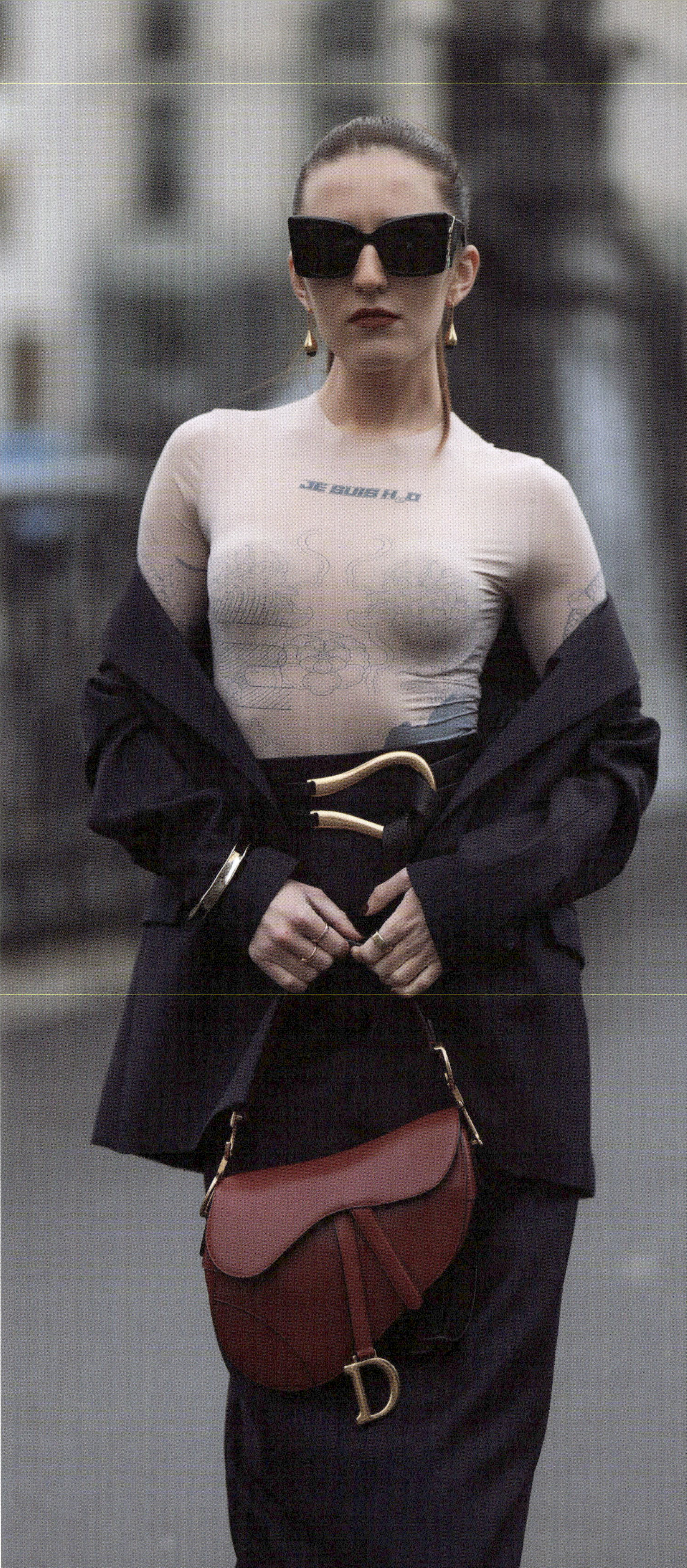

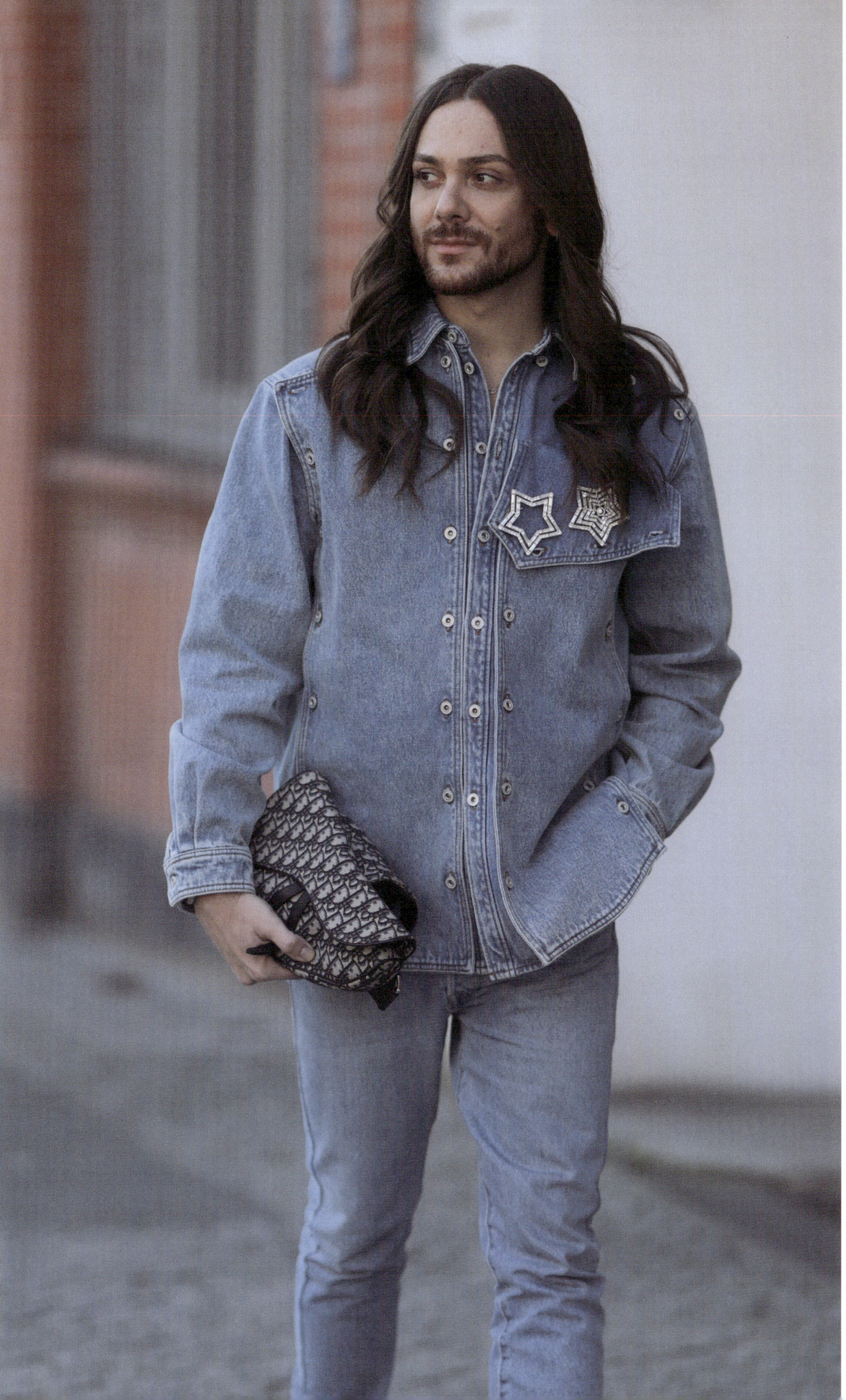

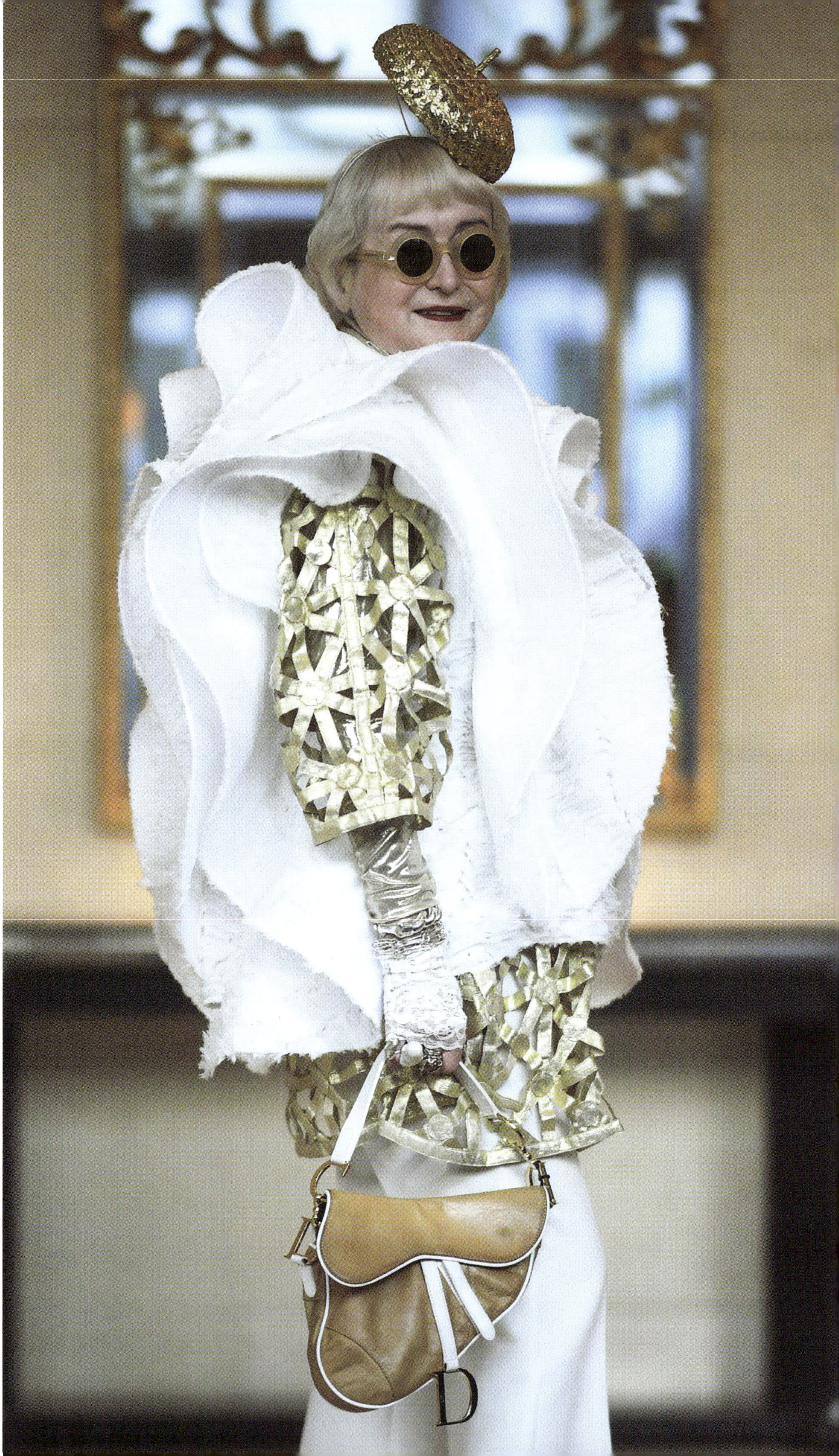

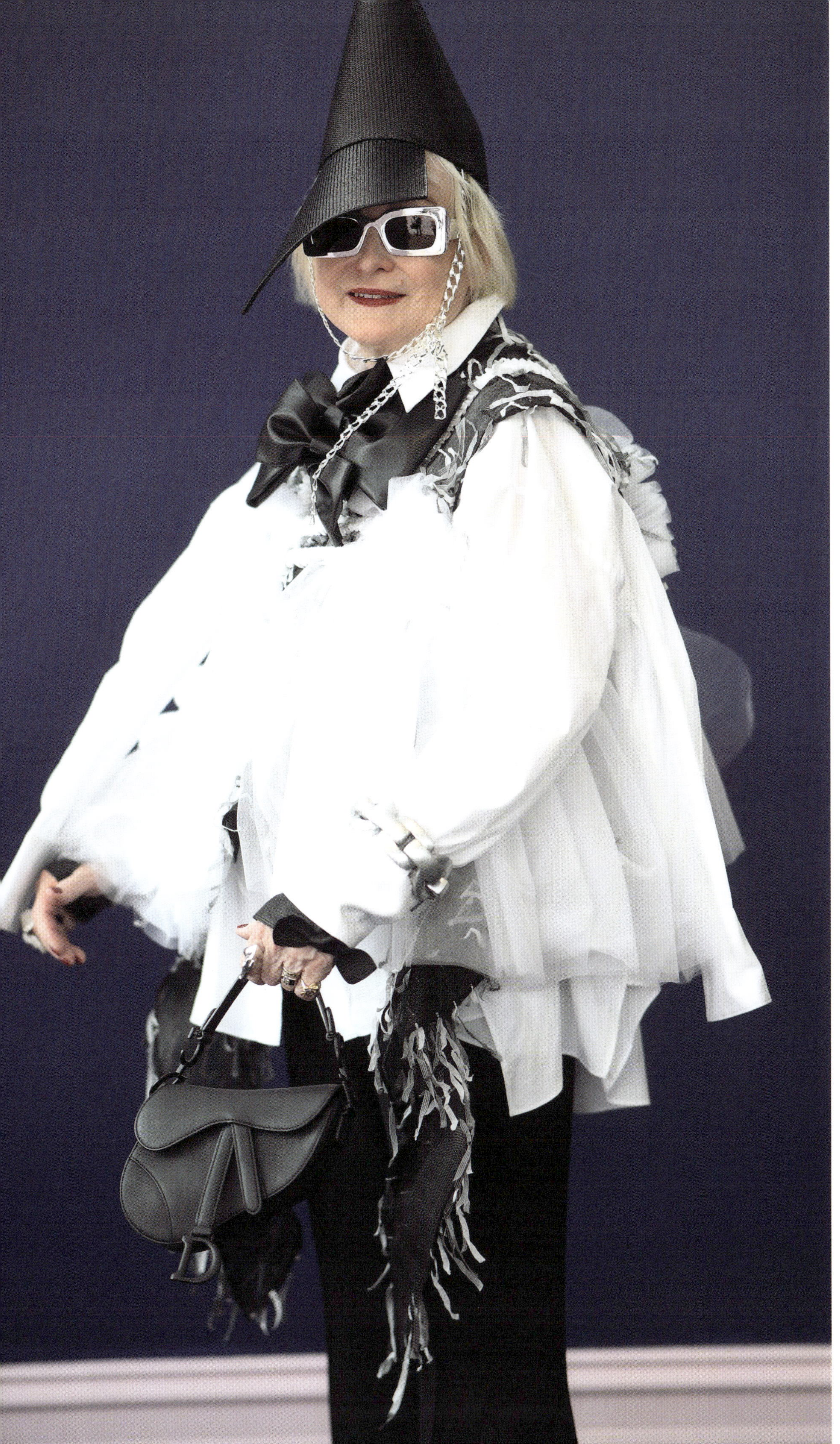

This page: Salome Chaboki showcases an *oblique* Saddle bag during Copenhagen Fashion Week Fall/Winter 2024

Next page: A guest dons a navy pleated dress, a silver belt, and a Dior Saddle bag paired with black leather boots outside Dior during Paris Fashion Week Fall/Winter 2024

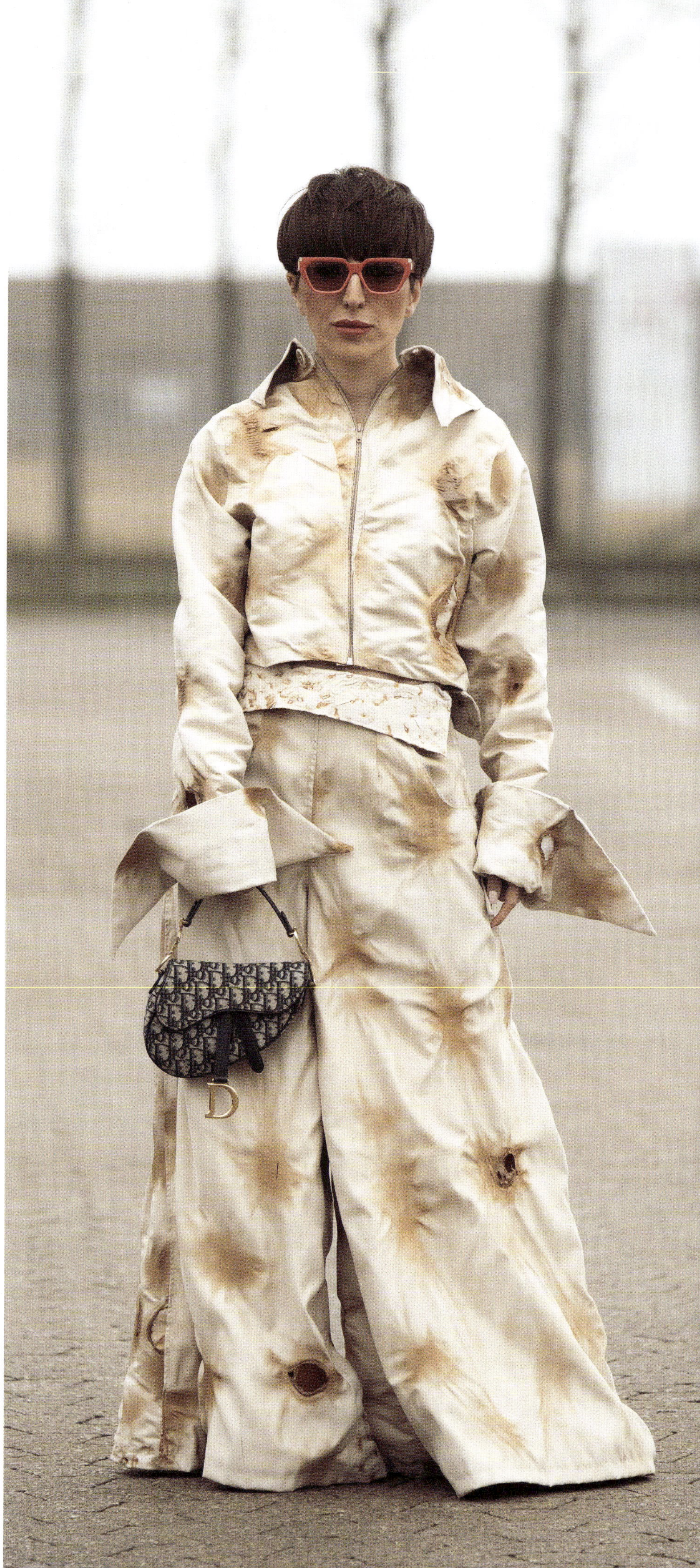

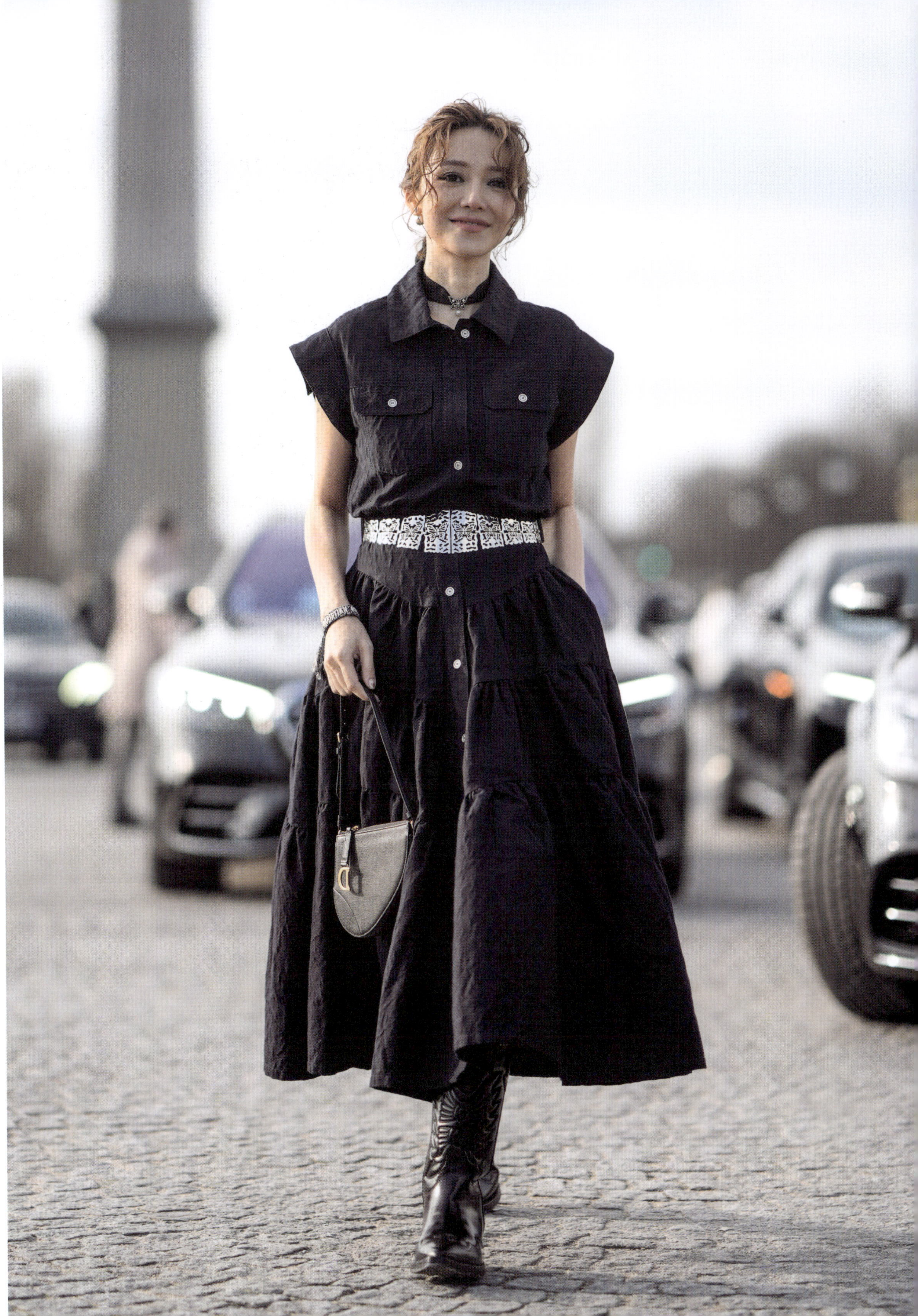

A model struts the runway in the Dior Pre-Fall 2024 show at the Brooklyn Museum in New York, 2024, showcasing a Saddle bag featuring a mash-up of the American and French flags, a motif originally created by Marc Bohan in 1966

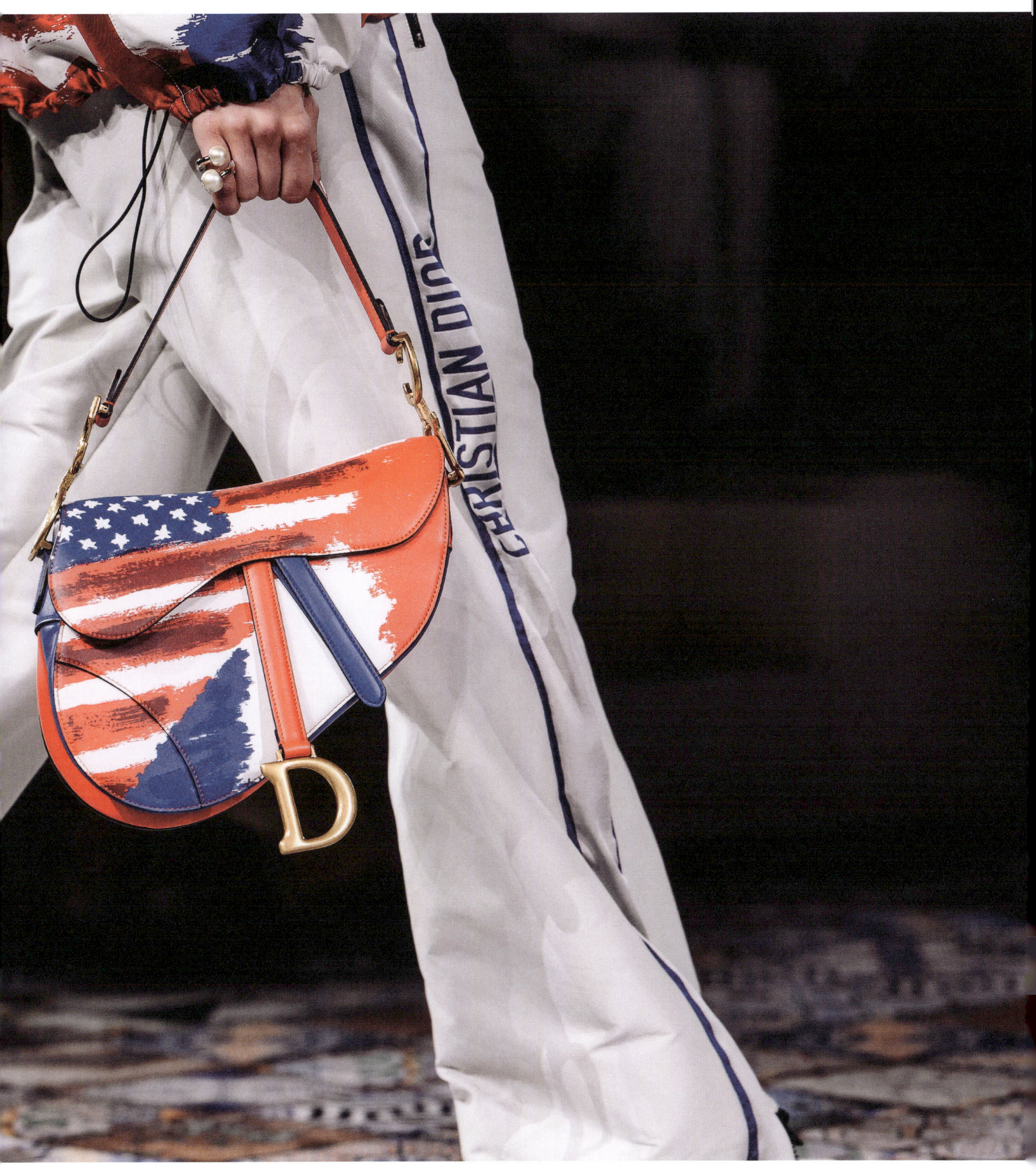
CHRISTIAN DIOR

BOOK TOTE

Fashion is often ridiculed for its less than practical approach to dressing, but the Book Tote is the perfect counterargument. It's an eminently pragmatic carry-all that combines the desirability of Dior and a designer fashion purchase with the usefulness of being able to access your belongings with ease and the ability to carry everything you might need for the day ahead.

The Book Tote was launched in 2017 as part of the Spring/Summer 2018 collection, designed by Maria Grazia Chiuri as a simple, structured tote. Chiuri took inspiration from a 1967 sketch by Marc Bohan found in the *maison's* archives. Apparently Bohan was influenced by students of that era, who gravitated to the bookstores, bistros and cafés of Paris to discuss their latest literary finds and philosophy. Bohan launched carefree canvas accessories to complement the mood of the moment. At its heart, the Book Tote is a simple bag designed to carry books—but it can do so much more.

Spring/Summer 2018 was the season that Chiuri showcased her fashion designs as a feminist manifesto. The iconic "We Should All Be Feminists" t-shirt with the title of Chimamanda Ngozi Adichie's seminal book appeared in the collection, as did a long-sleeve Breton style top worn by supermodel Sasha Pivovarova with the slogan "Why Have There Been No Great Women Artists?"—the name of a 1971 feminist art history essay by Linda Nochlin.

Beyond the pertinent political message, the bags are incredibly useful. They have a rectangular silhouette, easy open top (without a zipper or other fastening) and a capacious interior. While there are no pockets inside, devotees often use an insert to compartmentalize their items. Inserts are also useful to protect the interior of such a beautiful bag from accidental spills. But although the bag has a pared-back aesthetic, the details and artistic influences that create the design are so much more than meets the eye at first glance. The process to create a Book Tote starts in Dior's Italian *ateliers*. The embroidered version of the bag is a work of art that takes 37 hours of craftsmanship and over 1.5 million stitches to create. Every season, the studio brings out a reimagined version of the Book Tote with fabrics, colors and finishes that reflect the mood of the season. Some of the most iconic options include Dior's *oblique* house embroidery, camouflage embroidery, classic *toile de jouy* (a distinctive French pattern that features rural scenes), houndstooth, embroidered denim, velvet, fishnet, *bayadère* embroidery (a striped design that echoes Dior's spring 1967 haute couture collection), along with smooth or embossed calfskin styles. Rihanna has a khaki *oblique* embroidery Book Tote along with another in classic blue. Blue, black, *rose des vents* and Dior's signature gray are also go-to shades for the block-colored versions.

Next page: Sasha Pivovarova walks the runway with a Book Tote for Christian Dior at the Spring/Summer 2018 show in Paris

Page 80: A guest sports a blue Dior turtleneck, gray trousers, and a Dior Tote Bag outside Dior Homme Fall/Winter 2025 during Paris Fashion Week, 2025

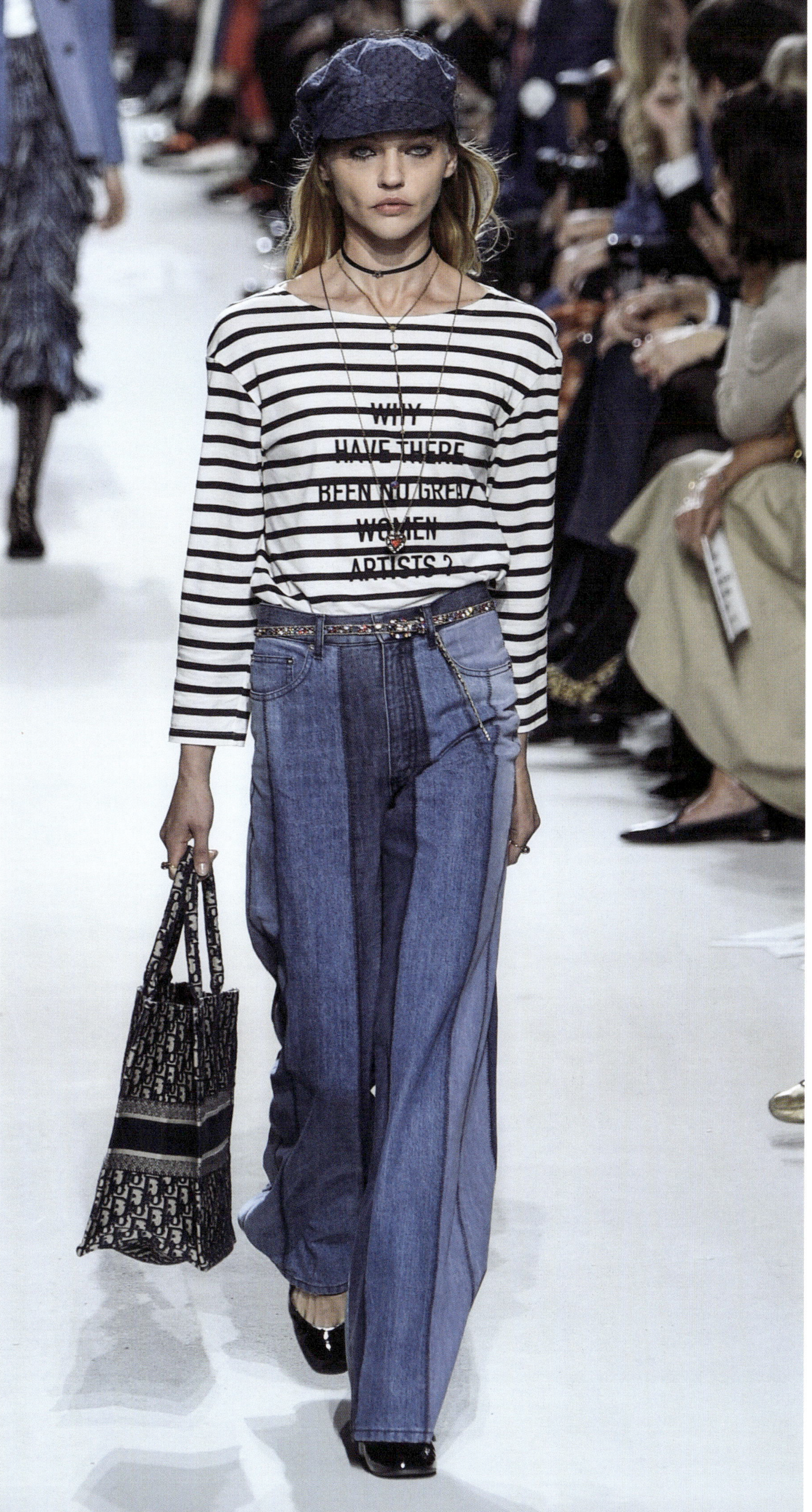
WHY
HAVE THERE
BEEN NO GREAT
WOMEN
ARTISTS ?

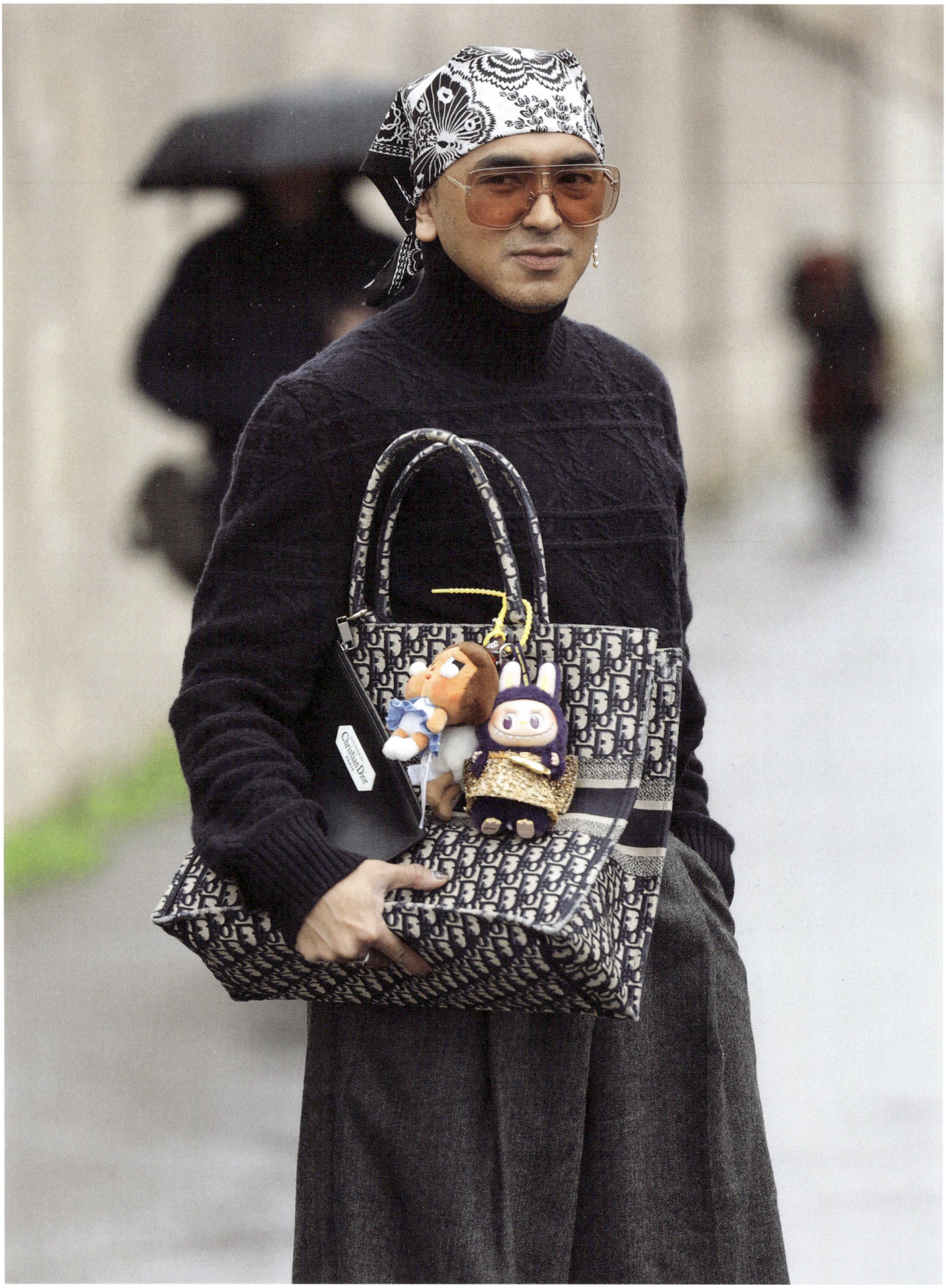

AT ITS HEART, THE BOOK TOTE IS A SIMPLE BAG DESIGNED TO CARRY BOOKS—BUT IT CAN DO SO MUCH MORE.

To create the unique and luscious textured finish, Dior uses an exclusive embroidery technique that is tri-dimensional. Each fabric is made by hand before being woven on top of the base textile, which creates an optical illusion of deeper texture to the embroidery. Every bag features loop handles, which allow the bag to be hand-held or nestled in the crook of one's arm, depending on size, along with a signature logo stripe, placed horizontally across the center of each bag.

Once the exterior design is completed, each bag is taken to Dior's in-house leather *ateliers* in Florence to be finished. Again, while the bag looks deceptively simple, the construction is remarkably study, which has led to the Book Tote being hailed as the ideal travel companion and carry-on style. The bags are also brilliantly light, as they are often made from canvas, which allows users to fill them with their belongings and not suffer the consequences.

For the Cruise 2024 collection, a new finish was introduced—*macrocannage* leather. *Cannage* is one of Dior's house motifs, replicating canework, but the *macrocannage* sees the detail supersized for a quirky look. The bags are also adorned with Dior's iconic charms—usually only attached to the Lady Dior—which elevate the casual vibes of the embroidered Book Tote to a sleeker, more city-appropriate look. If you are considering adding a Book Tote to your collection, it's important to note the appropriate size for your intended use. The first Book Totes that were launched were shown in a standard size, which has come to be known as the large option. A large Book Tote measures 42 × 35 × 18.5 cm. As soon as the bag hit the market, it was clear that customers would demand a wider range of sizes. Mini and medium versions came next, followed by the small size which was launched in 2022.

The medium Book Tote measures 36 × 27.5 × 16.5 cm while the small size is 26.5 × 21 × 14 cm. If you only need to carry the bare minimum, then perhaps the mini size is for you, clocking in at a petite 22.5 × 15 × 6 cm. A vertical Book Tote is available too.

Keen to offer shoppers another level of individualism, Dior also offers personalisation of the Book Tote where clients can have their initials or name added to their bag. It's not possible to put a long name on the smaller sizes due to space restrictions, but clients can play around with different iterations in store, and for certain styles ordered online, customers can choose a unique addition to their Book Tote. You can also customize the Saddle Bag, too, as well as Dior cushions and blankets.

Along with owning or carrying the Book Tote, Dior fans can take their dedication to the next level by watching The Dior Book Tote Club online, where short films showcase Dior ambassadors and friends of the house discussing the books that have changed their lives and sharing their love of reading. Natalie Portman, the face of Miss Dior fragrance and a long-term Dior muse, kicked off the series, but Rosamund Pike, Pretty Yende, Nine D'Orso and Beatrice Borromeo have also been filmed in their favorite bookstores and libraries around the world (with their Book Totes in tow, of course.)

Next page: Ellie Delphine combines a blue shirt and shorts co-ord with a small colorful Book Tote outside Rabens Saloner during Copenhagen Fashion Week, 2022

Pages 84/85: A guest showcases a lace midi dress complemented by a neon pink Book Tote outside Dior during Haute Couture Fall/Winter 2023

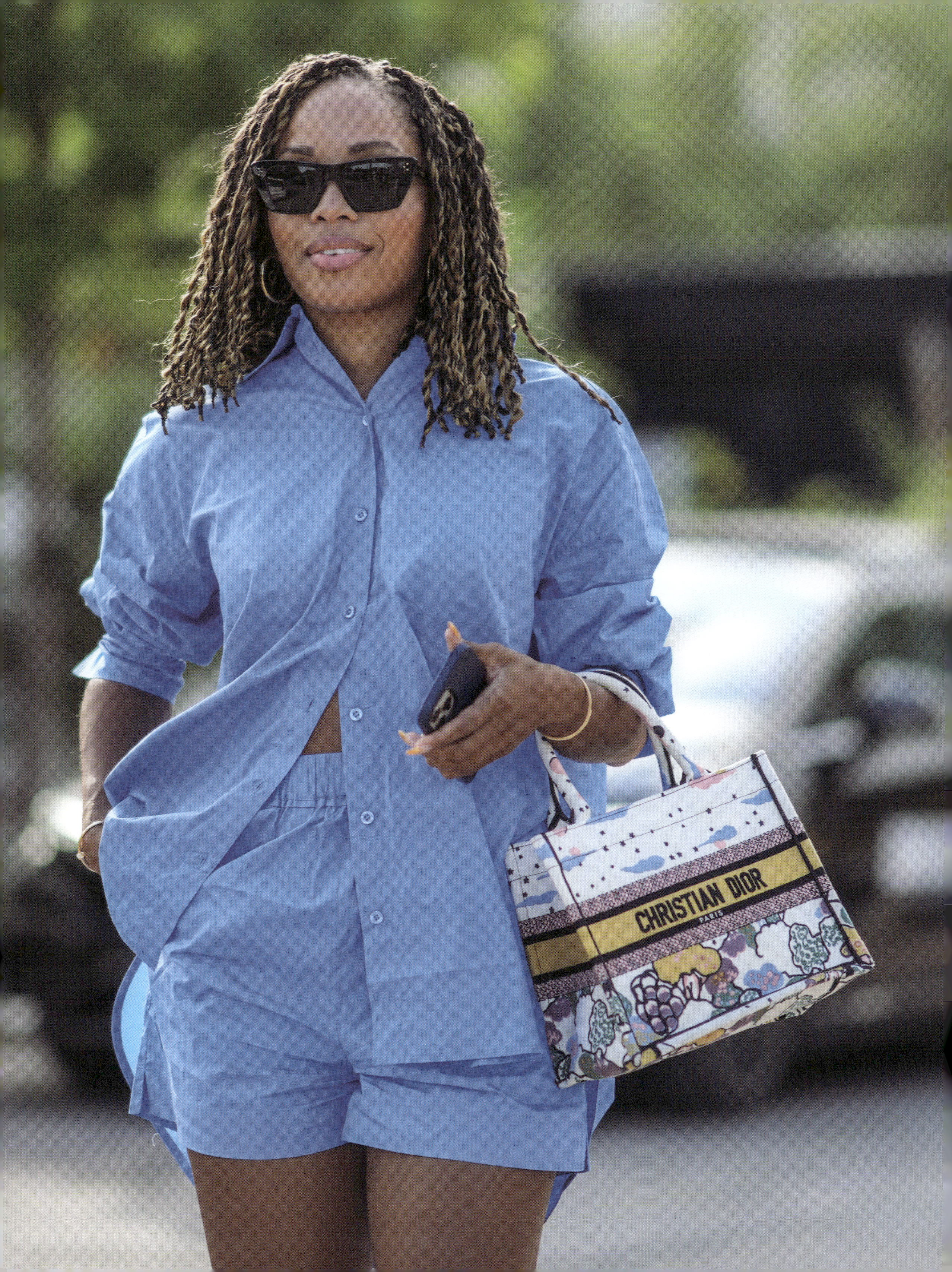
CHRISTIAN DIOR
PARIS

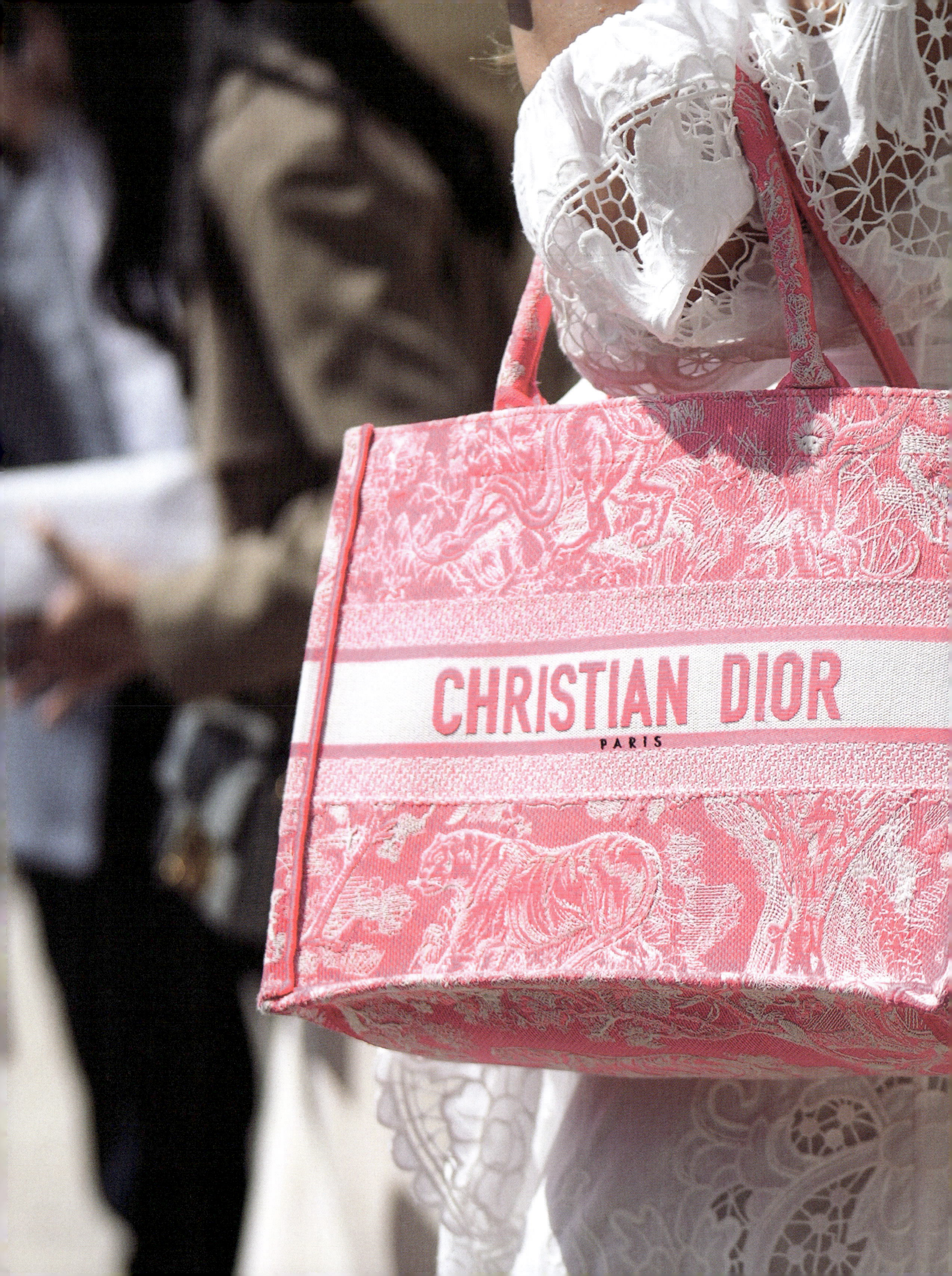
CHRISTIAN DIOR
PARIS

DIORAMA

A legacy from Raf Simons' tenure at the *maison,* the Diorama bag is a modern, slick and minimalist shoulder bag that echoes the designer's signature style. Dior have moved on from offering these bags at retail, but aficionados can find the styles on preloved and resale sites. Prices start from approximately £1200, depending on condition, material and size, and the bag remains a sleek option for those looking for a shoulder bag.

Distinctive for its rectangular shape, the Diorama combines Dior's elegant house DNA with a modernity that Simons wished to embody during his time at the *maison*. The bag has a shield-shaped clasp and a long chain and leather combined strap, so it can be worn shoulder-style or cross-body. The details are minimal and there is a geometric pattern across the exterior, which is sometimes embossed with a *cannage* design but is often presented in plain leather. The structure of the bag plays on architectural shapes—a subtle tribute to Simons' studies of industrial design and furniture design, which he pursued before moving into fashion.

Dior often includes plays on the house's name in their collections, and the Diorama offers a clever wordplay. A 'diorama' is a miniature theater scene or vignette, and the lines and graphic outline of the bag could suggest a stage set.

Rihanna was the bag's campaign star in its launch year of 2015. Obviously she had her pick of styles, but the multiple Grammy-winner seemed to be particularly enamored with the pale pink version, carrying it multiple times over the summer on a number of different occasions. The Diorama was also a favorite of French actor Marion Cotillard, famed for her portrayal of singer and fellow French icon Edith Piaf in the film *La Vie En Rose* (2007). Cotillard was the face of the Lady Dior bag, but was apparently equally enthralled with the Diorama, it would seem, and who could blame her?

Next page: The Secret Garden advertising campaign features Rihanna holding a Diorama bag in 2015

Page 88: The Diorama is showcased at Paris Fashion Week in 2016

Page 89: (Bottom) A black Diorama features an eyelet pattern, captured in Moscow, 2019 (Top) A silver Diorama is spotlighted during Milan Fashion Week, 2018

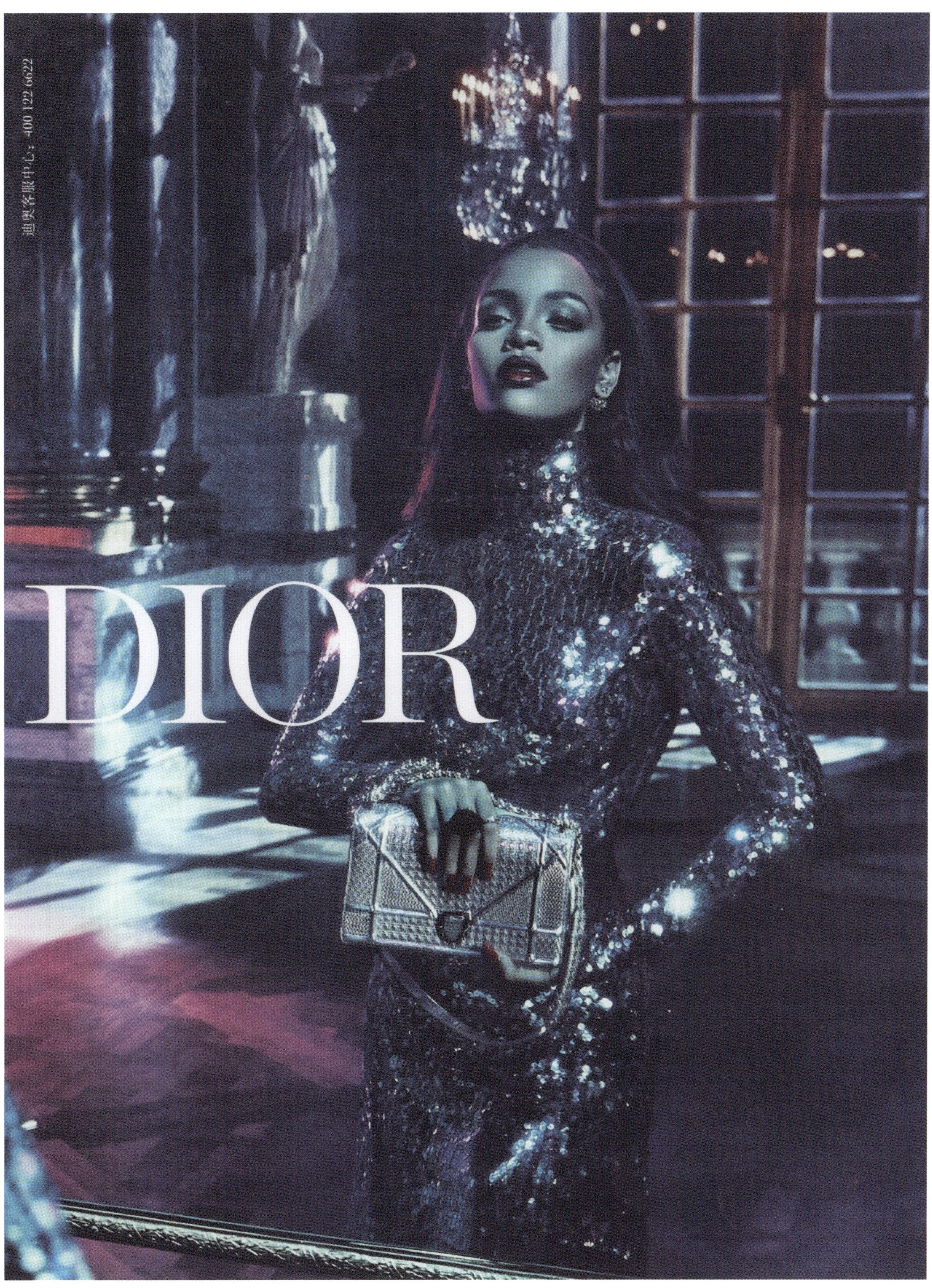
迪奥客服中心：400 122 6622
DIOR

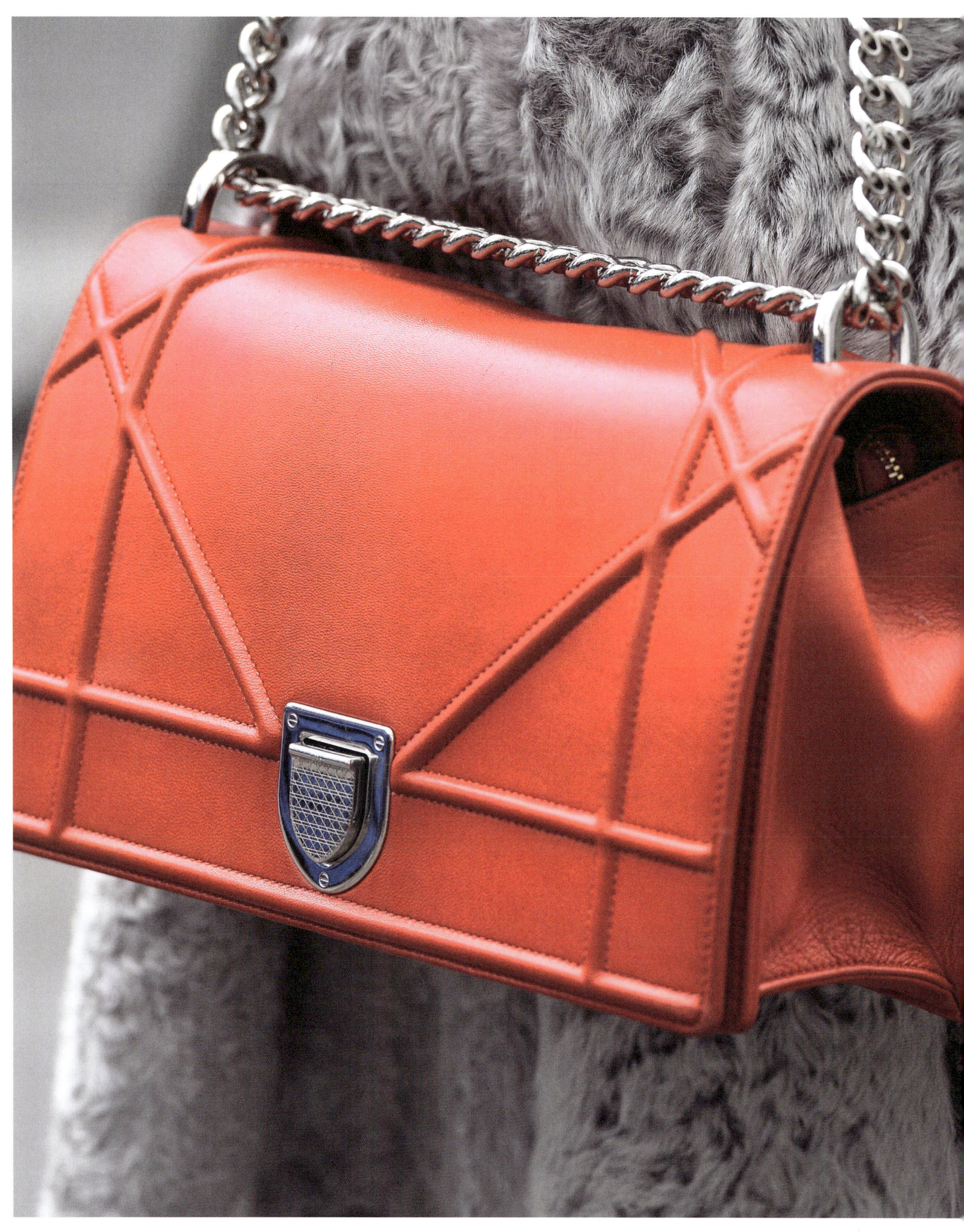

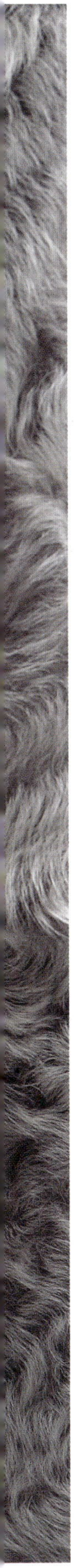

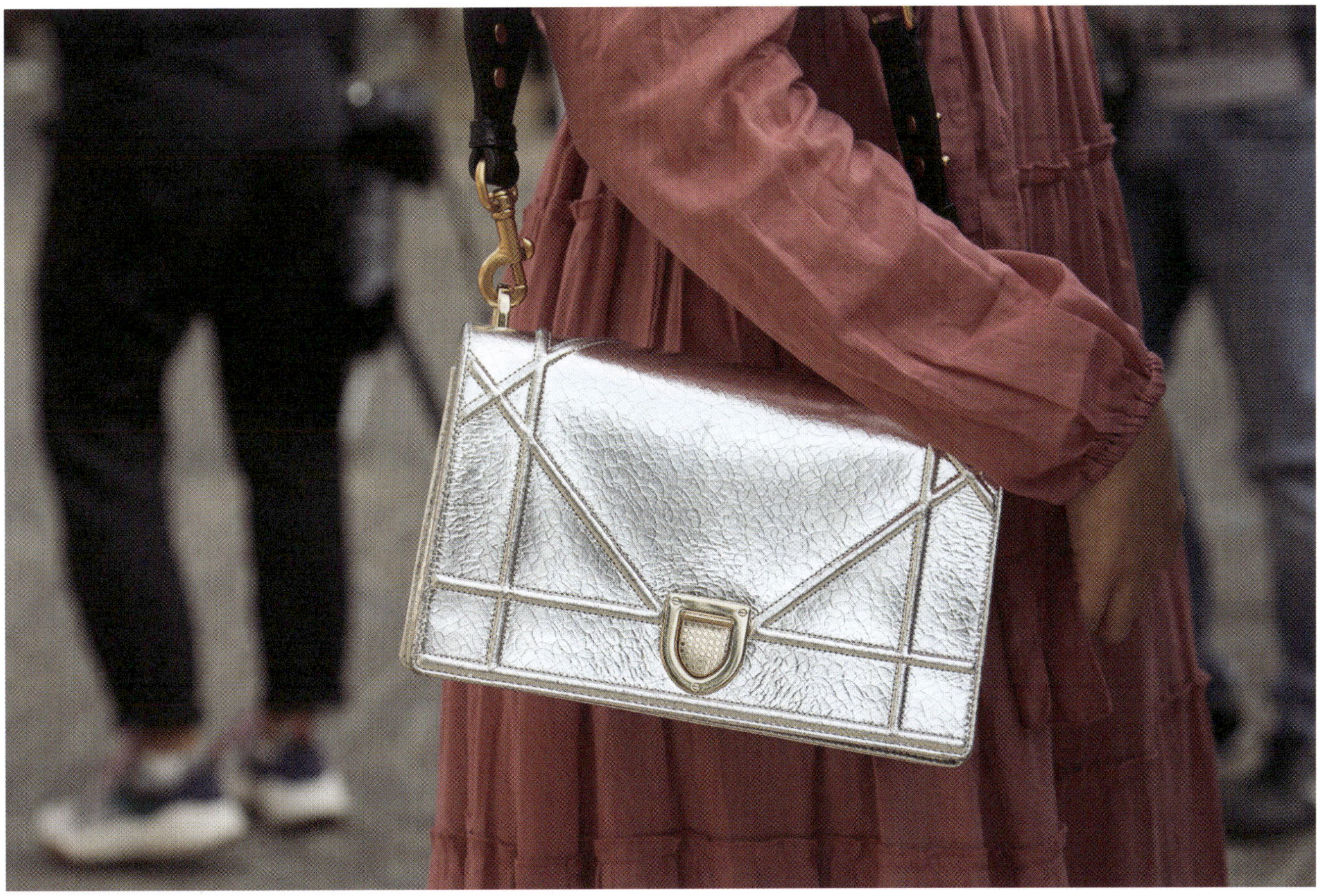

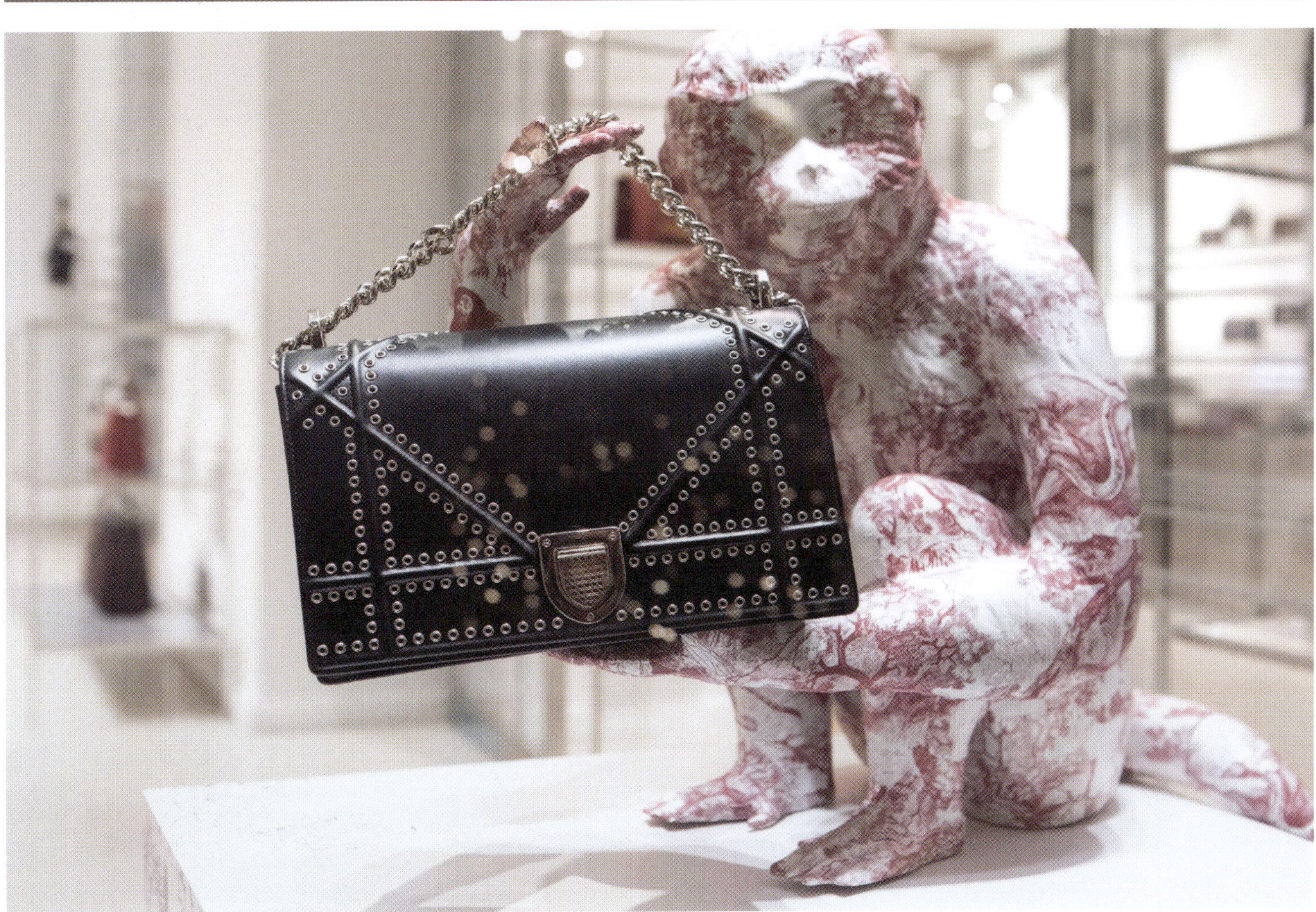

BOBBY

In the arsenal of bags, a saddle bag—that chic, yet carefree design—is an essential. Dior's Bobby bag, introduced by the *maison* as part of the Fall/Winter 2020 collection, is one such style. Not the *actual* Saddle Bag, saddle bags are equestrian-inspired without the literal look of a piece of horse tack. They are often worn cross-body with a traditional shape. Maria Grazia Chiuri is responsible for Dior's saddle bag style, which mixes the modernity of her vision with *Monsieur* Dior's original ethos. Named after Dior's favorite dog, Bobby has been the name of countless looks. Every season while he was alive, the designer would call one suit The Bobby. These styles were marked as the pieces that would make the biggest statement for each season and Dior wrote in his memoir that The Bobby suits would be "earmarked for success."

Bobby was not alone in being the object of Dior's affection. The designer also was a dog-dad to Sandale and Papillon, who lived with Dior's father, and Mirza (a wolf-dog) who resided at Dior's estate in the south of France. However, Bobby was the most famous, and perhaps most faithful, of Dior's collection of canines. While not part of the ready-to-wear collections, or indeed couture, the Bobby bag has certainly been a runaway triumph since it was launched.

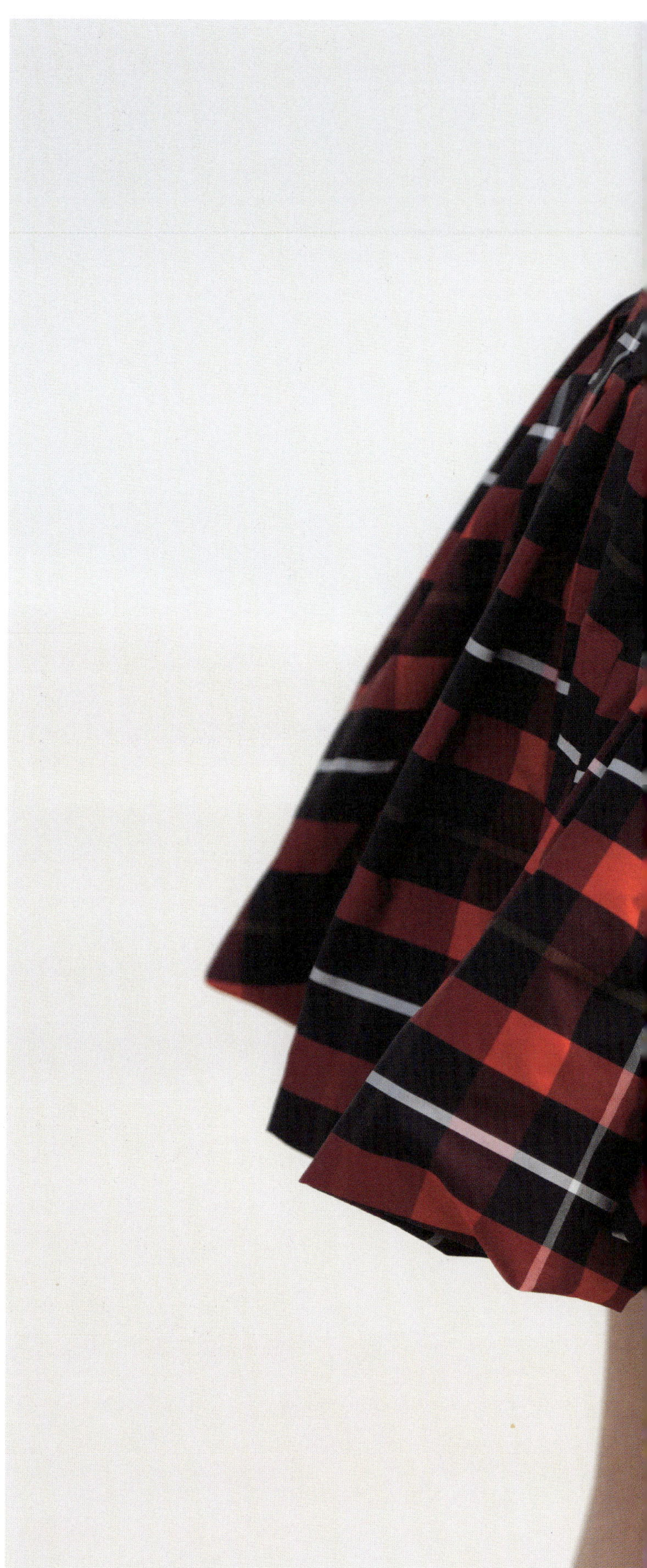

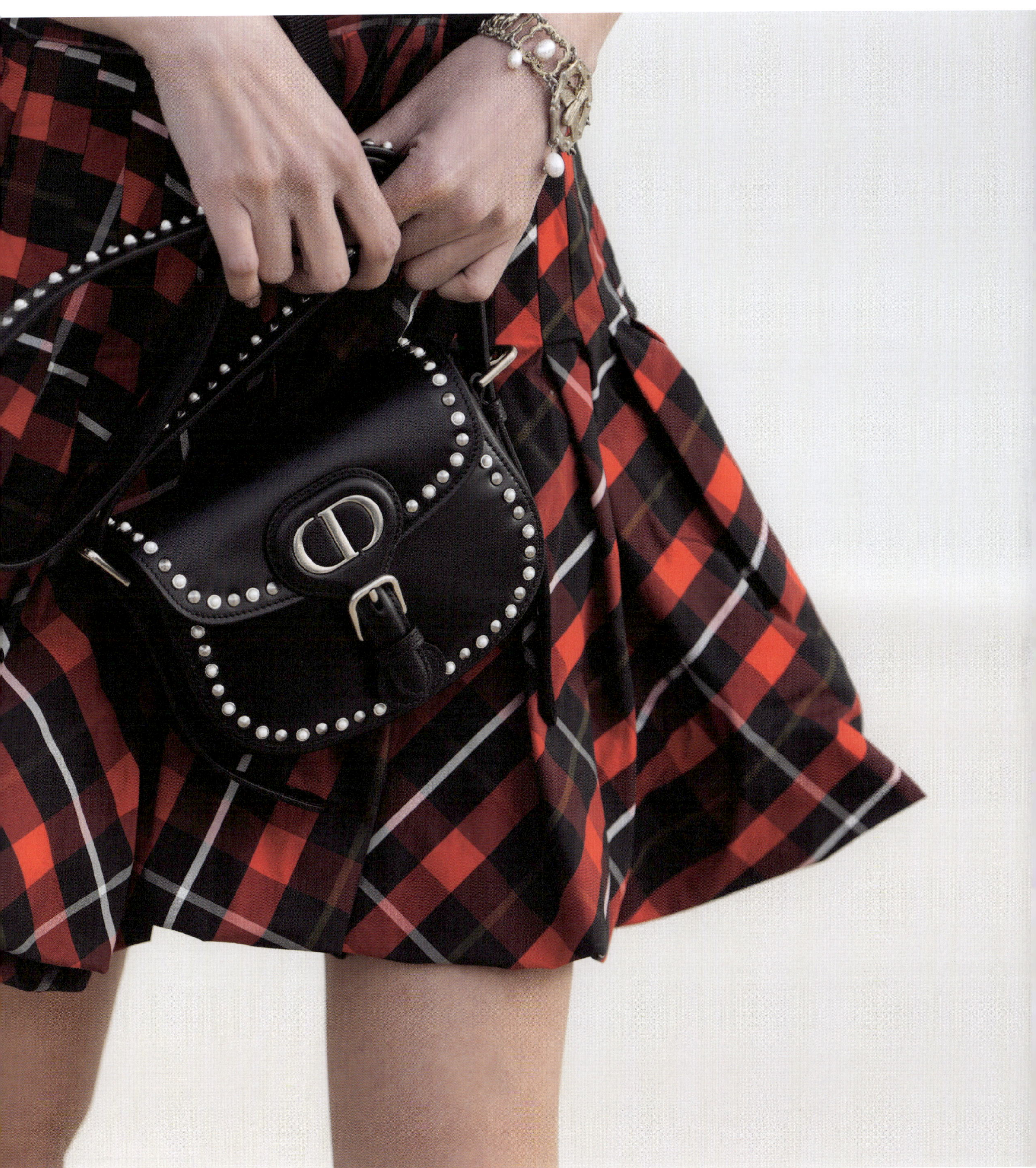

So many *maisons* play on their heritage, sometimes in very obvious ways (as Dior did with the relaunch of the Saddle Bag), but the Bobby looks back in a more subtle fashion. The Bobby bag has a curved silhouette that echoes the same lines and shape of Dior's own original couture clothing collections.

Each bag is finished with a CD logo over the buckle, which covers a hidden magnetic fastener for easy access to the bag's interior. The Bobby bag is also finished with a removable shoulder strap that you can switch out for the season's newest styles or a personalized version. Inside the bag you'll find a large compartment and a small pocket for your most precious items. At the back of the bag there is another useful pocket running the entire width of the bag; the address *30 Montaigne* is embossed halfway under the pocket.

30 Avenue Montaigne was where Dior founded his couture workshop. Dior employed 85 people in 1946, and his business swiftly expanded into the neighboring buildings. Still known as a destination for all things Dior, 30 Montaigne now includes a cafe, gardens and galleries as well as a boutique where Dior devotees can browse the ready-to-wear, accessories and *haute joaillerie* collections (designed by Victoire de Castellane) and revel in the *maison's* lifestyle proposition.

Getting back to the Bobby bag, it comes in three useful sizes: small, medium and large. Each season, an array of new materials, leathers and colors are added to the growing collection.

The small Bobby measures 17.8 × 14 × 6.4 cm. Medium Bobby bags measure 22.5 × 17.5 × 6.5 cm, while large ones are 27 × 20.5 × 8 cm. The New Dior Bobby Mini Bag has an elongated east-west silhouette introduced as part of the Cruise 2022 collection, and measures a neat 21 × 12 × 5.1 cm. Since its introduction, the Bobby bag has been an influencer and celebrity favorite. Charlize Theron and Heart Evangelista have both been spotted with the style.

Page 91: Kiwi Lee sports a small shiny black Bobby with studs during Paris Fashion Week in March, 2025

Next page: A street style favorite: the studded black Bobby as seen during Paris Couture Fashion Week, January 2025
A Bobby East-West bag is presented on the runway at the RTW Spring/Summer 2022 show in Paris, 2021; (Top) Models showcase Bobby bags from the Fall/Winter 2020 Womenswear collection in Paris, 2020

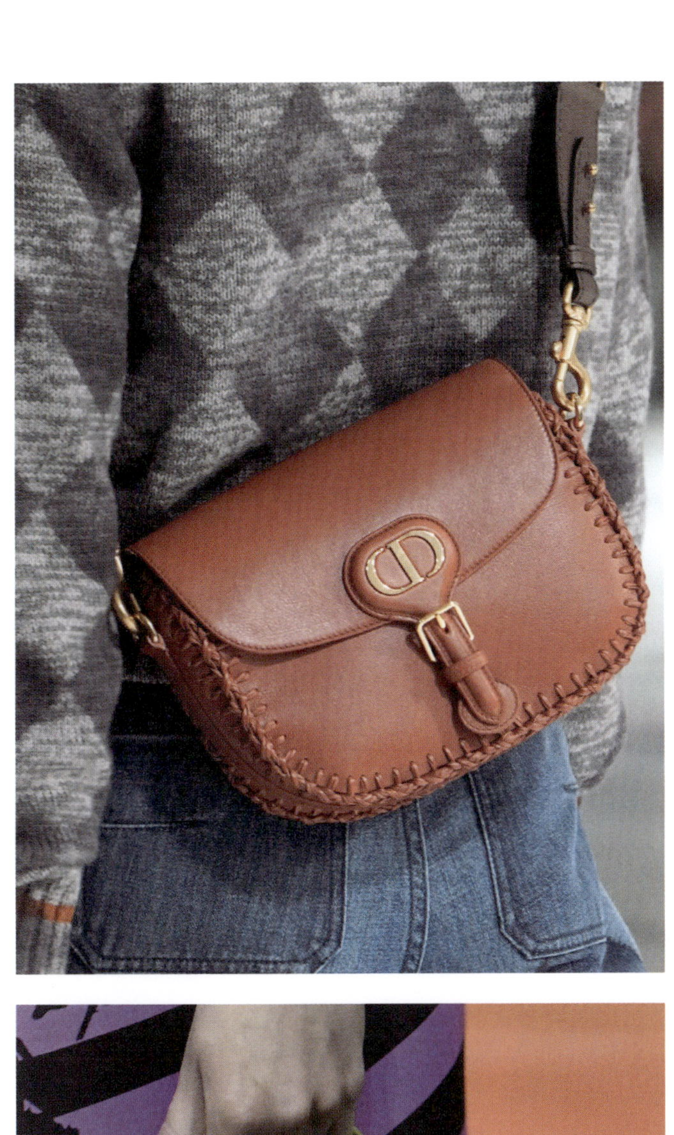

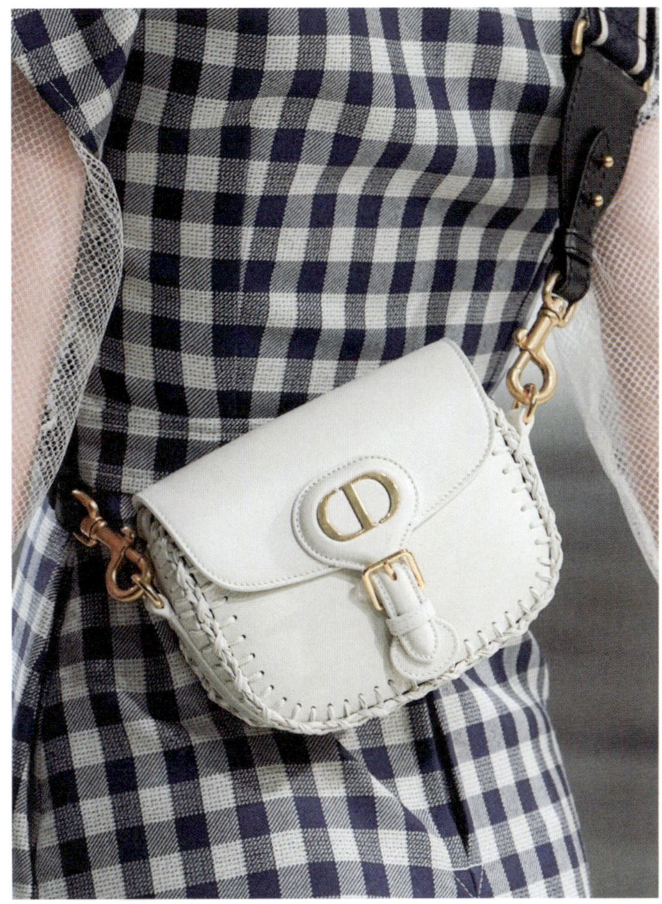

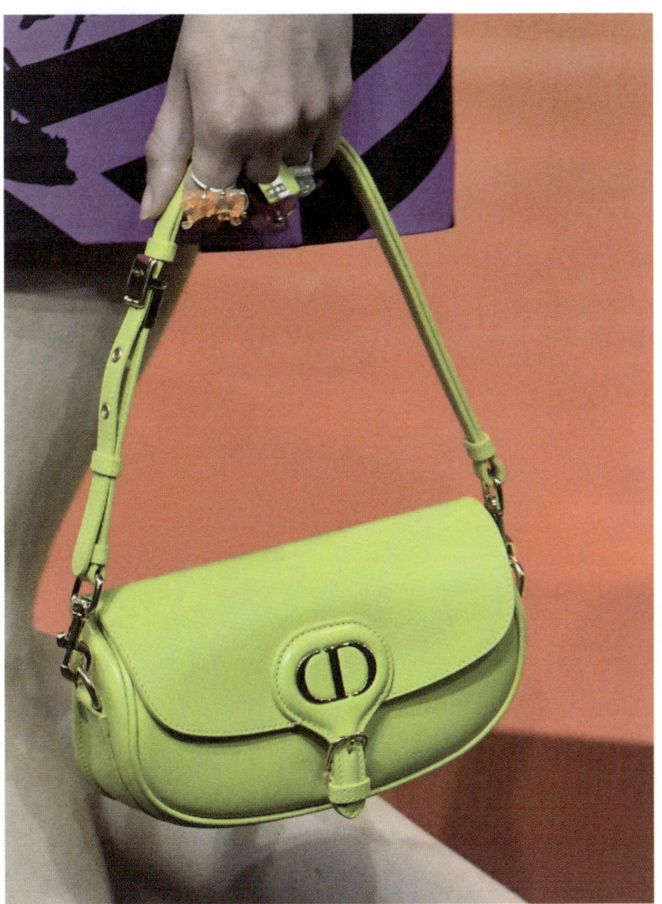

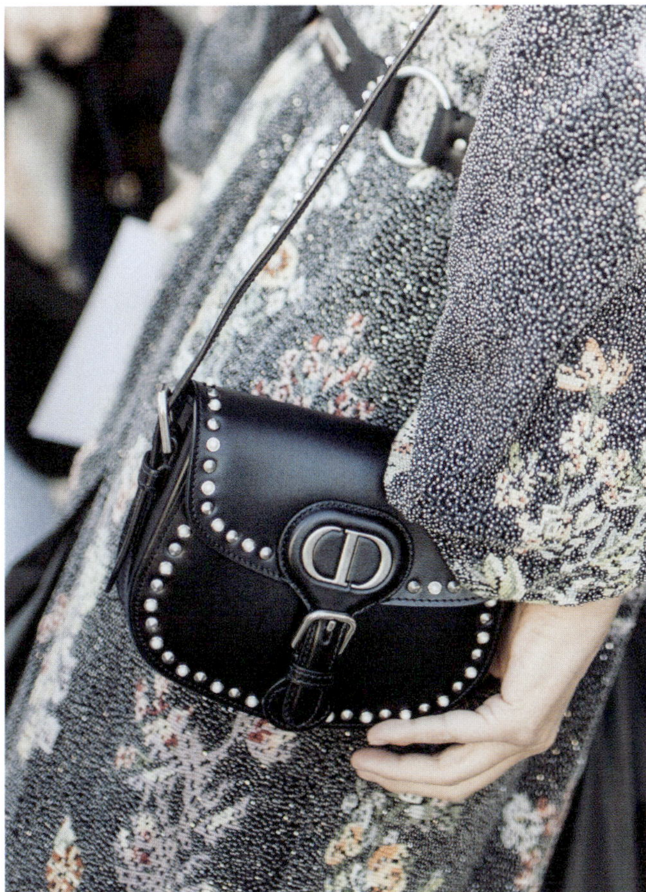

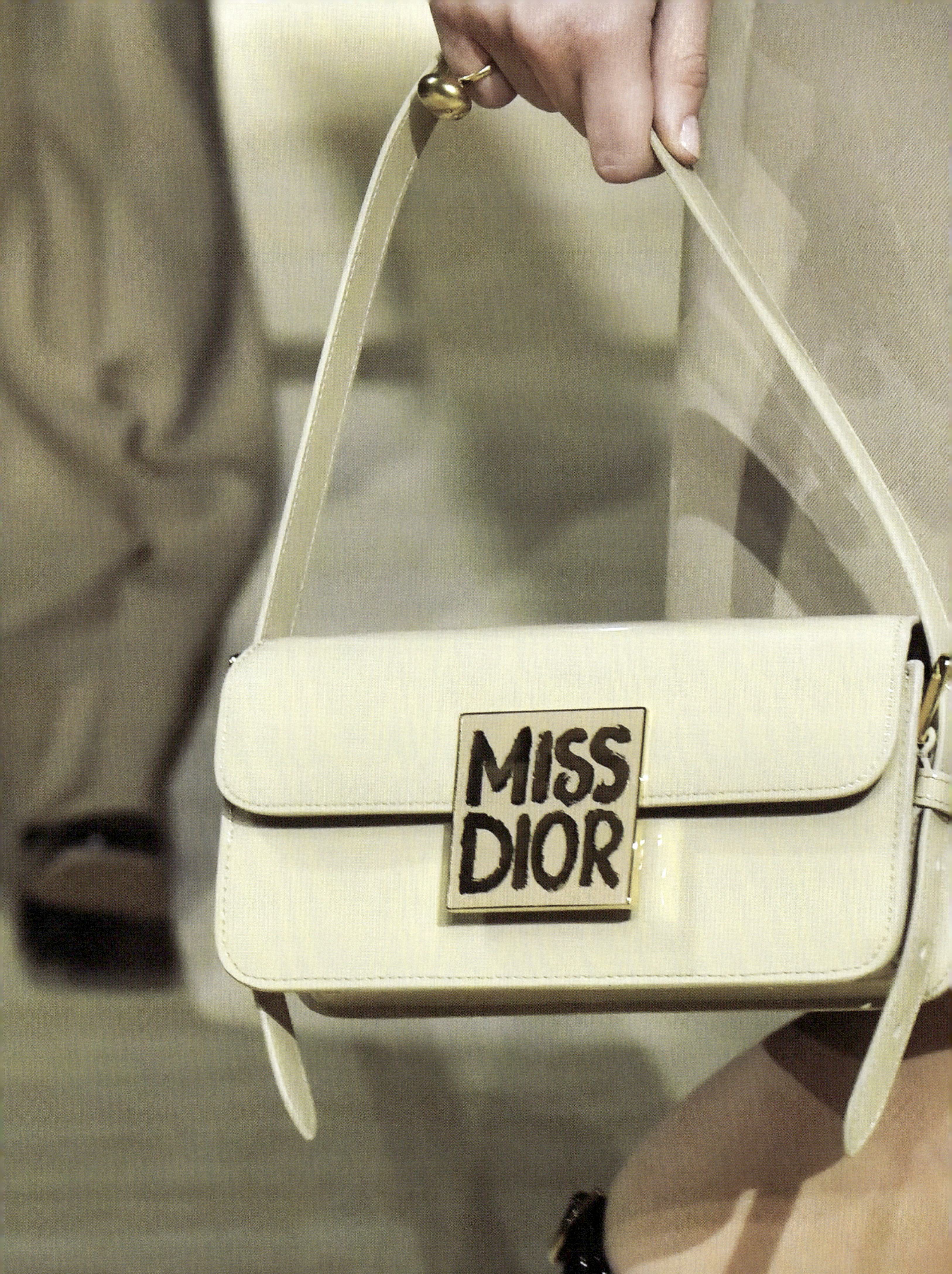
MISS
DIOR

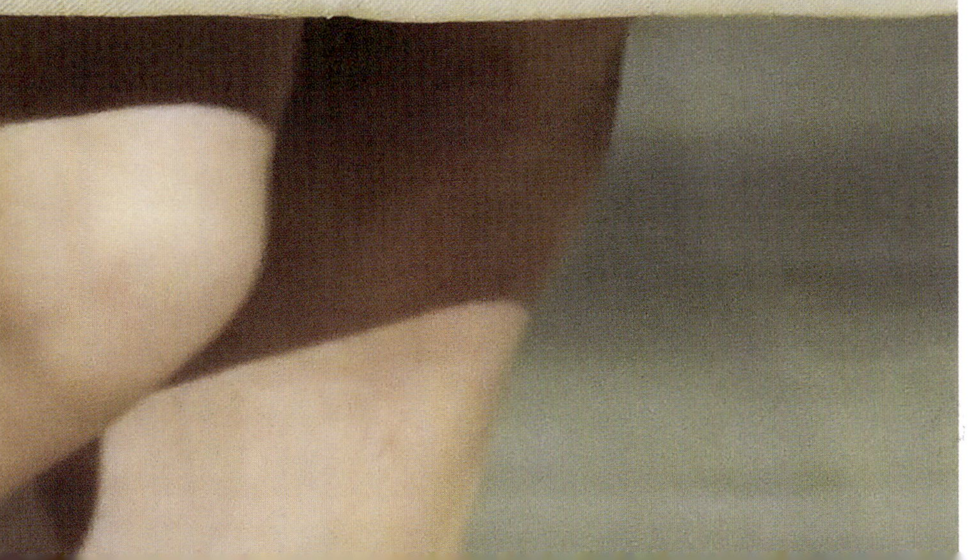

MISS DIOR

A model with a Miss Dior bag walks the runway at the Dior ready-to-wear Fall/Winter 2024 fashion show during Paris Fashion Week. The Miss Dior collection was first introduced in 1967 by Marc Bohan.

LADY D-JOY

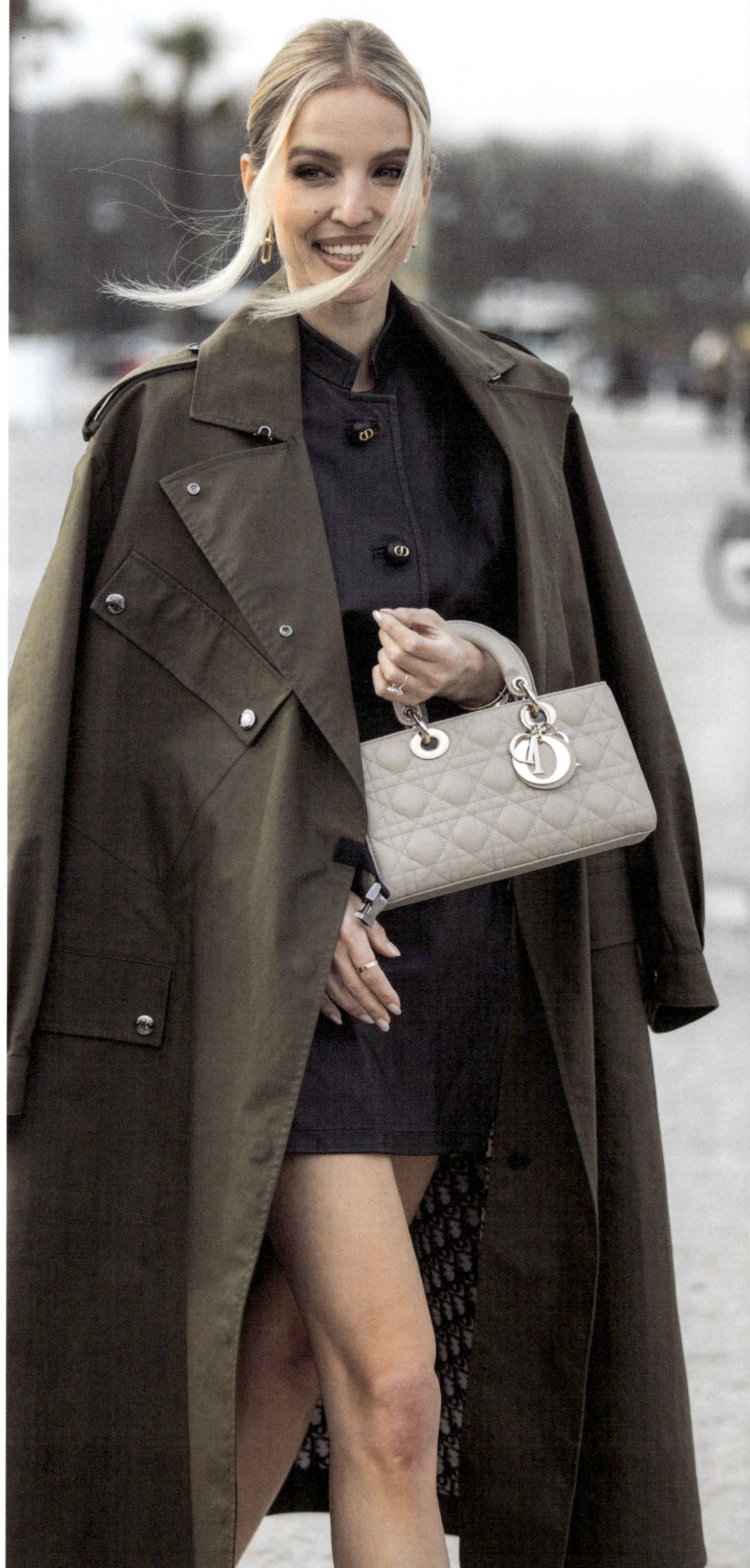

This page: Maria Grazia Chiuri reinvents the Lady Dior and introduces the Lady D-Joy with its elongated silhouette in the Fall 2022 collection. Leonie Hanne presents a cannage Lady D-Joy bag outside Dior during the Womenswear Fall/Winter 2025 show in Paris, 2025.

Next page: A visitor at New York Fashion Week showcases a Lady D-Joy featuring a floral print, 2025

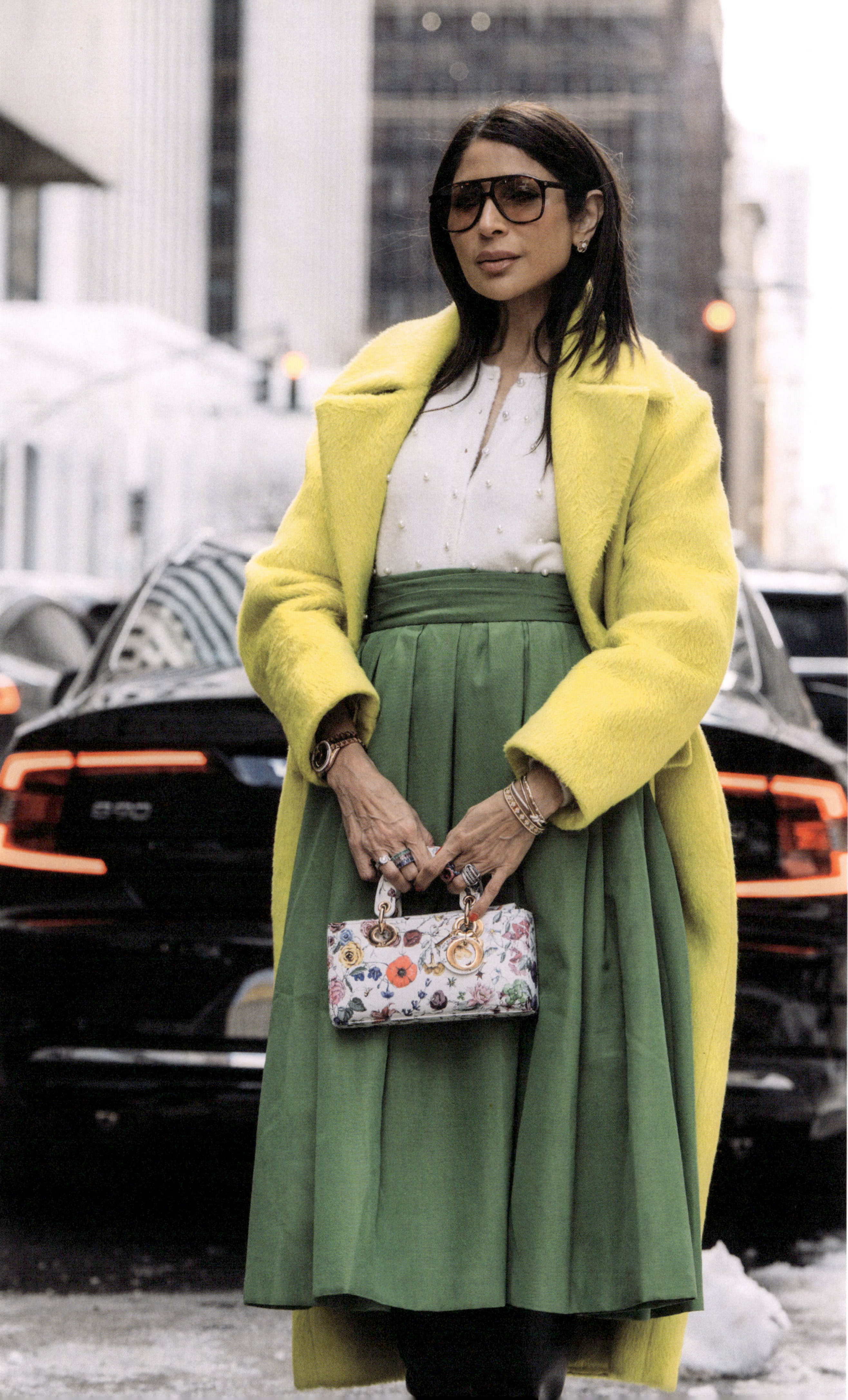

30 MONTAIGNE

30 Montaigne bags are displayed at a Dior store in Rome, 2020. This model is named after the address of the maison's first workshop.

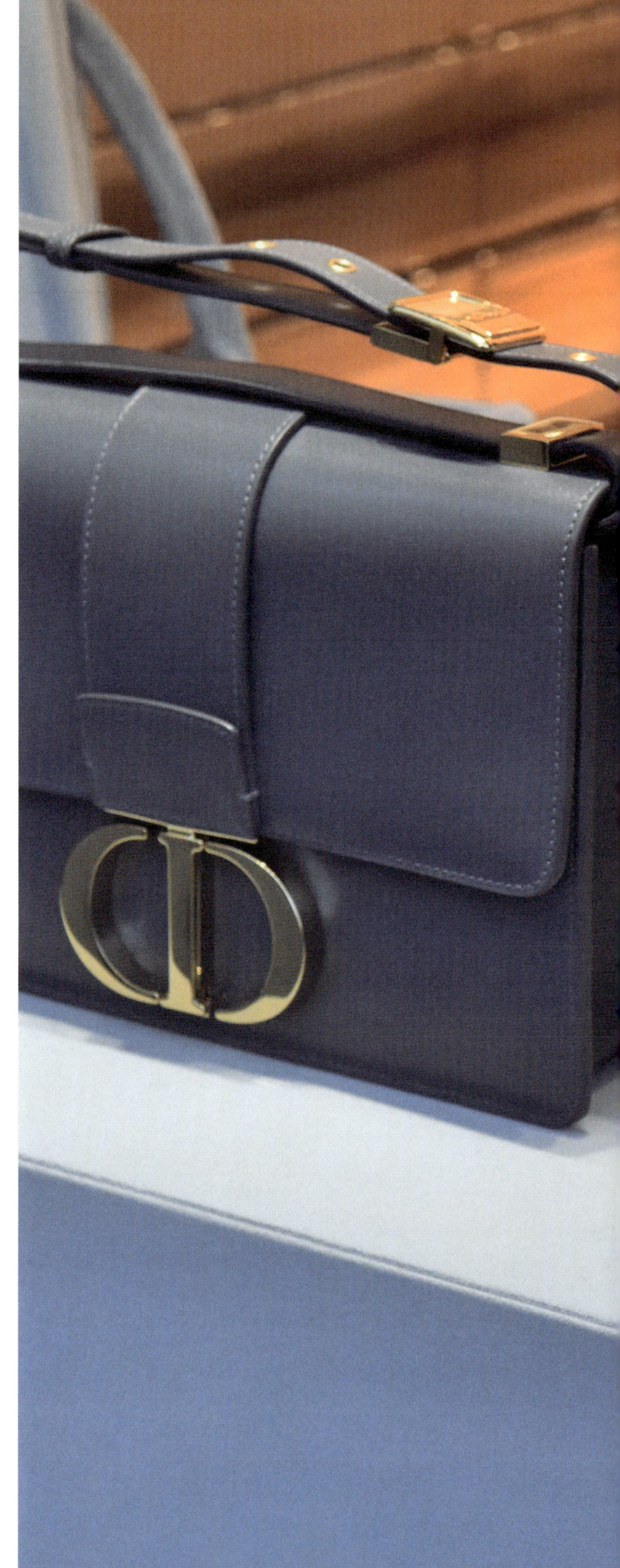

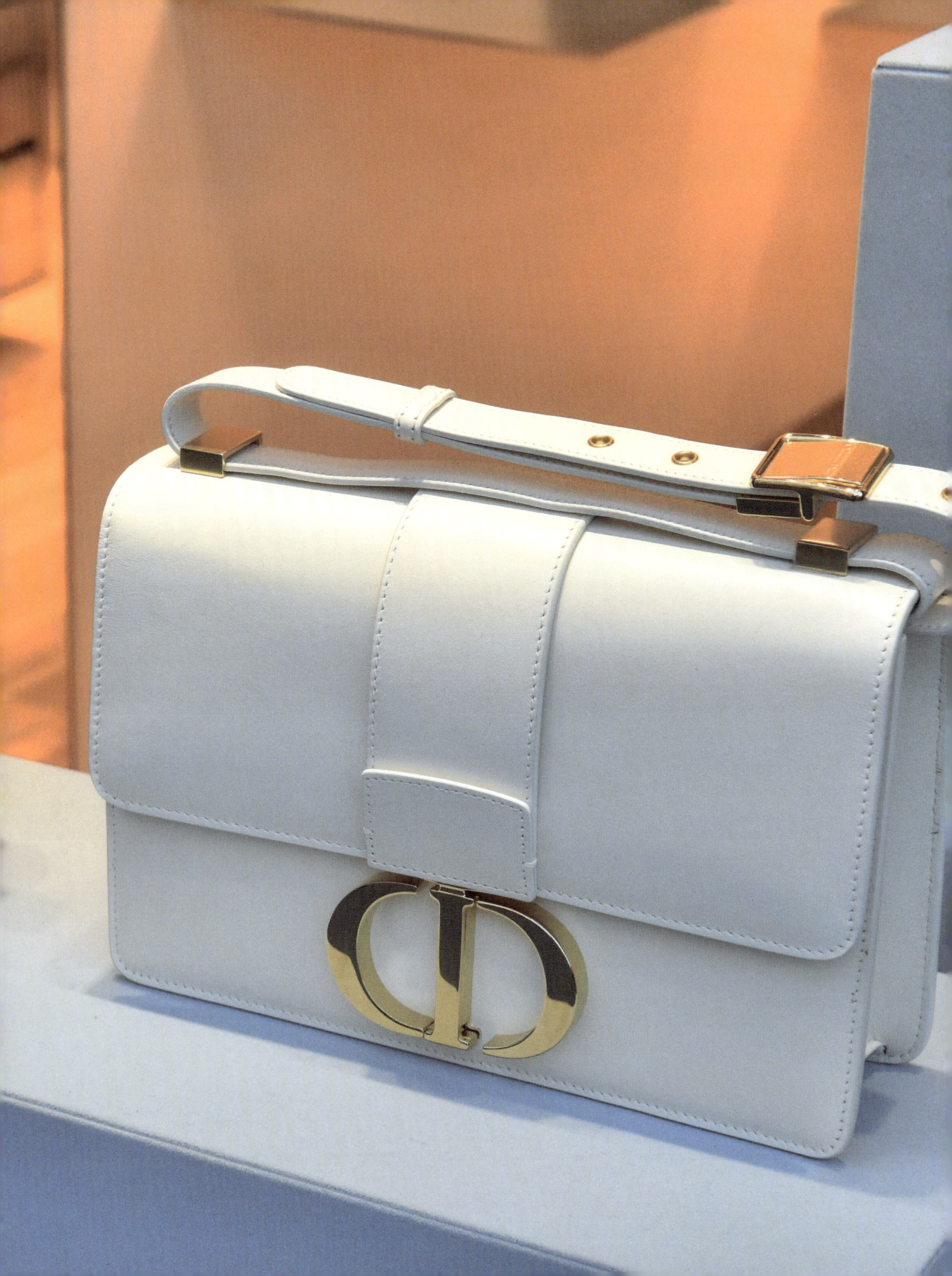

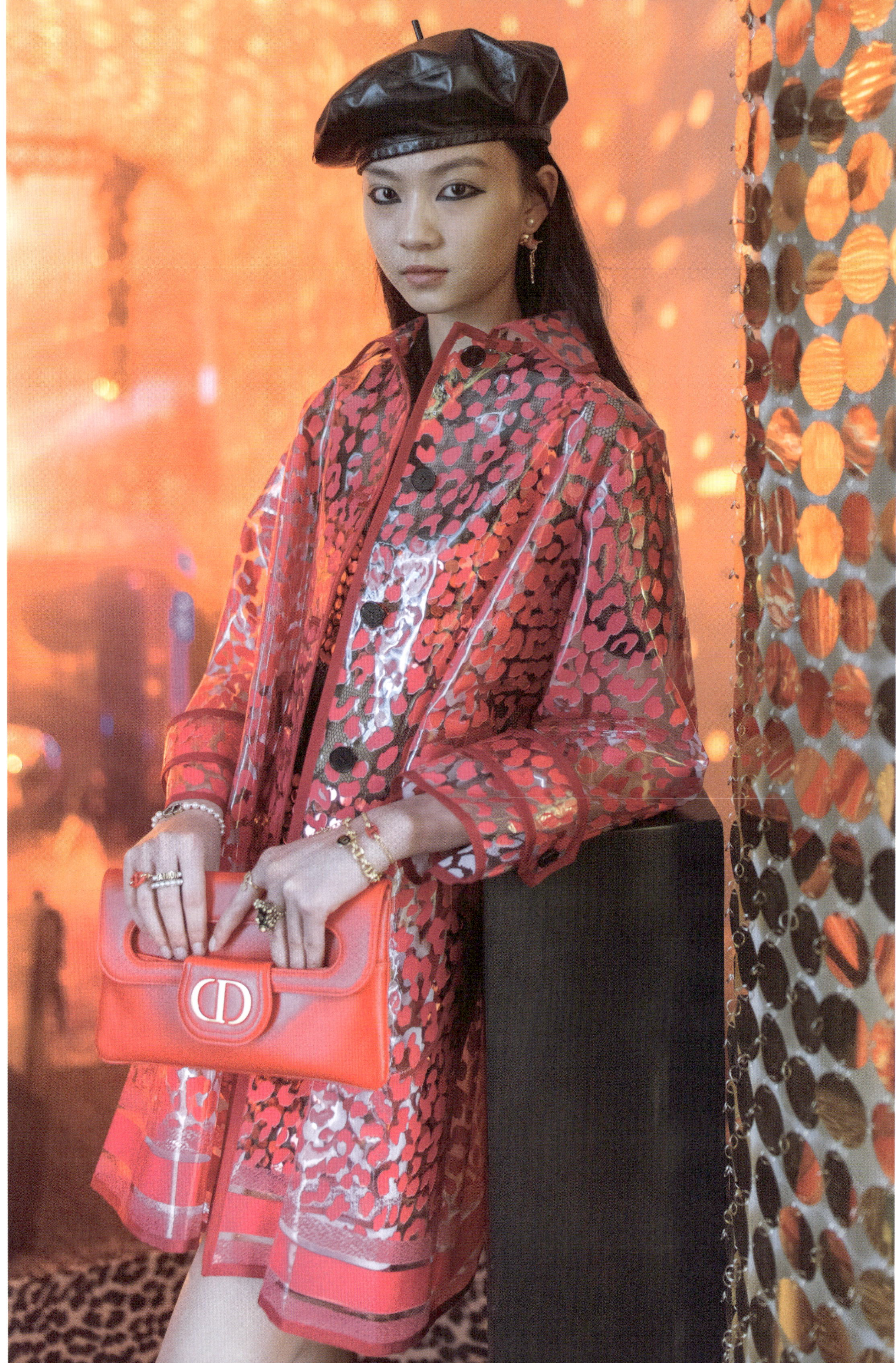

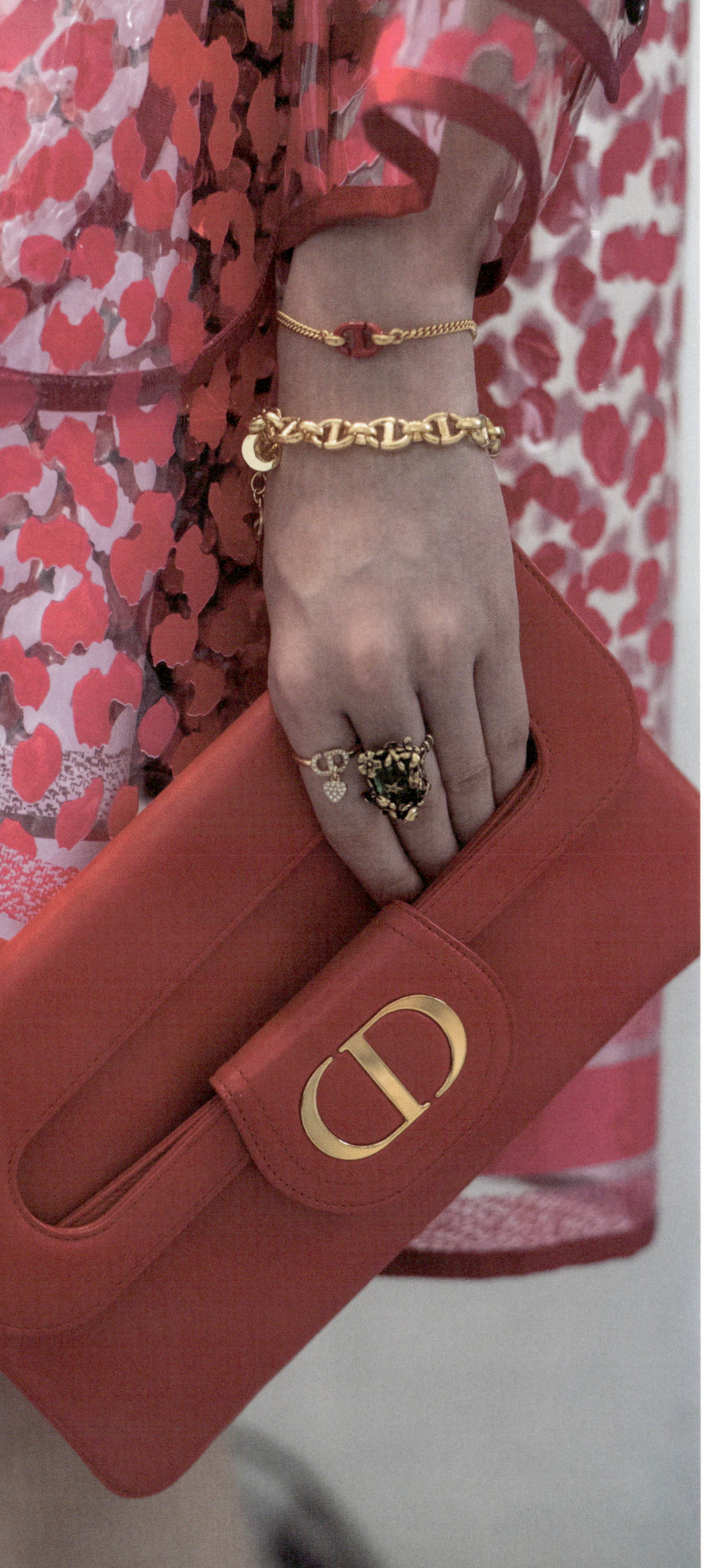

DIORDOUBLE

A DiorDouble is showcased at Shanghai Fashion Week 2021. This versatile bag can be used in three different ways: folded with a chain as a shoulder bag; folded without the chain as an elegant evening clutch; and when unfolded, it serves as a tote bag with a convenient leather handle

ST HONORÉ

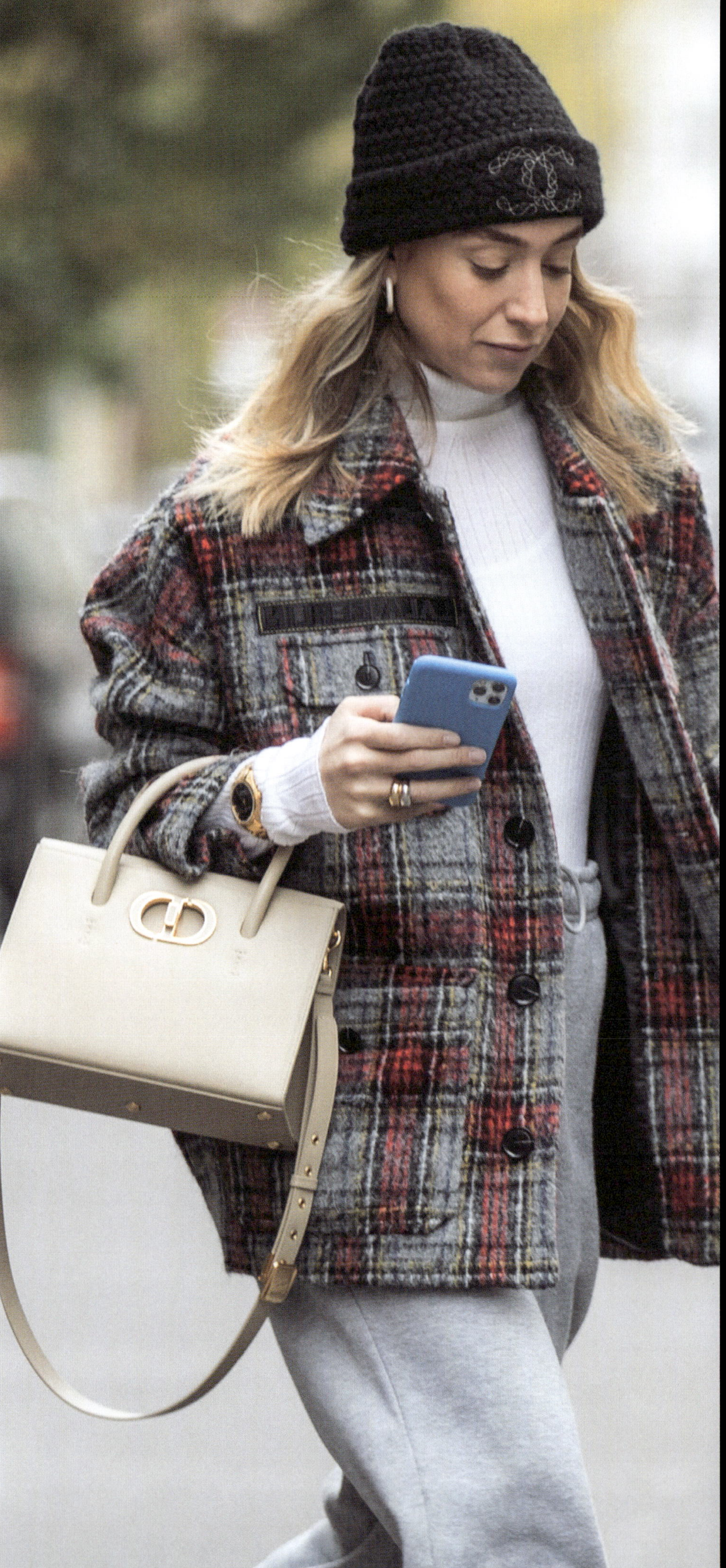

Sonia Lyson carries her St Honoré around Berlin on various occasions in 2020. The St Honoré debuted in the Cruise 2021 collection and is yet another It Bag designed by Maria Grazia Chiuri.

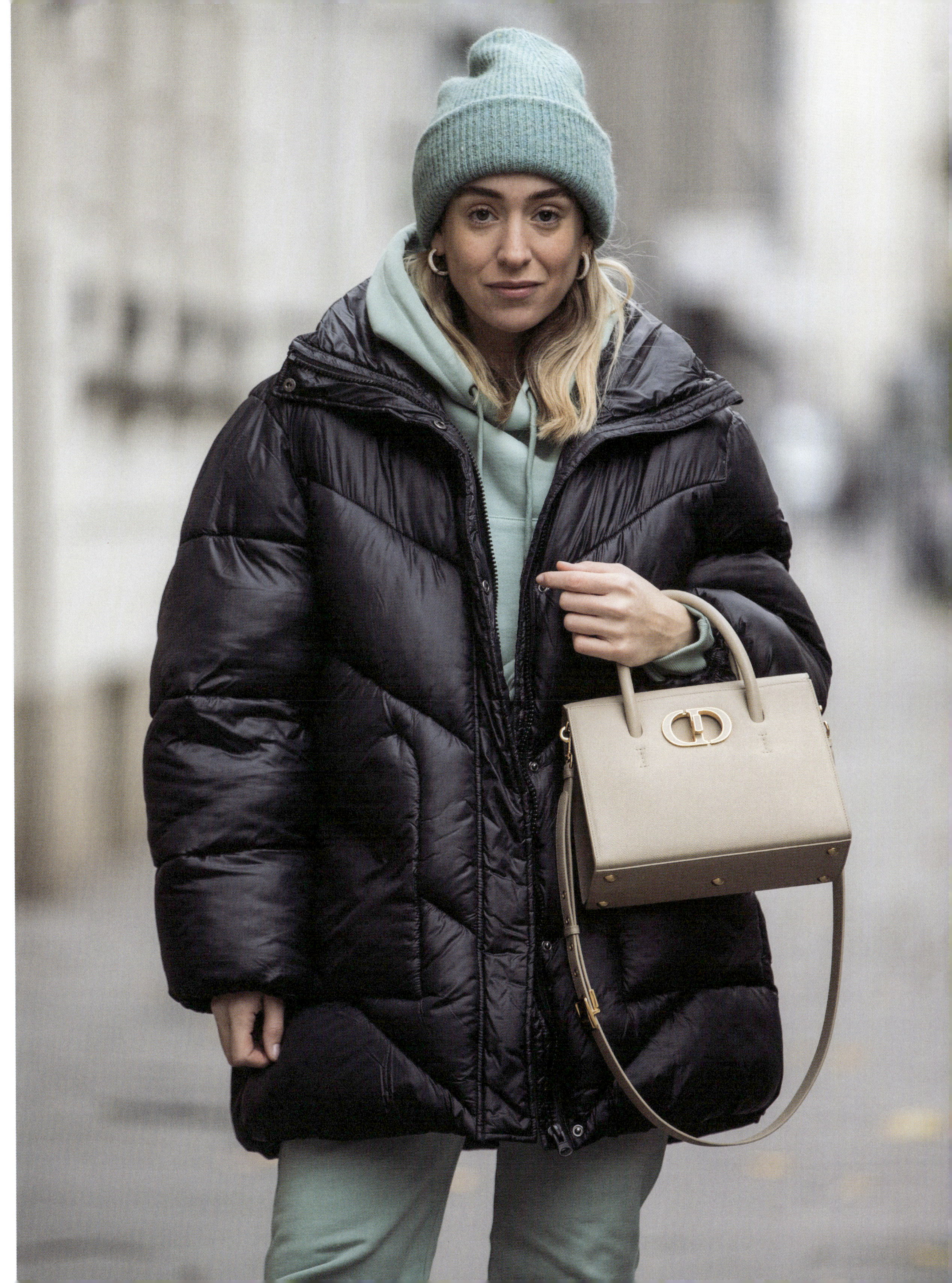

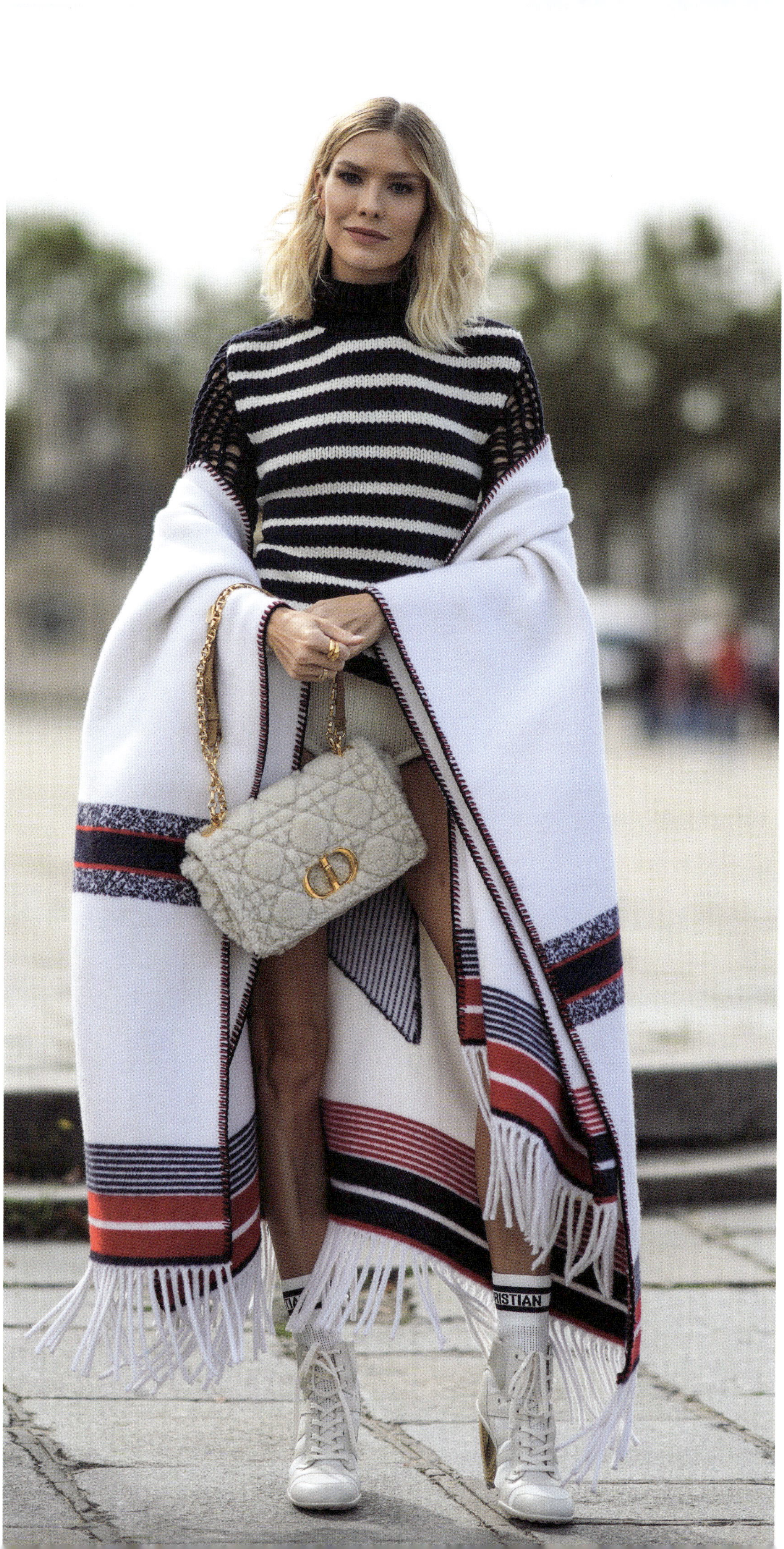

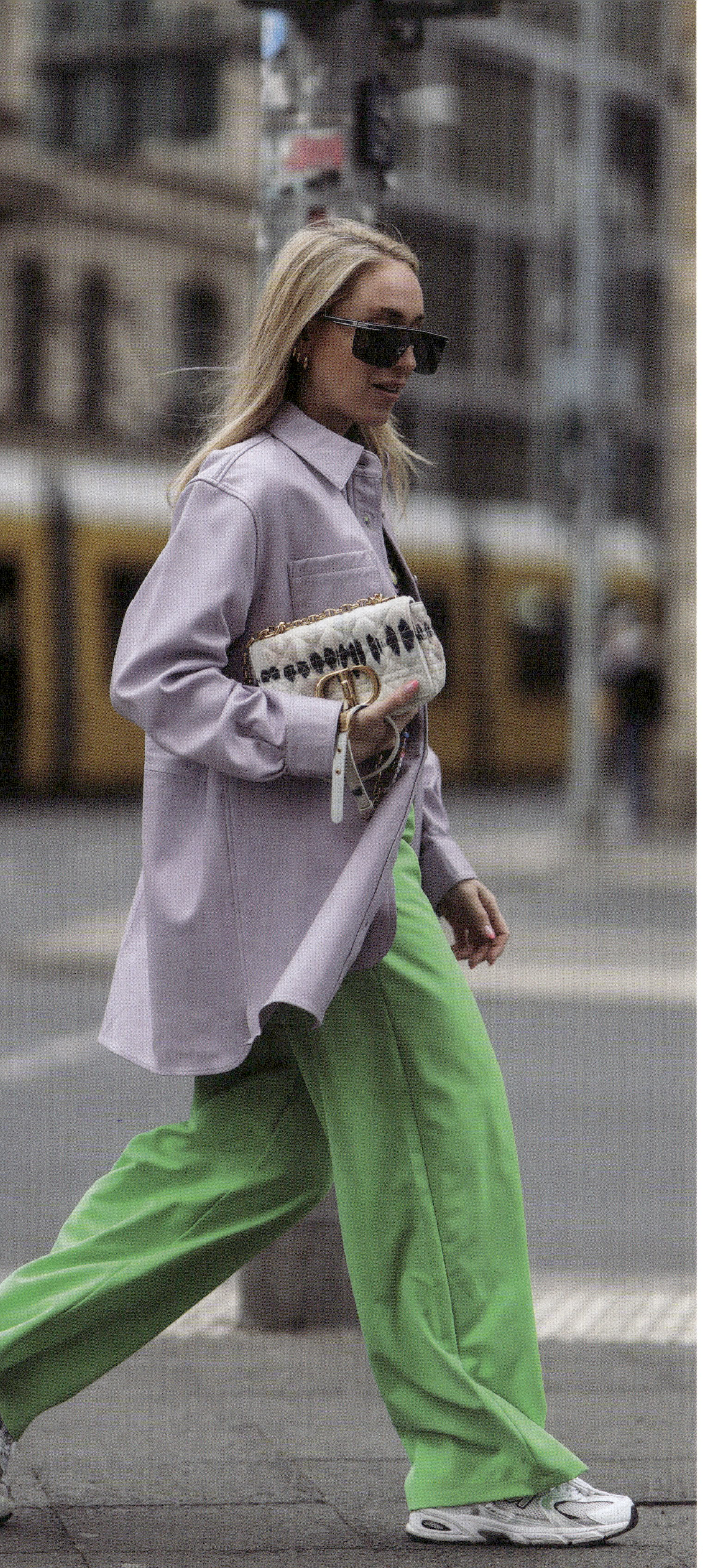

CARO

Previous page: Lena Perminova showcases a beige fluffy Caro handbag with a *cannage* design outside the Dior show during Spring/Summer 2022 Paris Fashion Week, 2021. Named after Christian Dior's sister, whose nickname was Caro, it launched on New Year's Day 2021.

This page: Sonia Lyson presents a small denim tie-dye Caro on her arm in Berlin, 2021

Pages 106/107: Lea Naumann carries her black leather Caro through Berlin, 2021

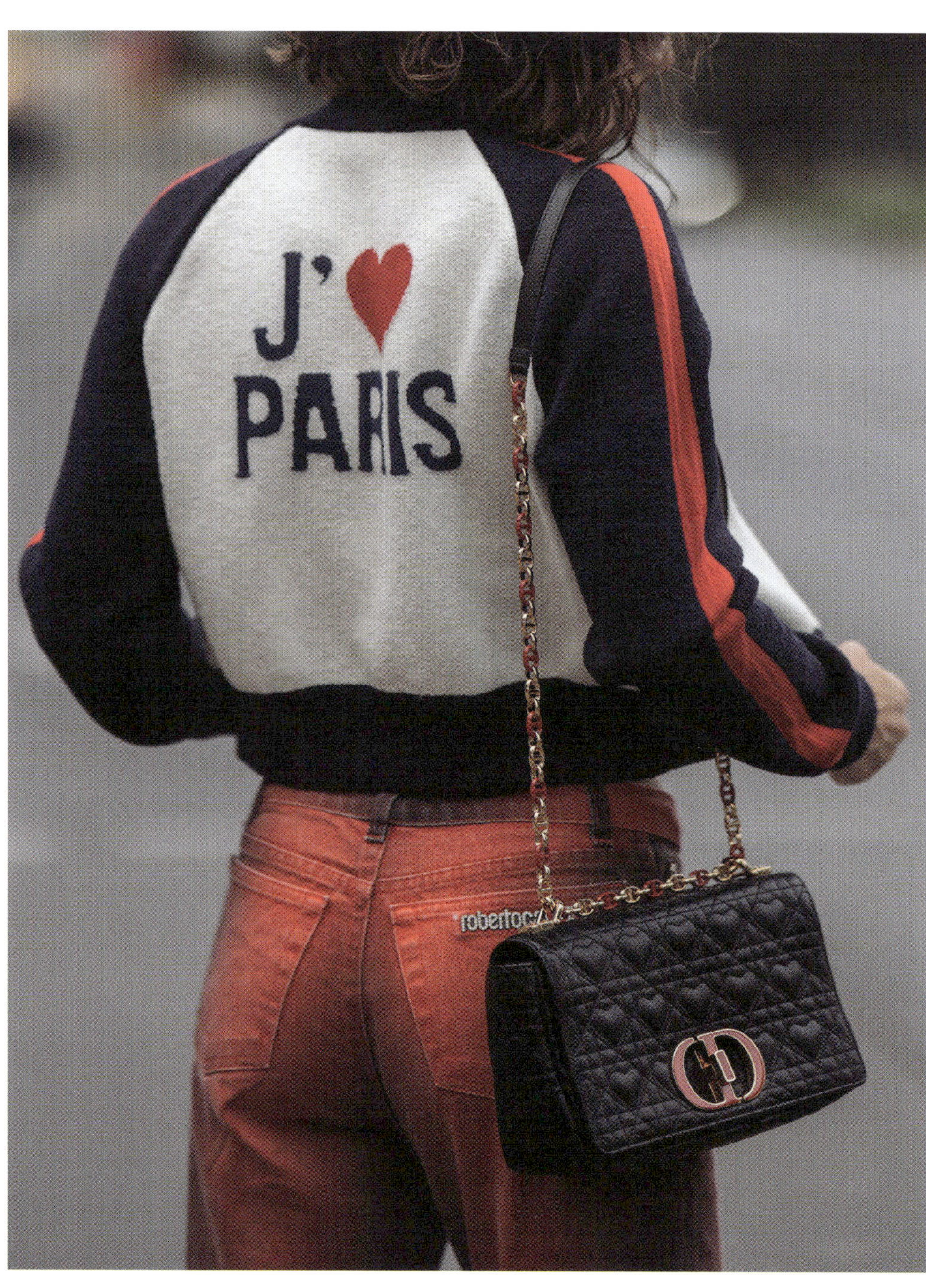
J’ ♥
PARIS

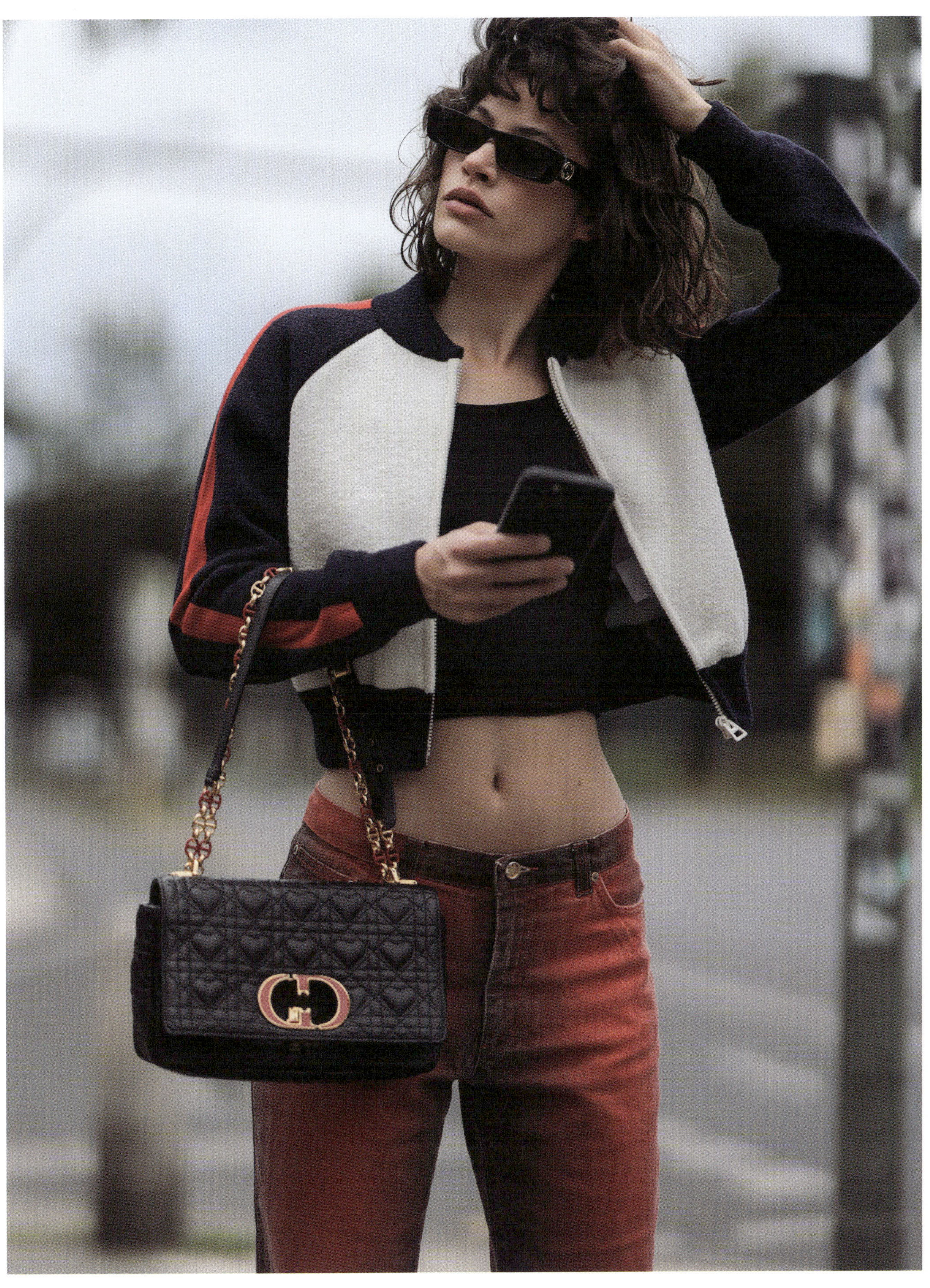

DIORISSIMO

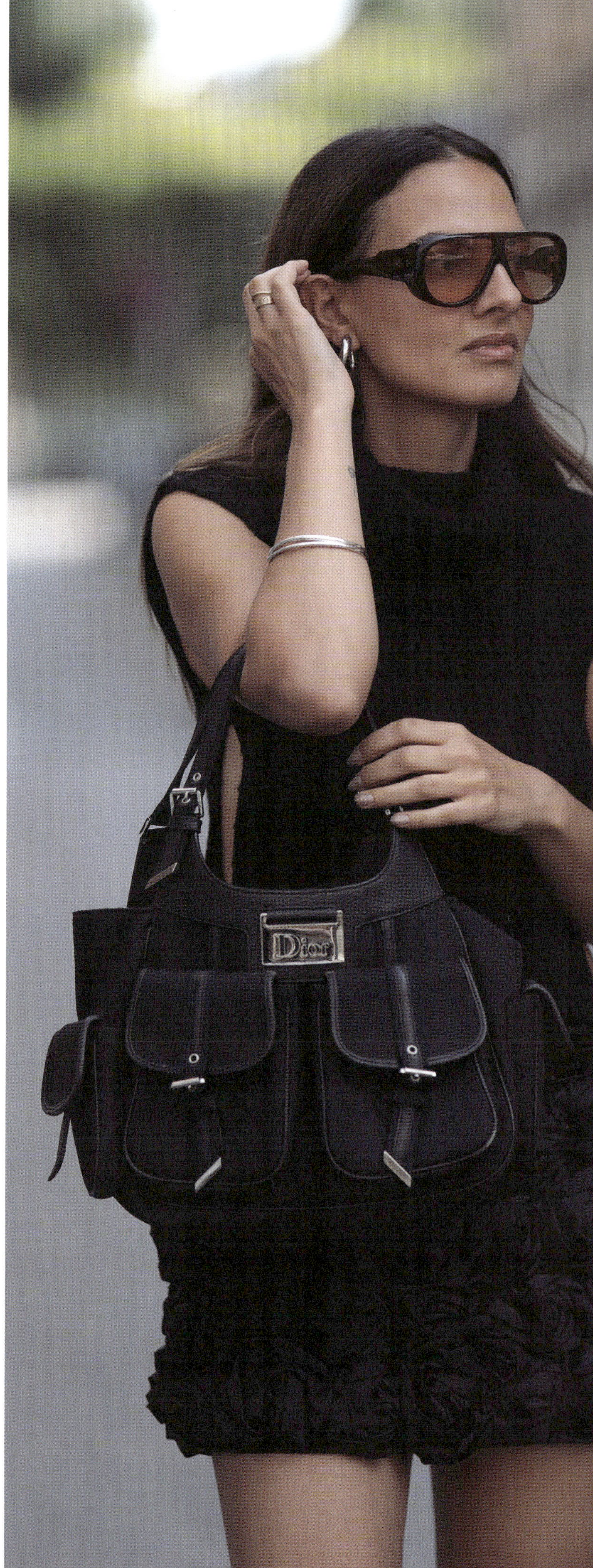

Anna Winter (left), carrying a Diorissimo multi-pocket shoulder bag, and Alessa Winter (right) attend Spring/Summer 2025 Copenhagen Fashion Week, 2024

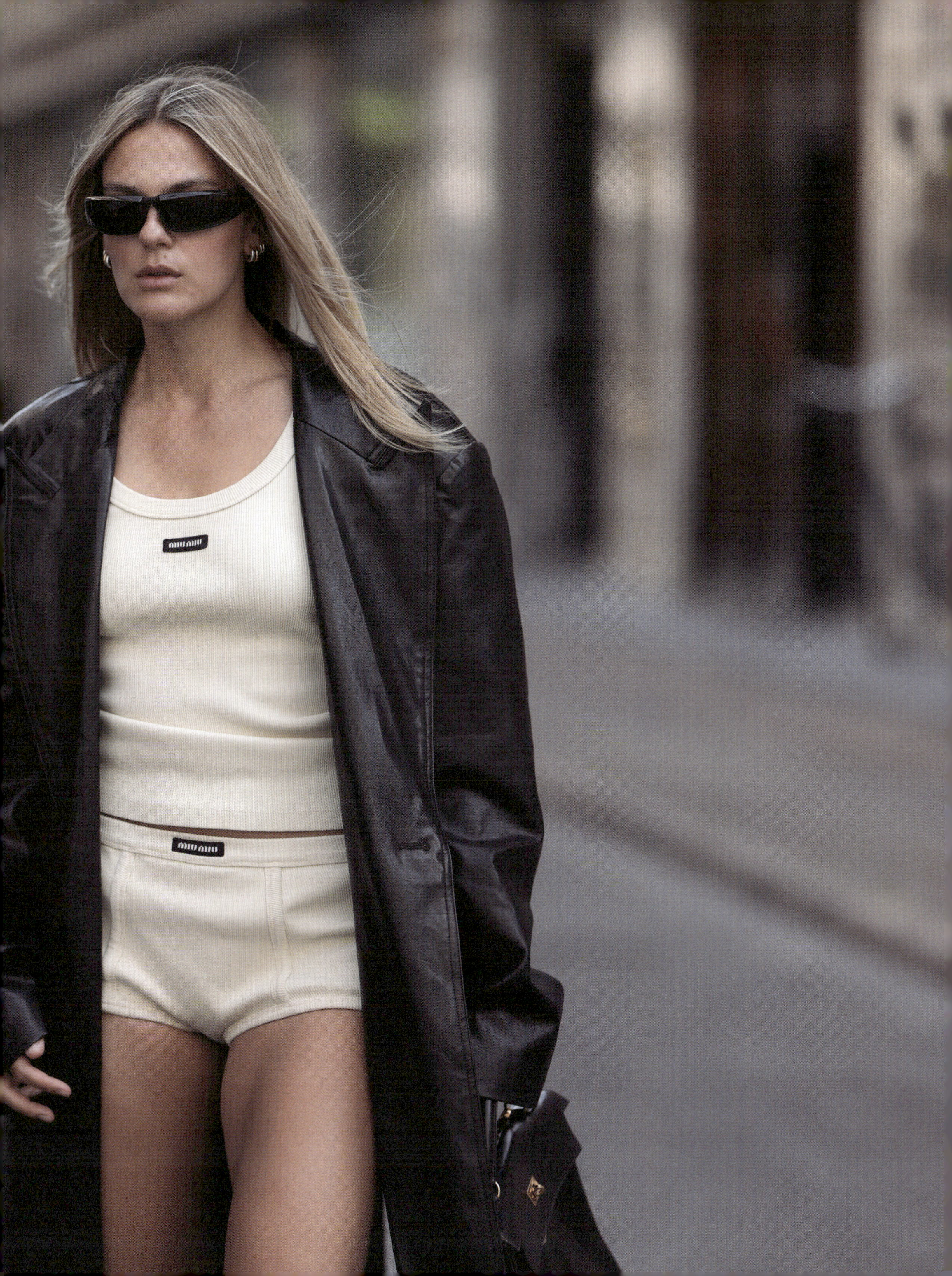
miu miu
miu miu

DIOREVER

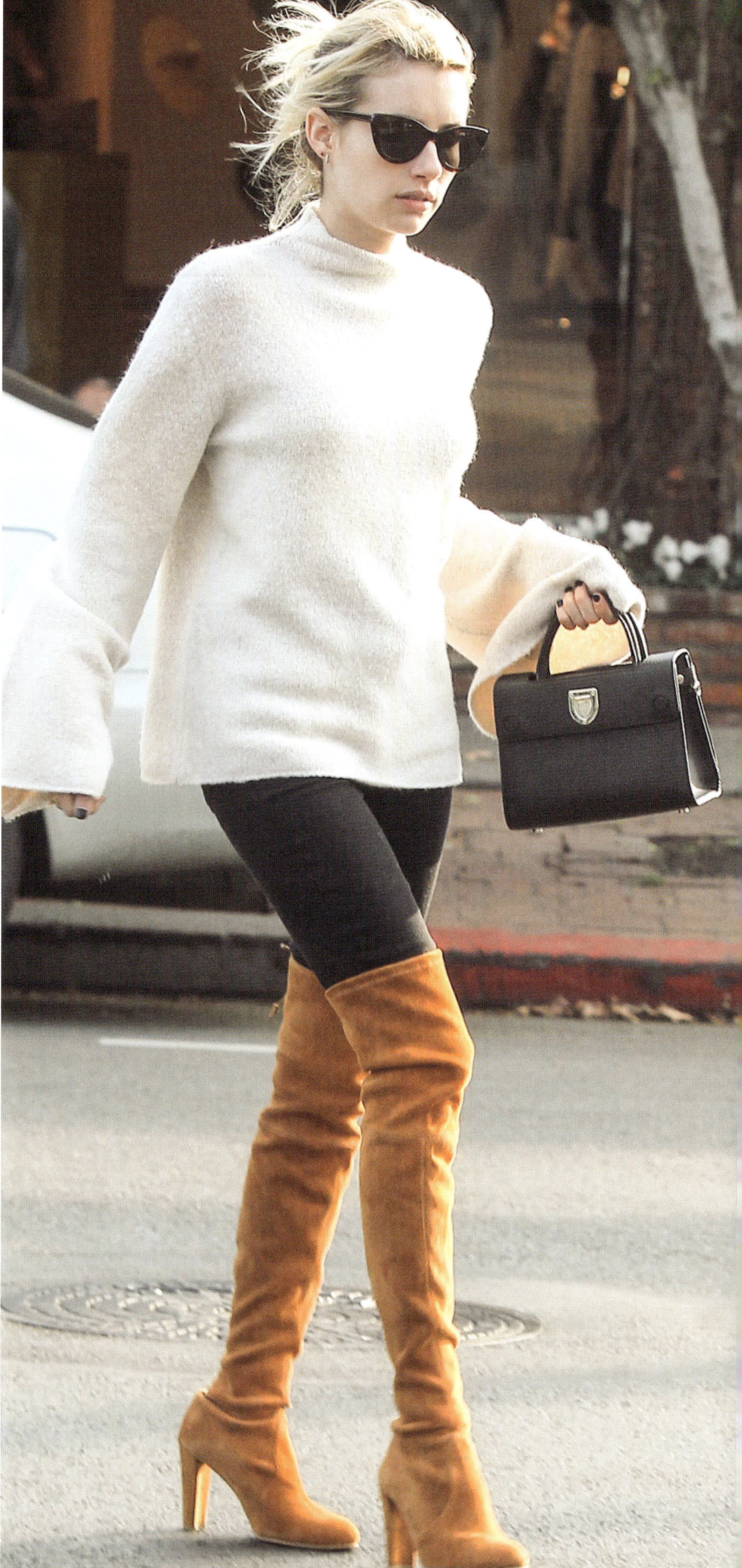

Emma Roberts is seen with a Diorever bag in Los Angeles, 2016. The Diorever was introduced in the Spring/Summer 2016 collection and rapidly gained popularity among celebrities; for instance, Rihanna was spotted with it while Jennifer Lawrence became the face of the Diorever advertising campaign.

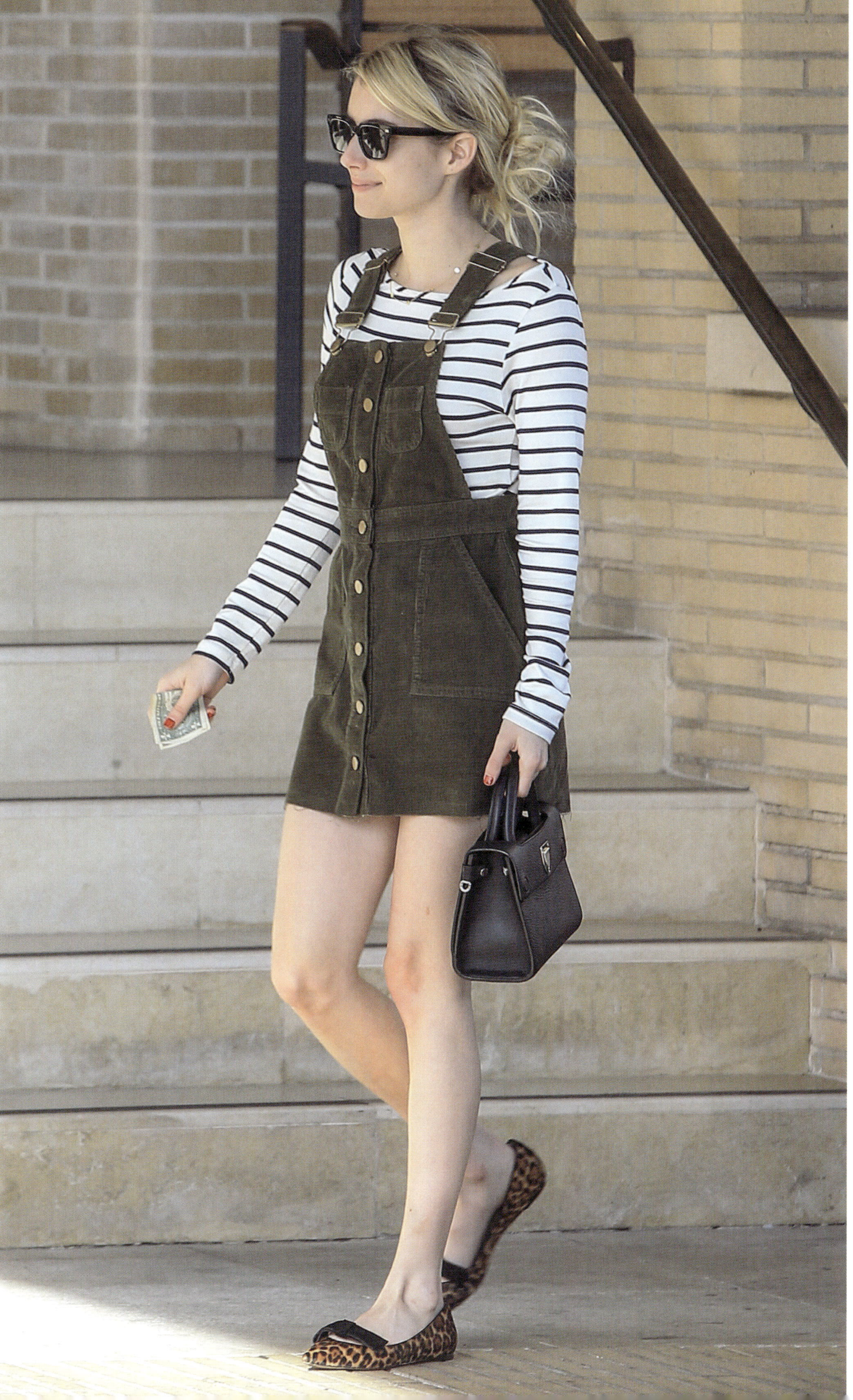

VIBE

Pages 113,115,119: Vibe bags designed by Maria Grazia Chiuri are featured at Dior's Womenswear Spring/Summer 2022 show in Paris, September 2021

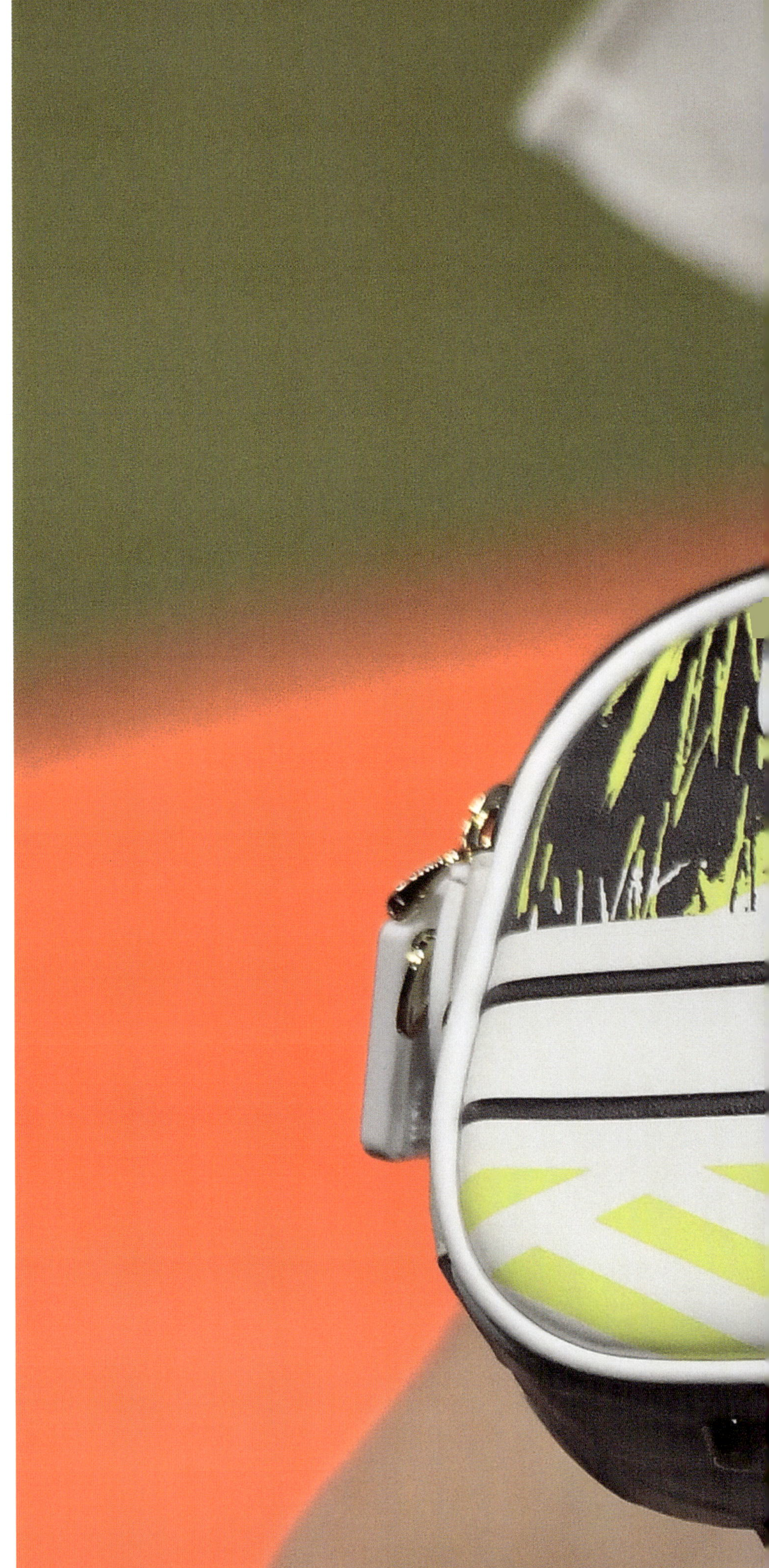

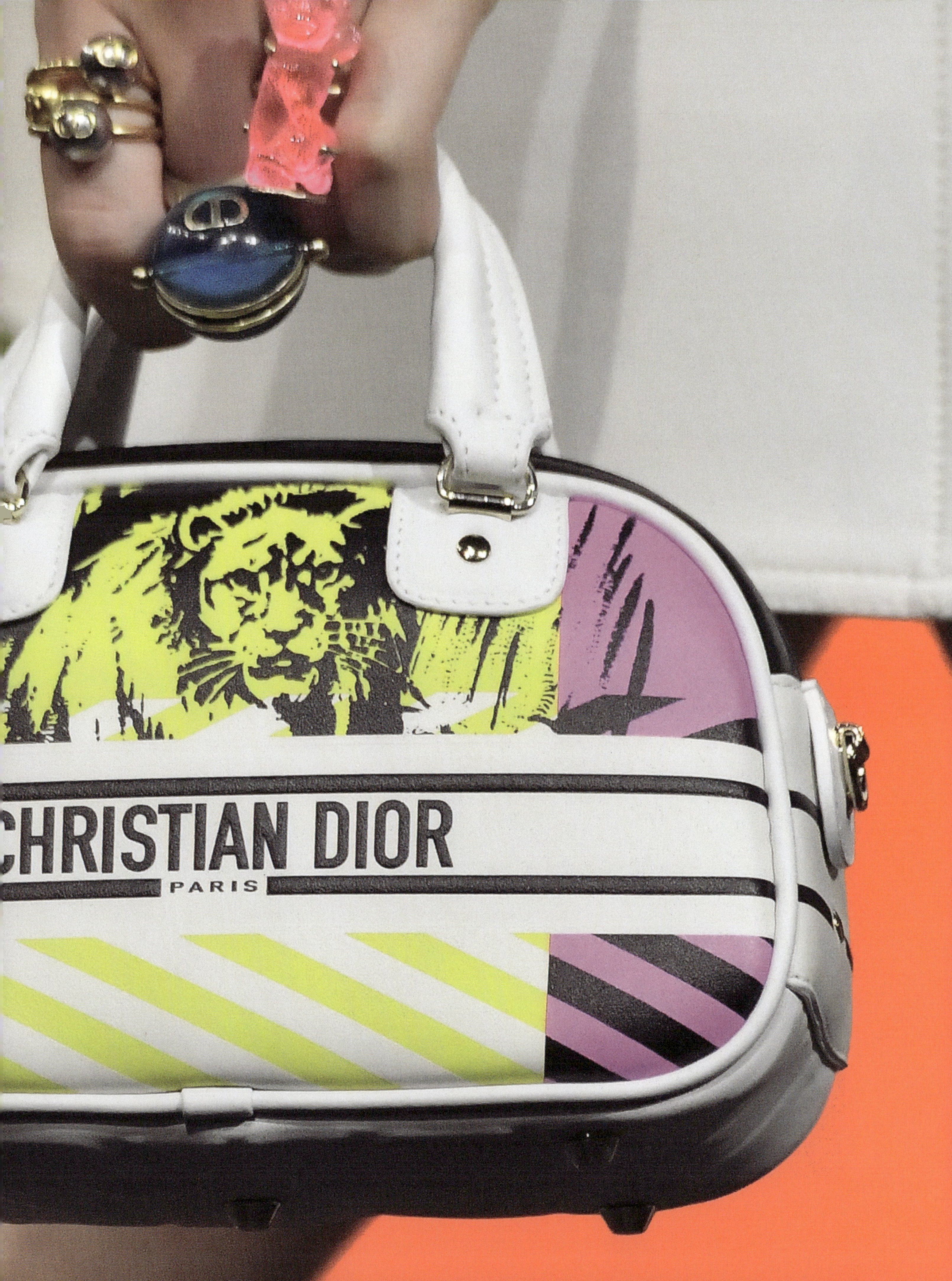
CHRISTIAN DIOR
PARIS

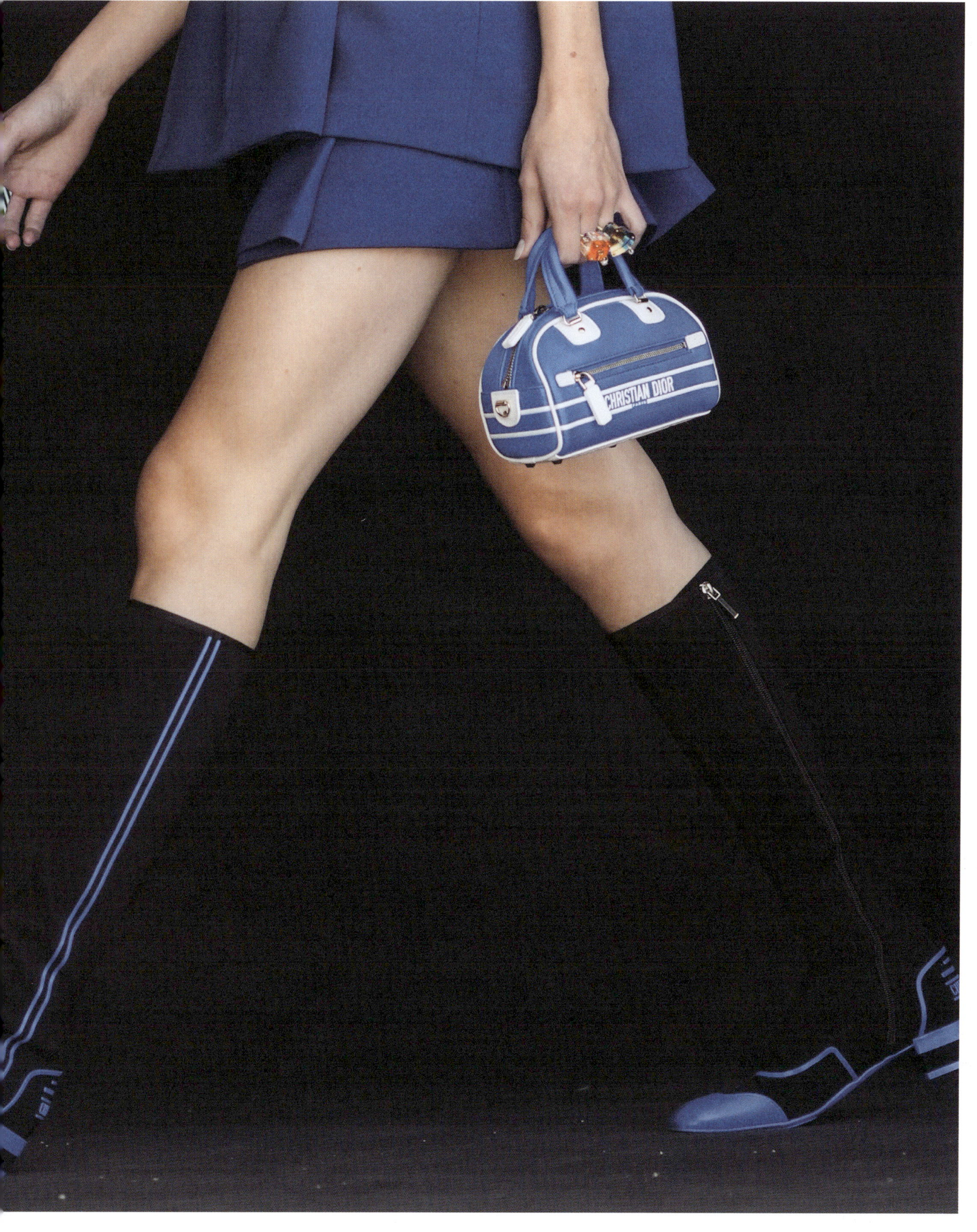
CHRISTIAN DIOR
PARIS

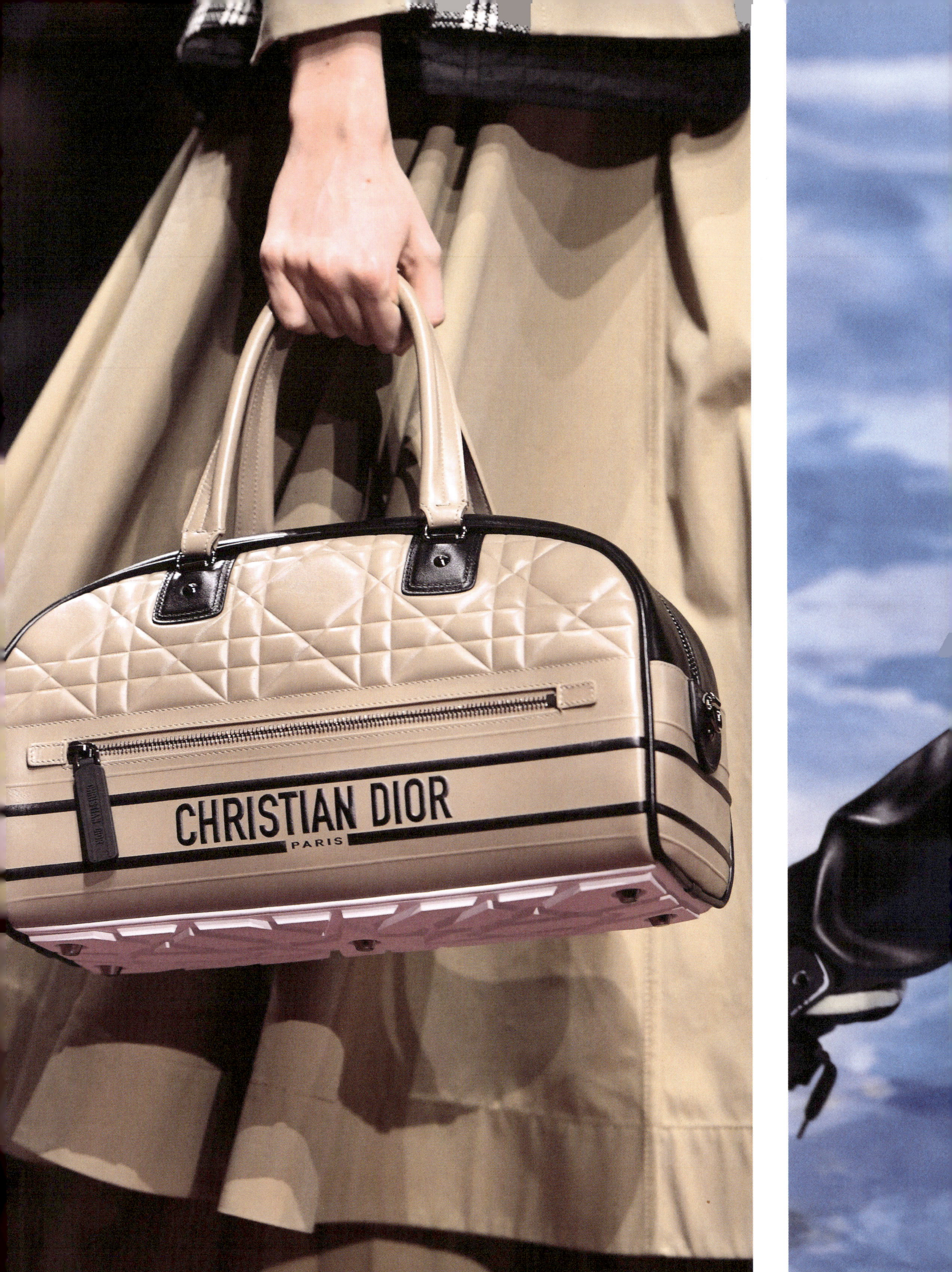
CHRISTIAN DIOR
PARIS

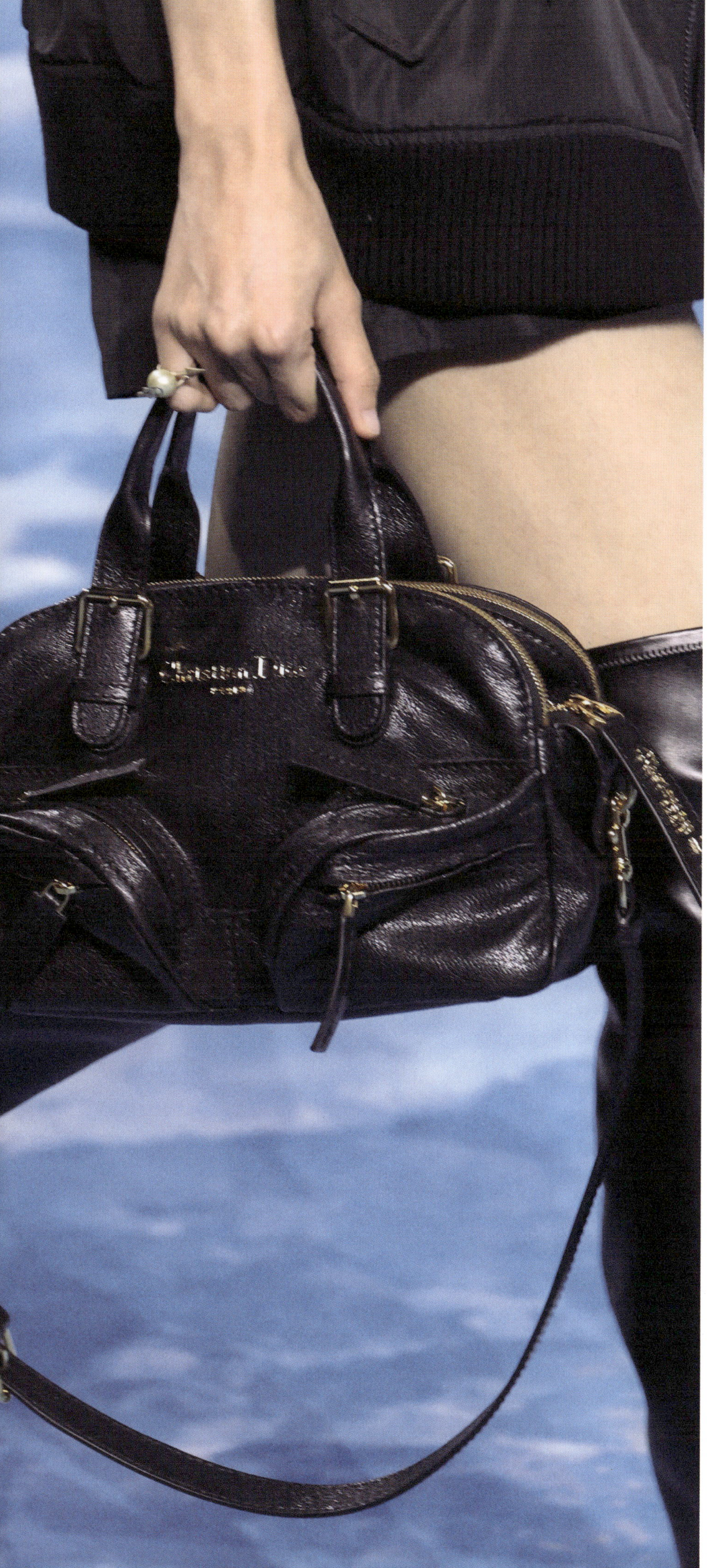

BOWLING BAGS

117

Previous page: A model walks the runway with a Vibe Bowling Bag during the Dior Womenswear Fall/Winter 2022 show in Paris, March 2022

This page: A small Grand Tour Bowling bag is showcased on the runway at Dior's Spring/Summer 2025 Womenswear show in Paris, September 2024

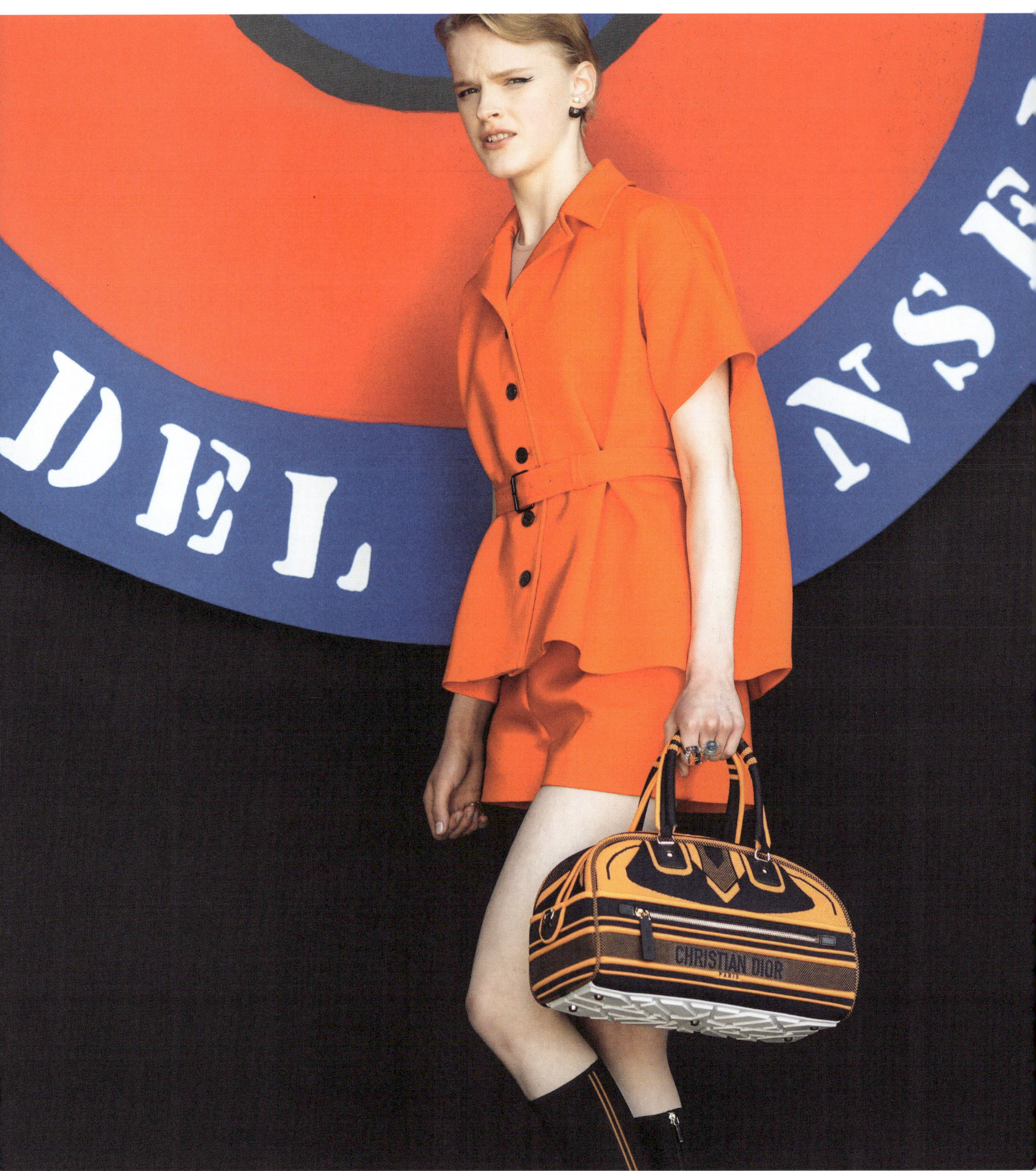
DEL
CHRISTIAN DIOR
PARIS

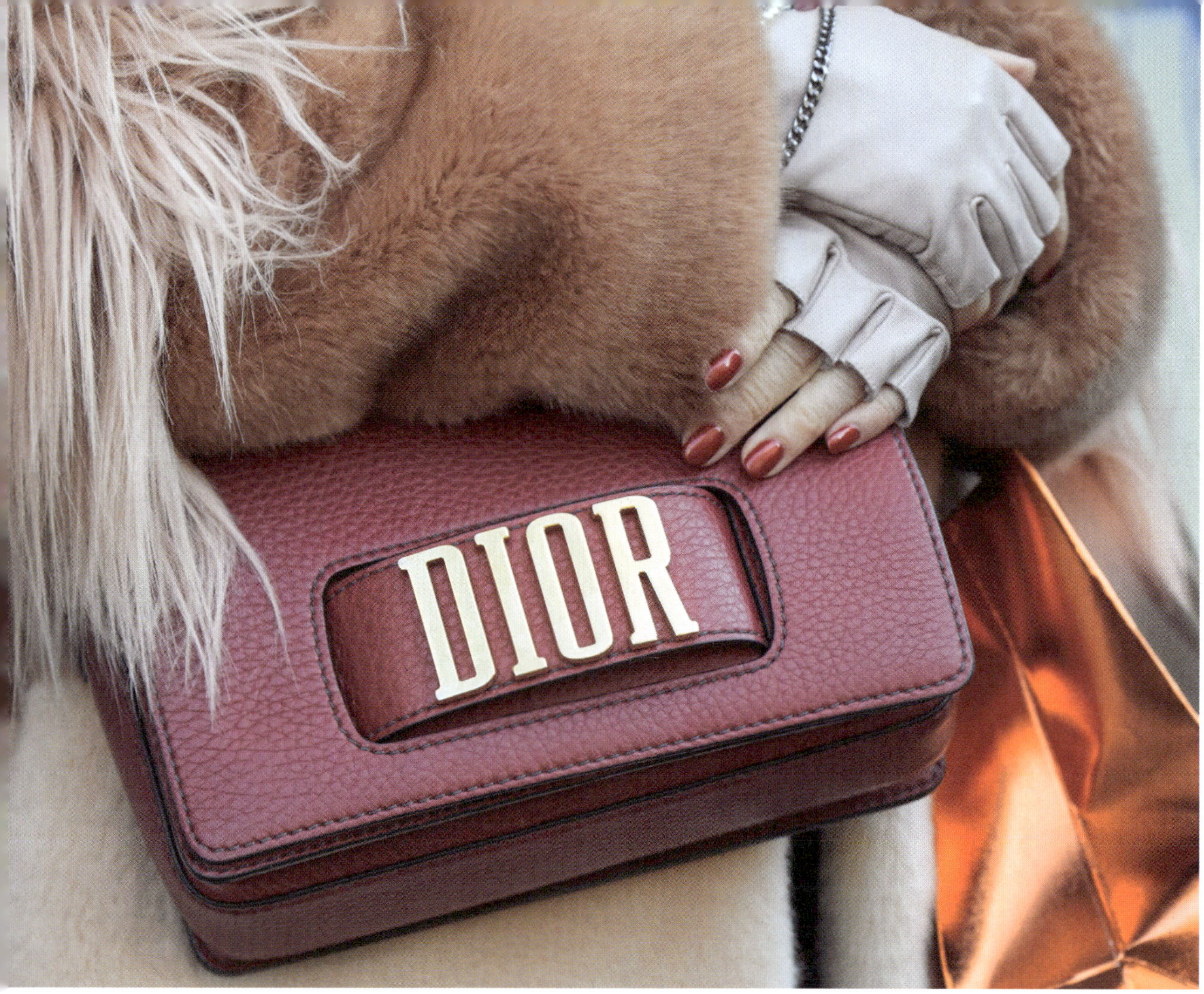

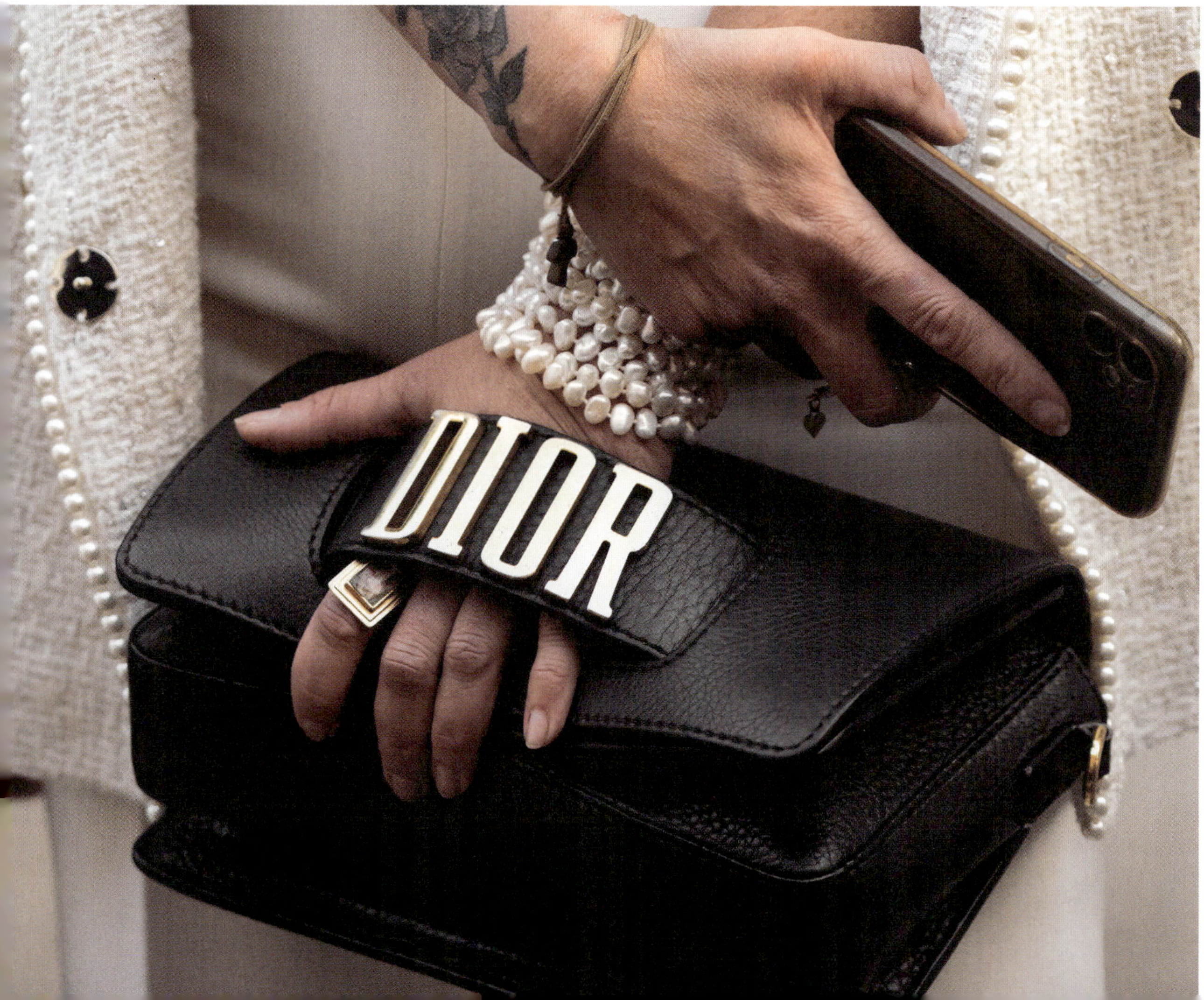

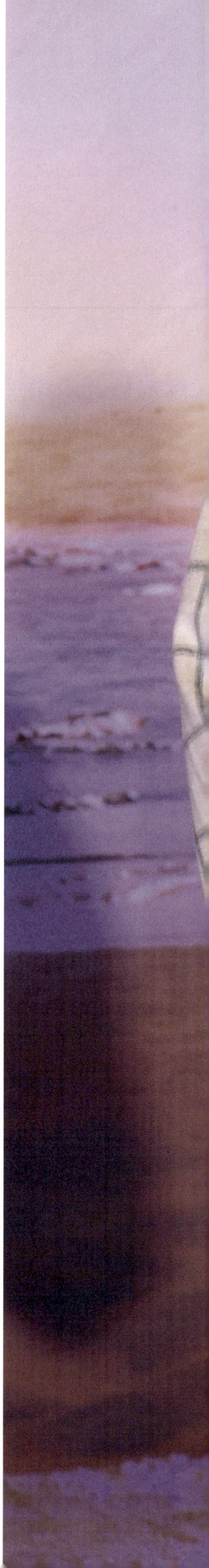

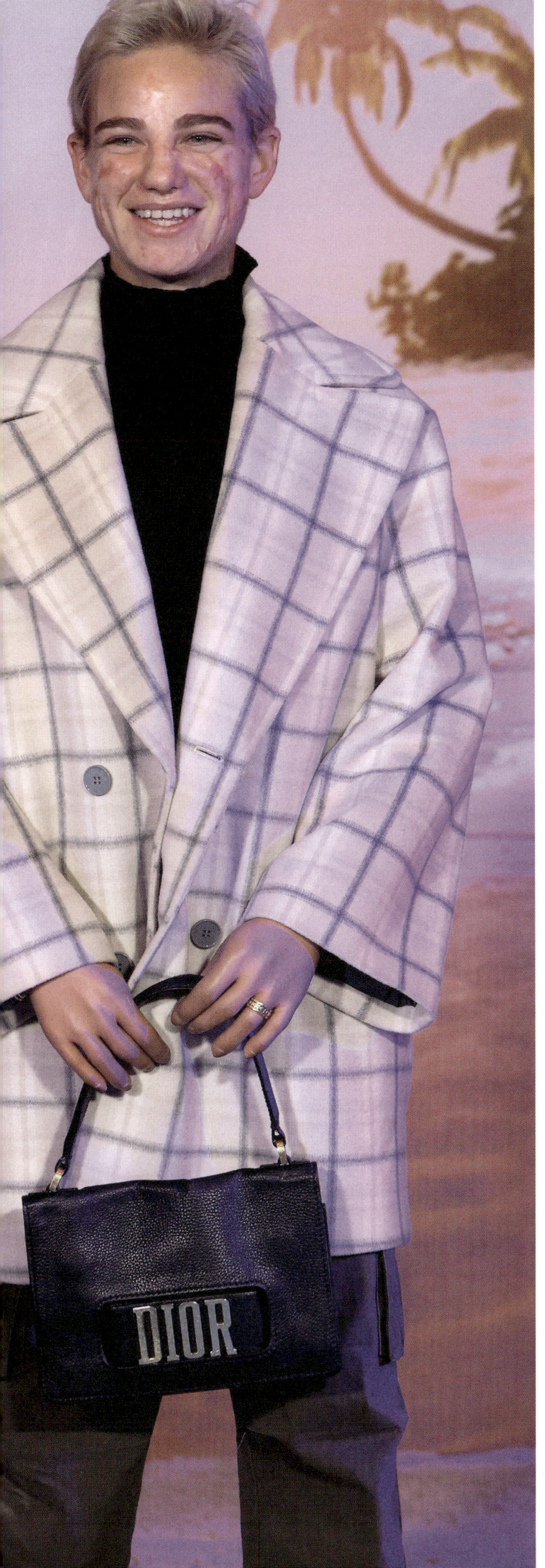

DIO(R)EVOLUTION

Previous page: Close-ups of the Dio(r)evolution are featured in Milan. The flap bag was first presented in 2017. Thanks to the slot handclasp, it can be worn as a clutch or as a shoulder bag with a strap.

This page: Bebe Vio attends the *Oceania 2* premiere at The Space Cinema Moderno, carrying a Dio(r)evolution in Rome, 2024

DIORADDICT

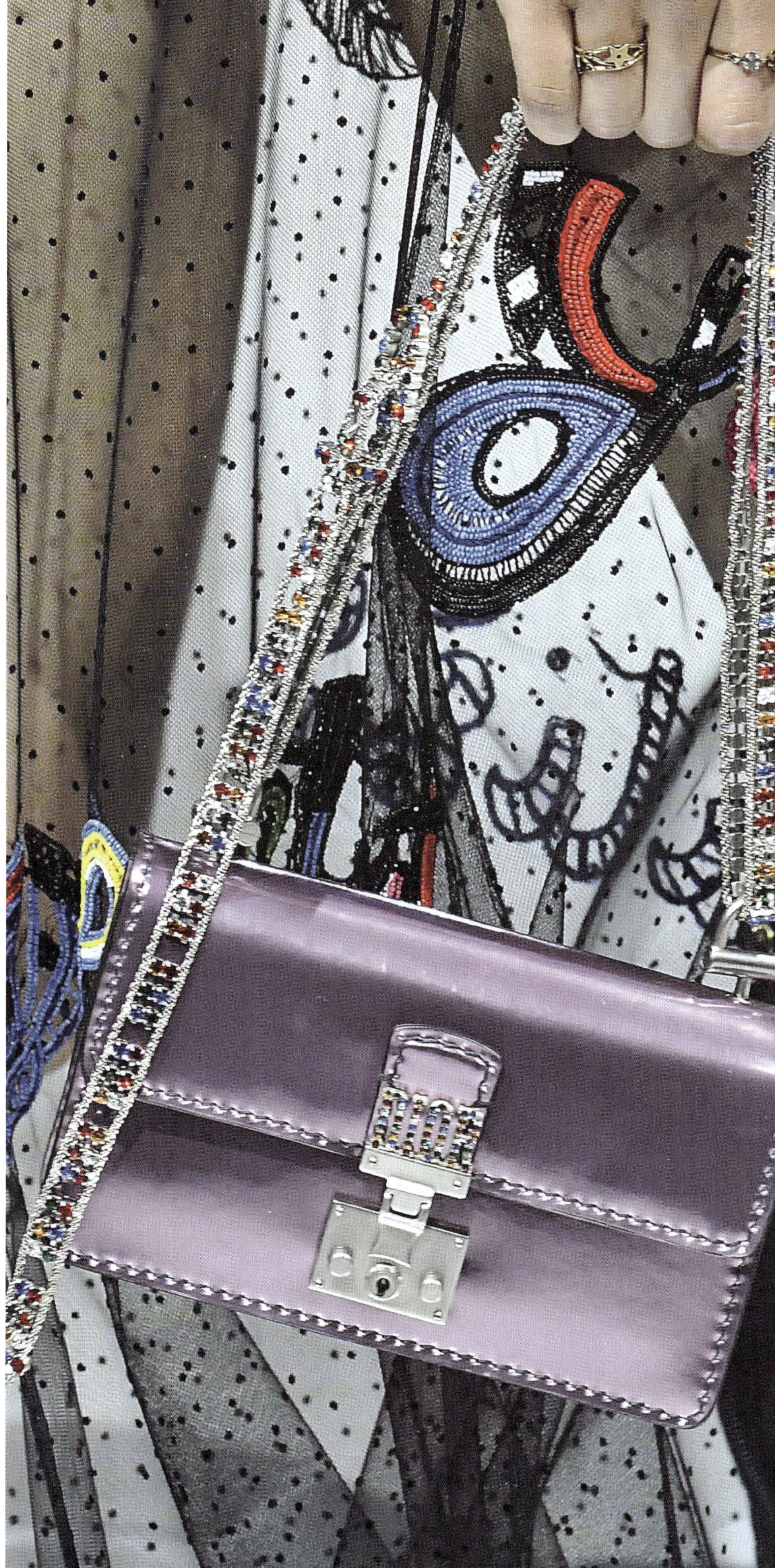

This and next page: The DiorAddict is available in a variety of shapes and materials, including oblique and cannage versions, as well as these two models presented at the Spring/Summer 2018 (left) and Fall/Winter 2018 (right) shows in Paris

Pages 124/125: A J'Adior bag is showcased during Paris Fashion Week, February 2018

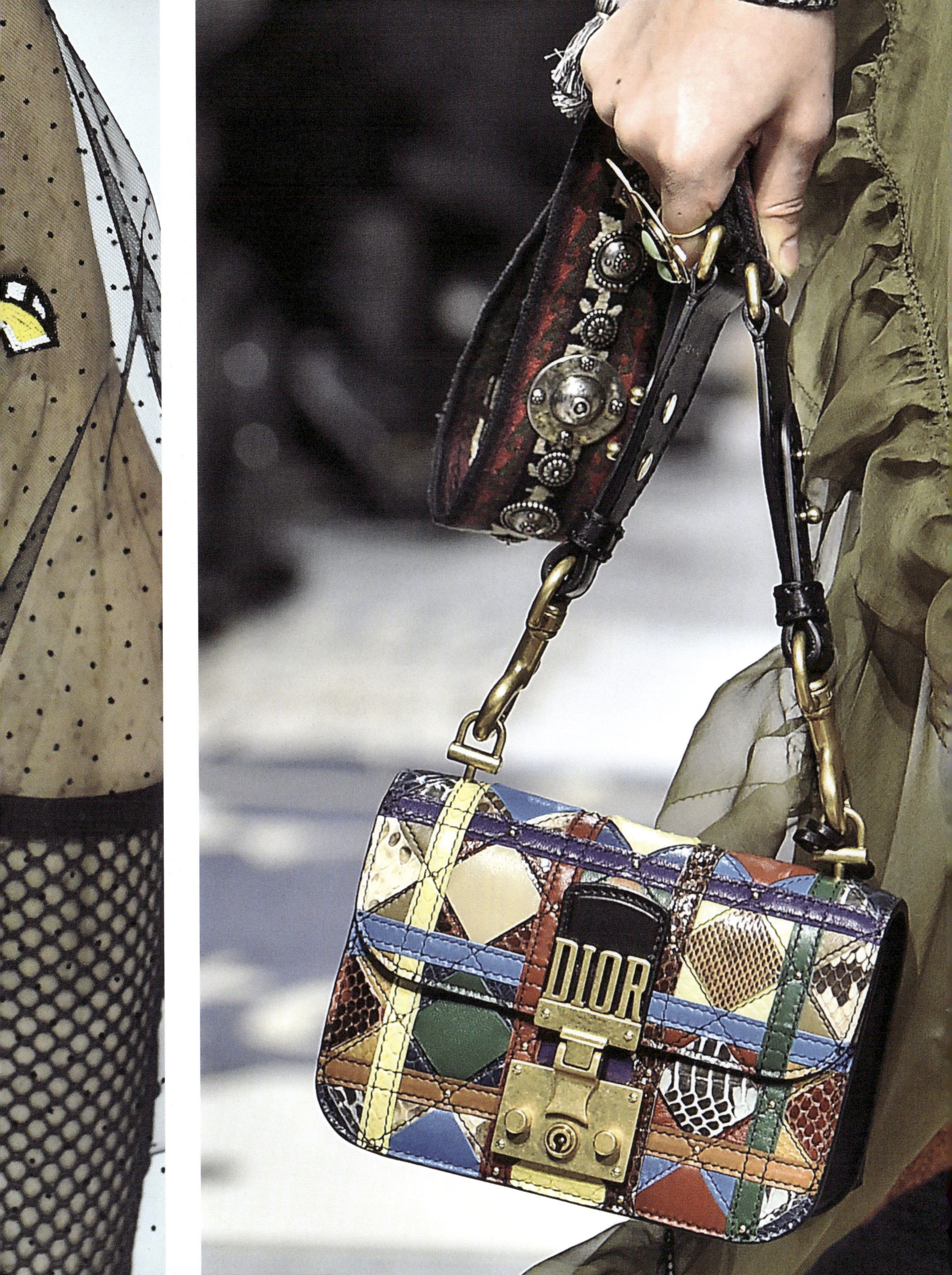
DIOR

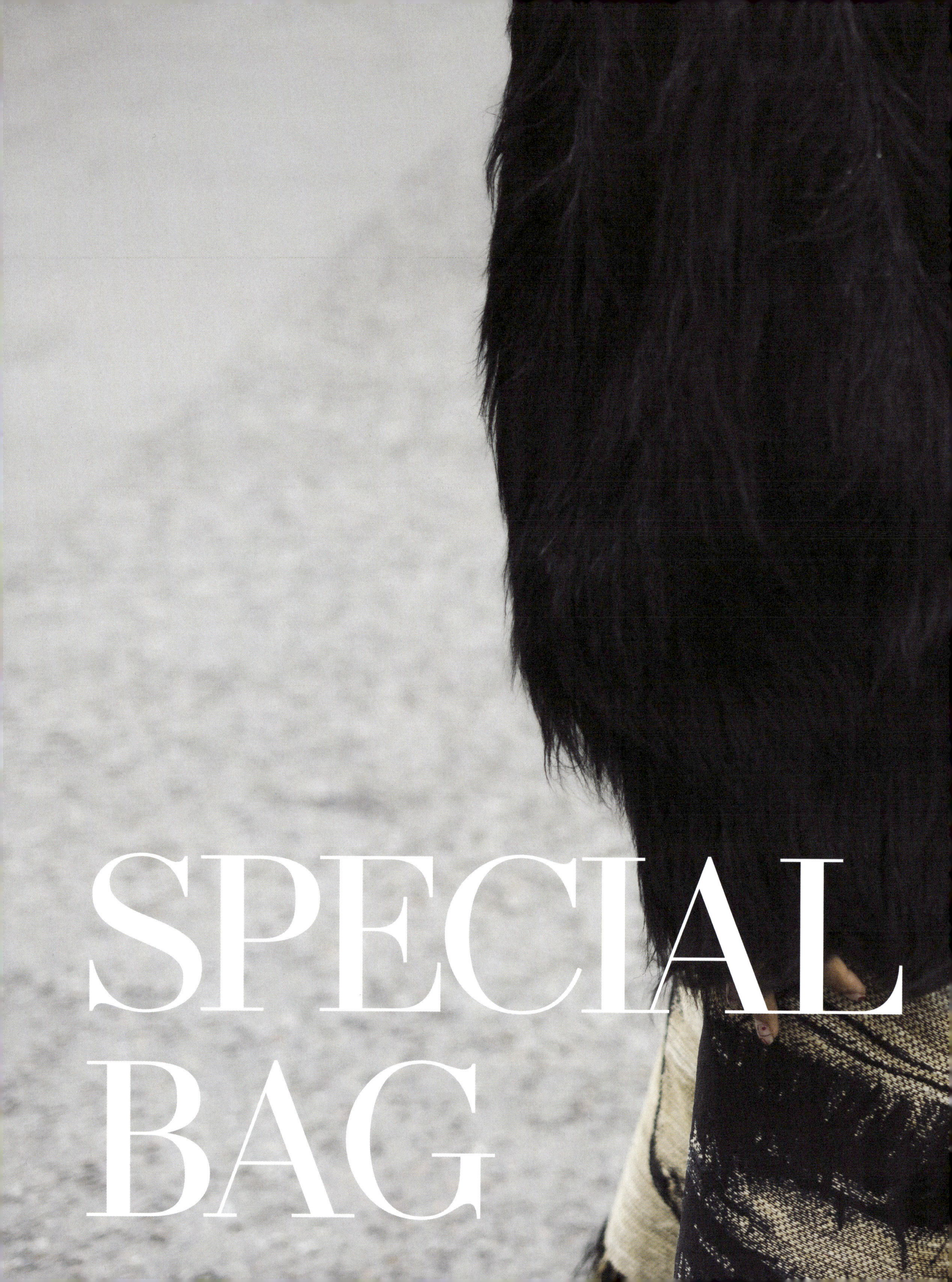

SPECIAL BAG

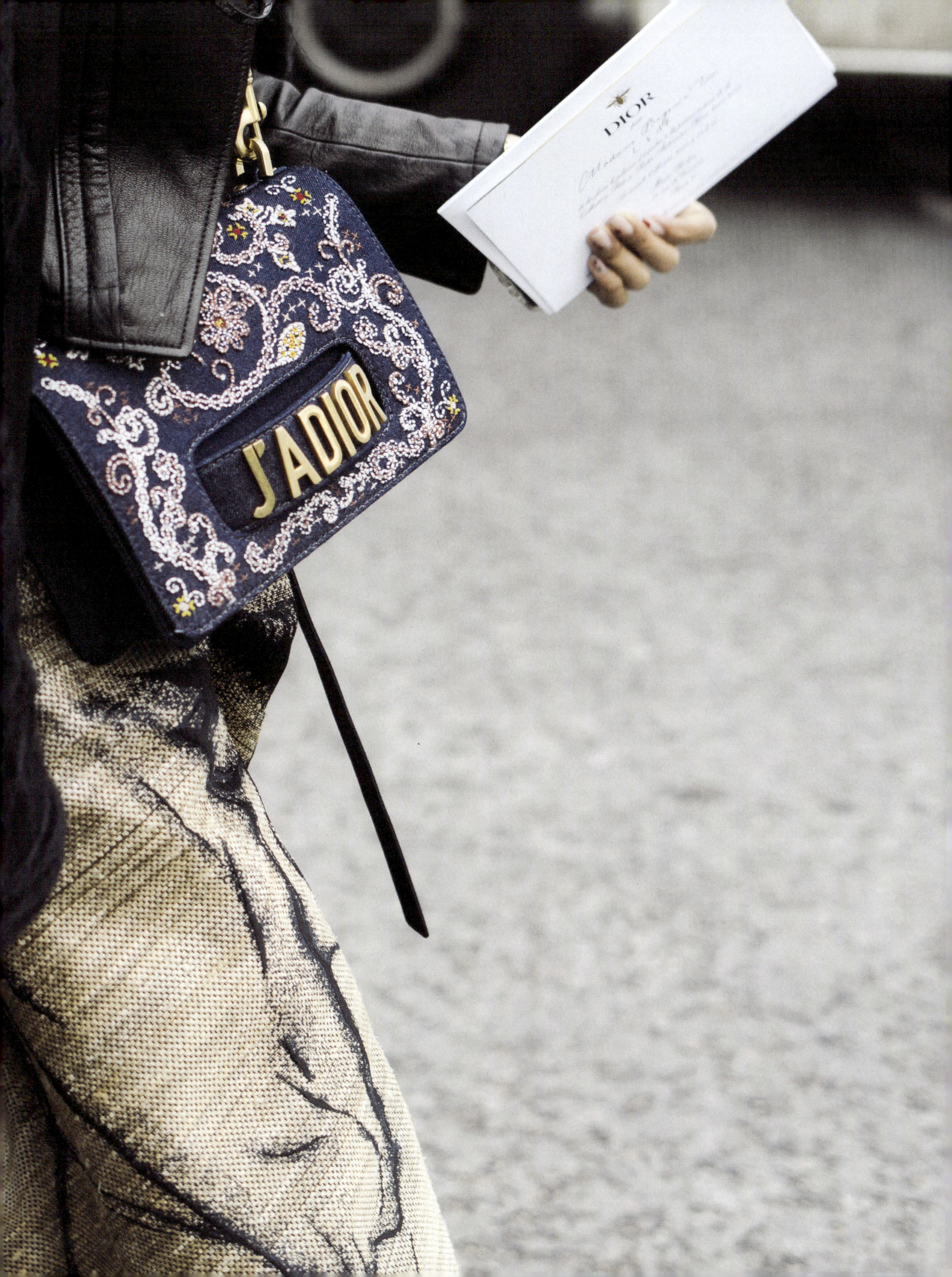
DIOR
J'ADIOR

J'ADIOR

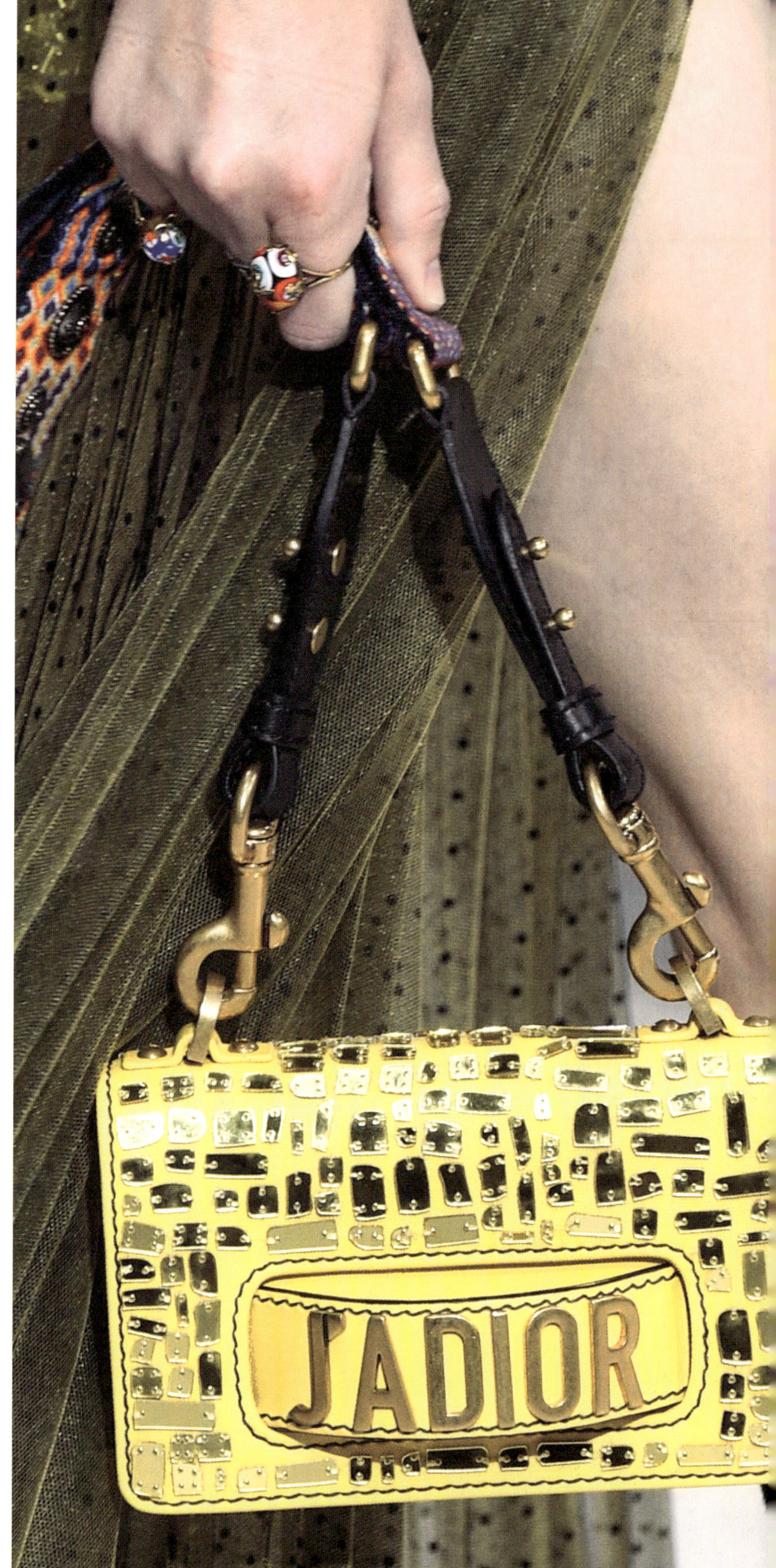

Pages 126–129: The J'Adior bag was one of Maria Grazia Chiuri's first creations for Dior in 2017. One of the early J'Adior bags is featured on page 128 at the Spring/Summer 2017 show. Similar to the Dio(r)evolution, the J'Adior can be styled as a clutch with the slot handclasp or as a cross-body or shoulder bag with chain or leather straps. It boasts many prominent fans and has been produced in various different versions, as shown in the following pages. Its discontinuation has only heightened its appeal.

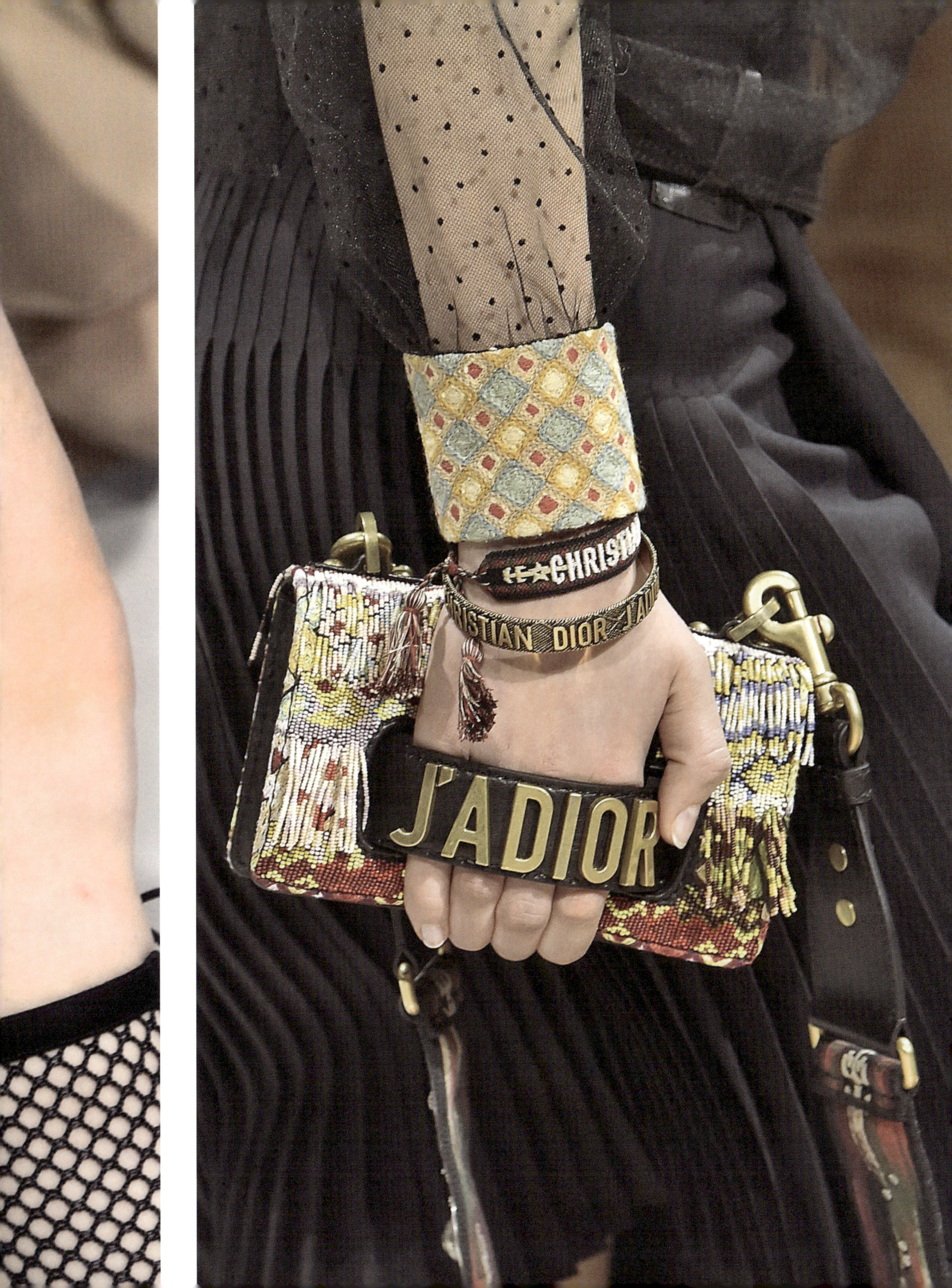
J'ADIOR

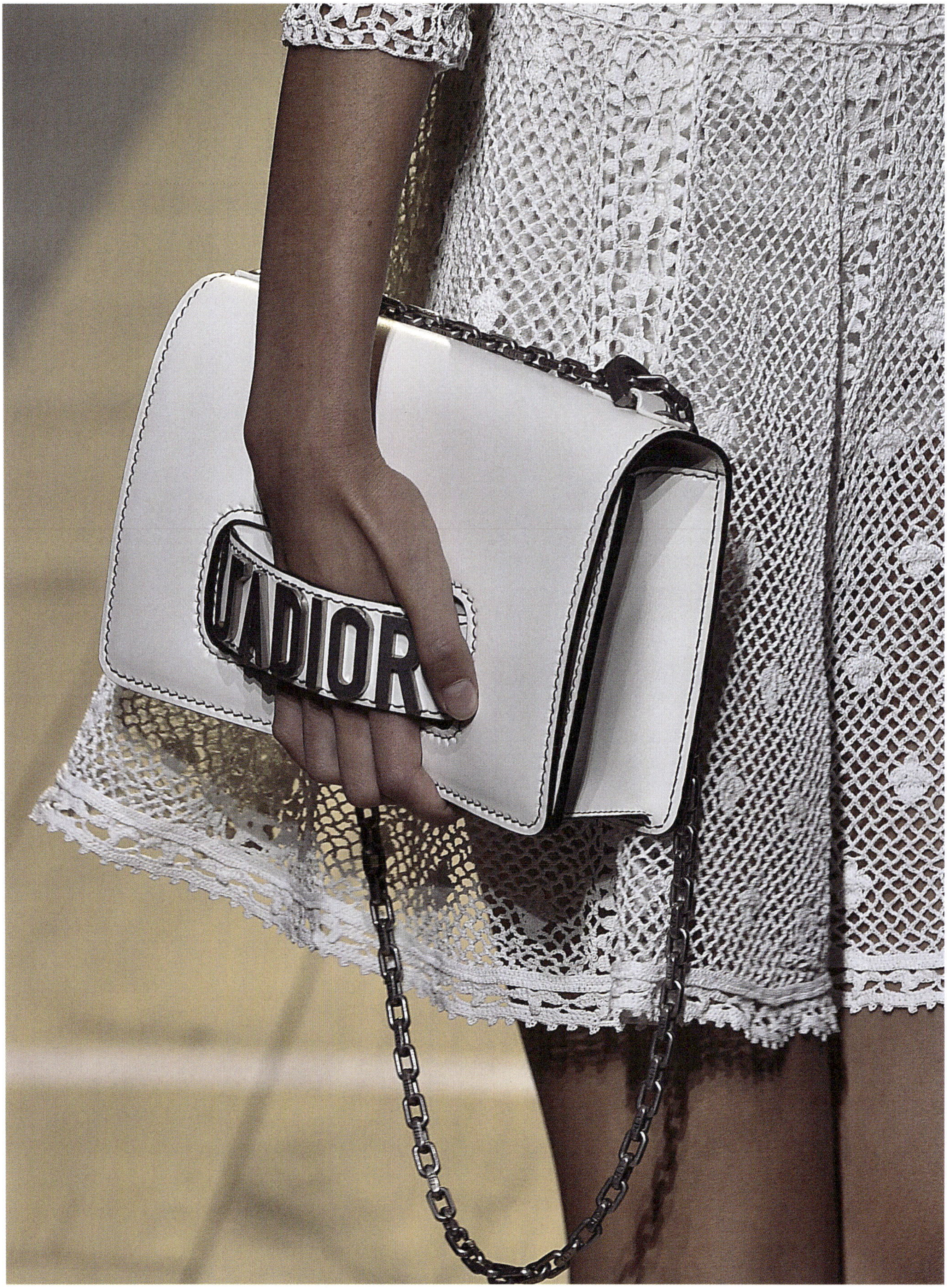

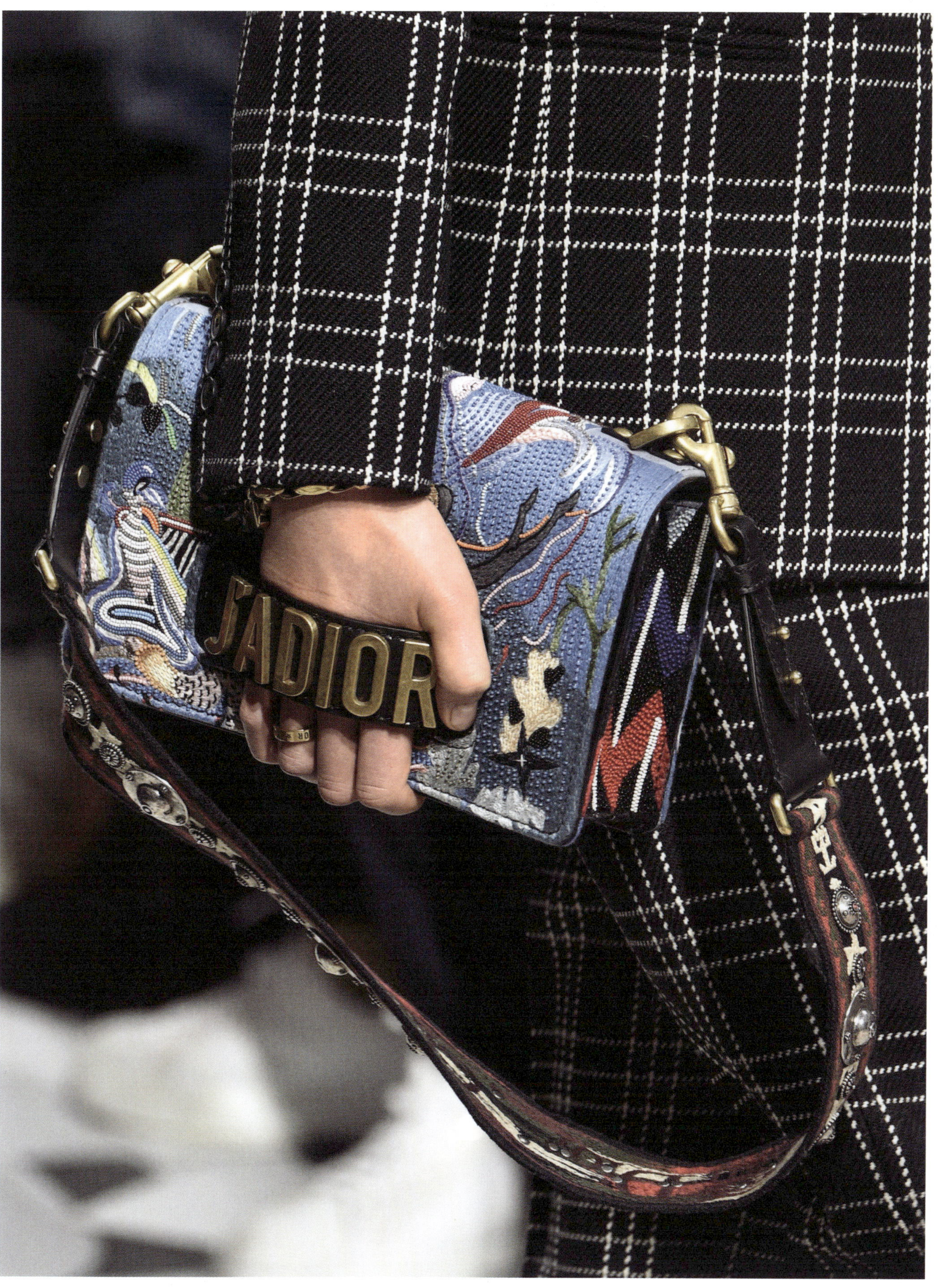
J'ADIOR

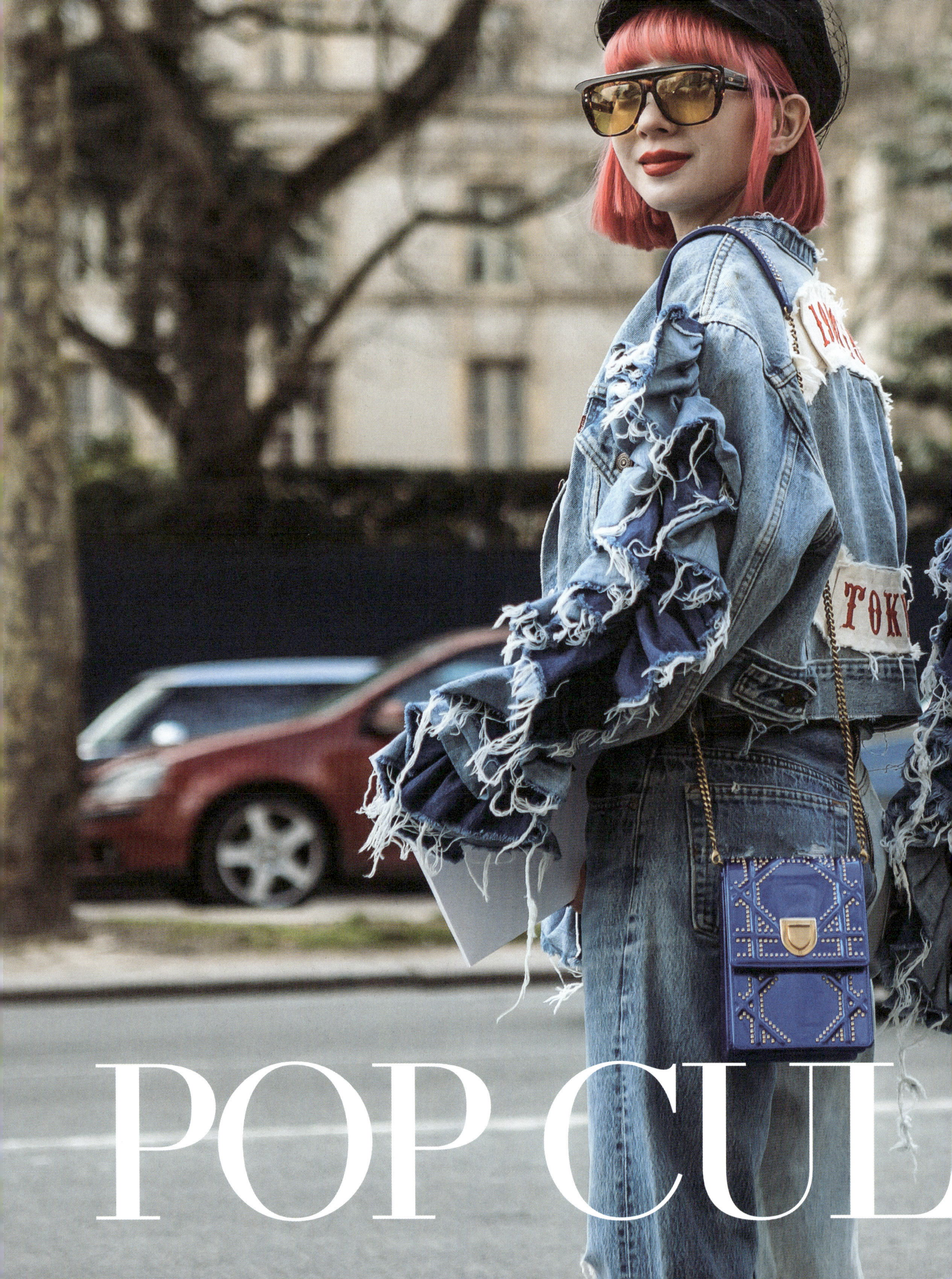

POP CUL

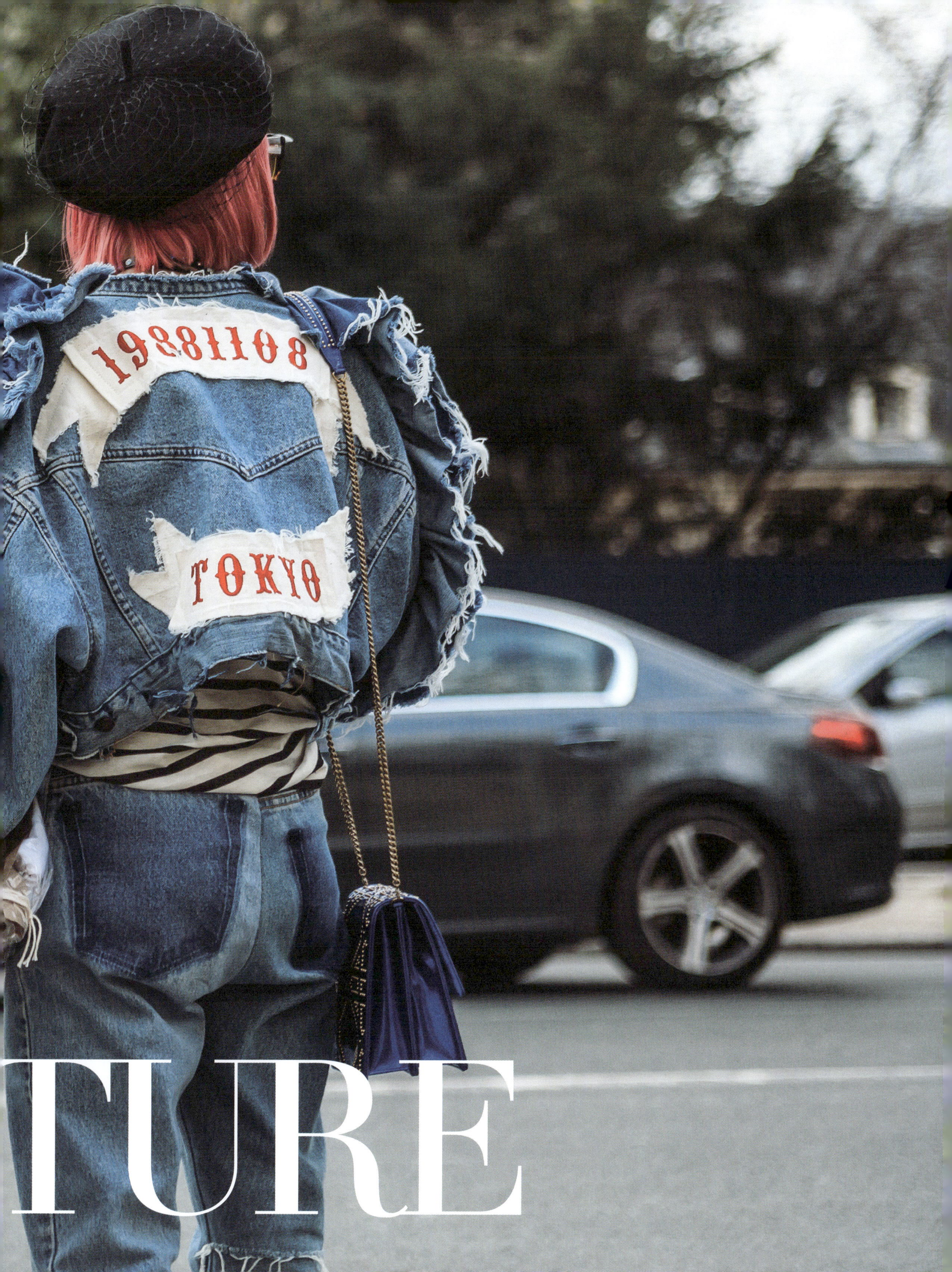
19881108
TOKYO
TURE

ON STAGE AND SCREEN

Throughout the history of the house, Dior has seen the direct influence of celebrity patronage and how the impact of popular culture could transform its reputation and desirability. In the early days of Dior's own creative direction, the *maison* was a favorite with the British Royal family and enjoyed repeated moments in the spotlight. Princess Margaret, sister of HRH Queen Elizabeth II, chose a divine Dior gown in white tulle covered with embroidery, sequins and pearls for her official 21st birthday portrait. The photo, taken by Cecil Beaton, was reproduced in the press around the world, helping to seal Dior's position as a household name and reiterate the notion that Dior was *the* high society couturier of choice. Princess Margaret regularly traveled to Paris to visit Dior's *ateliers* to choose *costumes* for her appearances. The *maison* was also favored by novelist Nancy Mitford, The Duchess of Marlborough and an array of upper class girls who would commission Dior to create their 'coming out' debutante gowns (a traditional ceremony that would launch aristocratic girls into society). Decades later, another royal beauty, the Princess of Wales, would help bring Dior's designs to the forefront again with her patronage of one specific handbag... The Lady Dior bag has since become one of the most famous handbags in the world; in a wildly meta moment, the bag was carried by Elizabeth Debicki as part of her portrayal of Diana in the Netflix TV series *The Crown* (2022). Next-generation fans of Dior include Meghan Markle and Lady Amelia Windsor.

Well beyond the bounds of British aristocracy, the modern iteration of the *maison* has also found favor with Princess Charlene of Monaco, Queen Mathilde of Belgium and Queen Rania of Jordan, taking Dior's fame global.

In addition to setting up enterprises in London and New York while he was alive, Dior presented his own collections in Japan in 1953 and subsequently partnered with an exquisite Kyoto-based silk workshop on couture fabrics. In 2025, Maria Grazia Chiuri chose Kyoto as the show location for the Pre-Fall 2025 collection, adding the destination to a variety of show locations including Athens, Seville, Edinburgh, Mumbai and Mexico City, all of which were chosen to celebrate the craft of artisans local to that area.

Pages 130/131: Aya and Ami Suzuki are photographed with Diorama bags outside the Dior show during Paris Fashion Week, Womenswear Fall/Winter 2018

Next page: Marlene Dietrich is seen wearing a Christian Dior design in 1950

Page 134: Princess Diana is captured with her Lady Dior in Birmingham, 1995

Page 136: Elizabeth Taylor wears Dior Couture at the 33rd Annual Academy Awards in 1961

Page 138: Jane Wyman and Marlene Dietrich appear on location in London, circa 1950, in suits by Christian Dior

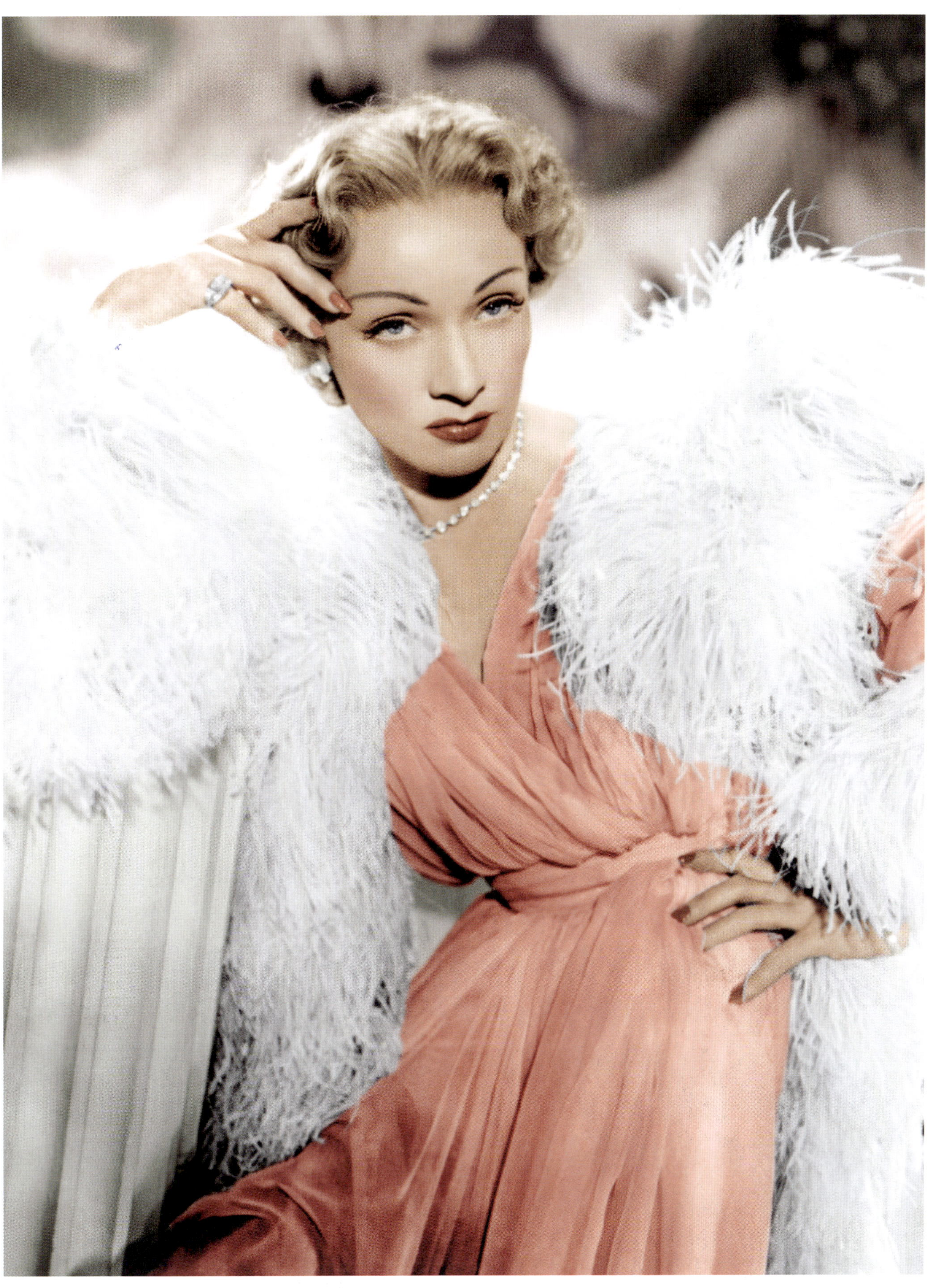

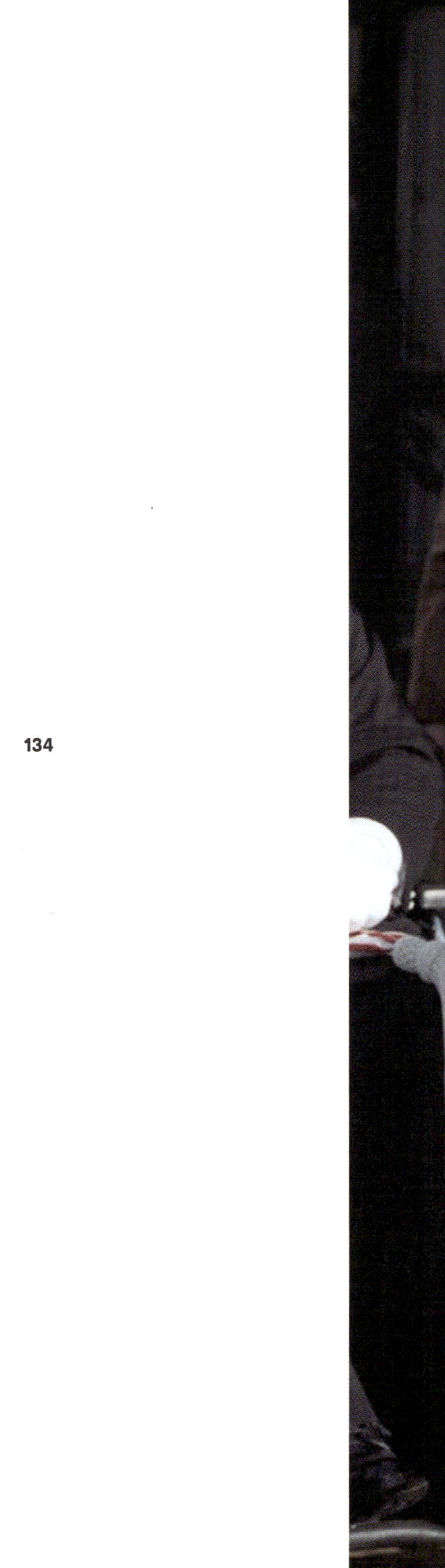

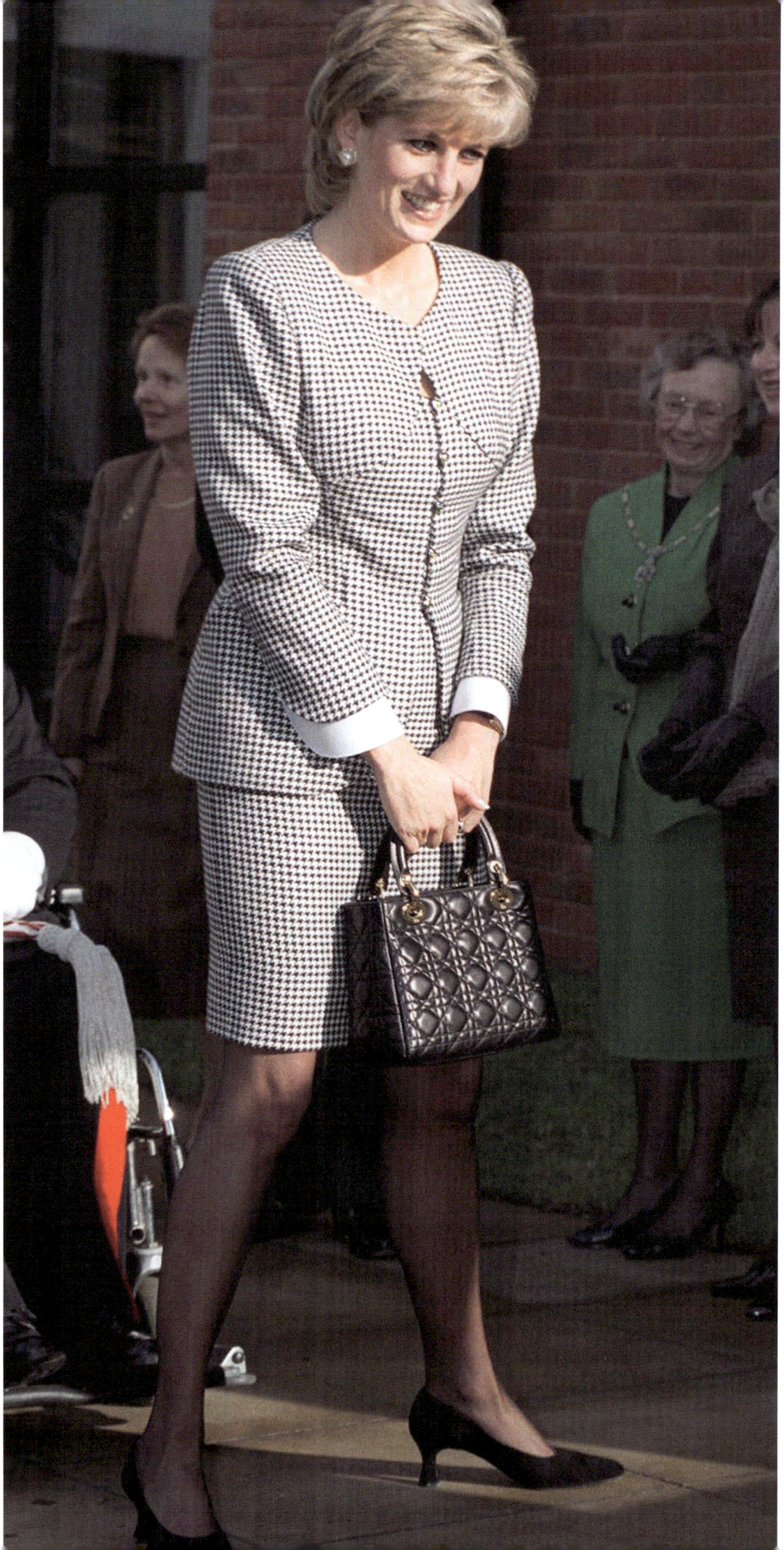

While he was alive, Dior was an astute publicist of his own work. Early in the *maison's* history, he cottoned on to the exposure that Hollywood could bring to his collections. Marlene Dietrich was both a friend of Dior and a fan of his work, exclusively wearing Dior in *Stage Fright* (1950) and *No Highway In The Sky* (1951). Ava Gardner and Olivia de Havilland both wore Dior in their respective films *The Little Hut* (1957) and *The Ambassador's Daughter* (1956). In addition to these on-screen appearances, Dior was on call for the stars of the silver screen for gowns to wear on the nascent red carpet scene, at premieres and at award ceremonies, too. Elizabeth Taylor, Rita Hayworth, Marilyn Monroe and Sophia Loren were all loyal to the *maison* throughout their lives. When Grace Kelly announced her engagement to Prince Rainier III of Monaco, she did so in Dior. The special relationship between the *maison* and movie stars continues today. The Academy Awards have grown from an intimate industry ceremony to one of the most watched spectacles in the world. In 2025, almost 20 million people tuned in to the event. But beyond the accolades, the red carpet is the biggest draw for viewers who enjoy the glam and create their own best dressed lists. Celebrity ambassadors are often contracted to wear the designs of a certain house for big events, so it's no surprise that Anya Taylor-Joy and Natalie Portman have made multiple appearances in Dior on the red carpet. It's also natural that Jennifer Lawrence (the face of the Joy fragrance and Dior Addict makeup line) would wear Dior. Lawrence chose a floral gown by Raf Simons when she won her Best Actress Award in 2013, famously tripping on the floor-skimming hem of the dress as she made her way to the stage to collect the golden statuette. Likewise, Charlize Theron, who is the current face of the Capture Skin Collection and has worked with Dior for the past 21 years, often appears on the red carpet in Dior.

In a reversal of influence, Dior's couture collections provided inspiration for Paul Gallico's novel *Flowers for Mrs Harris* (1958) about a London charwoman (a cleaner) who travels to Paris to buy her dream dress from Dior. The book was adapted into the film *Mrs Harris Goes To Paris* (2022), and costume designer Jenny Beavan used archive items in the production, along with reimagined replica pieces, to create an authentically retro look.

Beyond cultivating cinematic relationships, Dior also is closely aligned with the world of music, and some of the biggest mega-stars of the moment are ambassadors for the house. Rihanna was announced as the new face of *J'adore* fragrance in 2024, although she has been building a relationship with the *maison* since 2015. The singing superstar apparently took home a $75 million paycheck for her appearance in the perfume campaign shot by similarly stellar photographer Steven Klein at the Palace of Versailles.

Dior has long been name-checked in hip-hop tracks and in rap, as its exclusive and expensive brand image evokes symbolic wealth and status, which is so often a subject of the genre. In the early 2000s, John Galliano was openly inspired by Lauryn Hill, Foxy Brown, Lil' Kim and Mary J Blige—who likewise become members of the Dior fan club, appearing in the *oblique* monogrammed pieces and Galliano's Y2K take on Black Seventies style. Foxy Brown performed at the re-opening of a New York Dior boutique, in 1999, wearing a denim print silk slip dress, *oblique*-print boots—and a Saddle Bag, of course. More recently, Taylor Swift and Ariana Grande have both made appearances in Dior at awards ceremonies and on the red carpet, while Lady Gaga and Celine Dion were both dressed in Dior Couture for their appearances at the opening ceremony of the 2024 Paris Olympics.

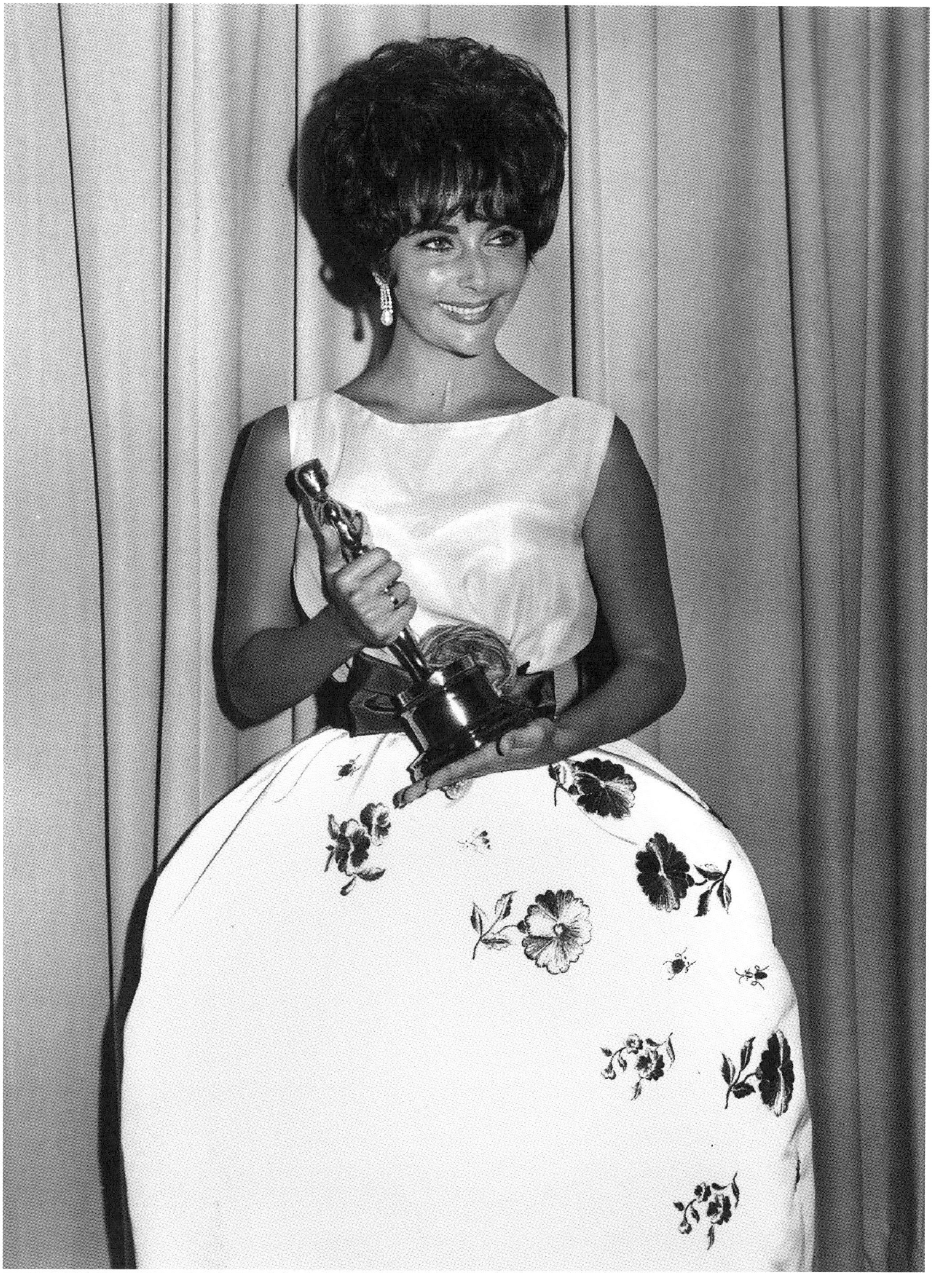

Today, Dior is building strong partnerships with sports personalities to reflect the building synergy between the two disciplines. Paris was host to the most recent Olympics, which put the focus on French talent, but across the world—and across sports—fashion is realizing the incredibly broad reach that sports stars can have. Jamaican sprinter Elaine Thompson-Herah, American soccer player Alex Morgan, Olympic medalist and surfer Carissa Moore, boxer Estelle Mossely, skateboarder Louise-Aina Touboulet and French gold medalist judoka Clarisse Agbegnenou were all named Dior ambassadors in the runup to the 2024 Olympic Games. Tennis players Emma Raducanu and Zheng Qinwen have both been named Dior ambassadors as well.

As it becomes more and more common for reality stars to morph into bonafide celebrities, Paris Hilton is one of the stars most noted for her love of all things Dior. From her early days appearing in the docusoap show *The Simple Life* and her adoration of the Saddle Bag to her more recent incarnation as a mom (with a Dior baby stroller, of course), Hilton is a huge Dior devotee. Kim Kardashian has also remained loyal to the *maison* throughout her career, even treating her daughter North West to an estimated $1,250 worth of jewelry on a shopping spree in Beverly Hills for North's 10th birthday in June 2023.

And although Dior blends beautifully with other elements of popular culture, it's clear that the fashion house has just as much power all on its own. The description of the 'New Look' and its stylized silhouette became a common cultural touchstone as it defined the 1950s style of feminine fashion, while Dior's particular shade of pale gray, known as either Montaigne or Trianon, is the default when describing that most elegant of French colors. *Monsieur* Dior was also known for his superstitious nature and believed the number 8 to be especially significant. The house of Dior was founded on October 8th, 1946 and the *maison* was located in the 8th *arrondissement* (district) in Paris. Dior also created the *En Huit* line (eight in French), which accentuated the wearers' hips with the clean lines of the outline of a number 8, as part of his 1947 debut. Even Christian Dior's love of the lily of the valley flower is noted today. *Monsieur* Dior used to add a stem of the flower into the seams of his dresses for good luck, and the flower's fragrance is included in Dior's signature perfumes today.

As fashion had become a pillar of popular culture by the 2010s, the fall of John Galliano was given a great deal of attention in the global media and entertainment press. Galliano went on a drunken, antisemitic rant in a Parisian bar in December 2010, and once video of the event spread, Galliano was suspended, and the process to dismiss him began. Antisemitism is illegal in France; in court, Galliano's lawyer defended his clients' actions, attributing them to "work related stress and multiple addictions." Galliano was found guilty and given a sentence that included a € 6000 fine. Since leaving the *maison,* Galliano went clean and sober, designed Kate Moss's wedding dress in 2011, and was appointed creative director at Maison Martin Margiela in 2014—a position he held for the next decade. Galliano was effectively canceled before cancel culture even existed, but he has worked his way back into the public eye. As today's young designers take their cues from the previous generation, Galliano's Dior design legacy is relevant once more.

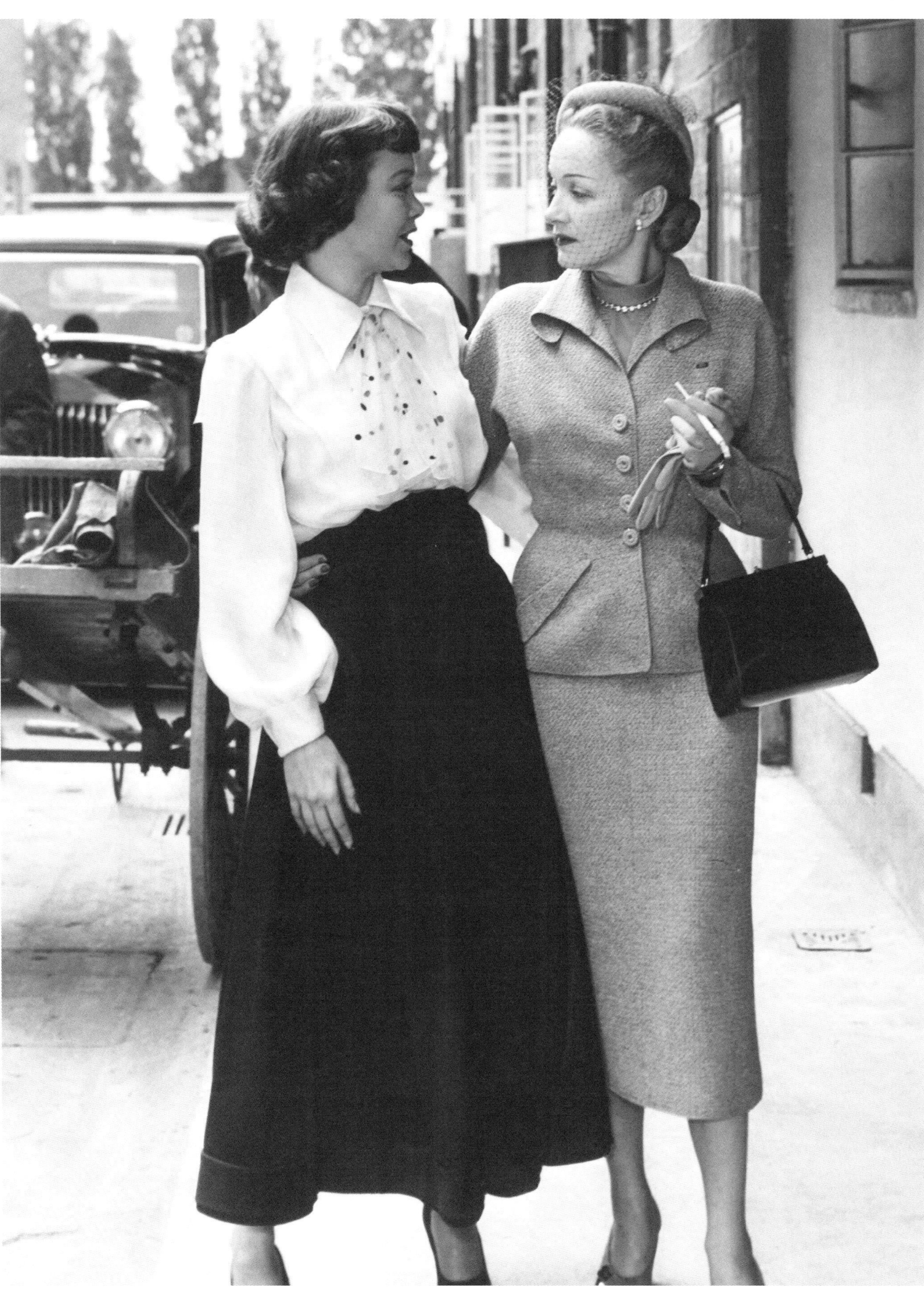

MARLENE DIETRICH WAS BOTH A FRIEND OF DIOR AND A FAN OF HIS WORK

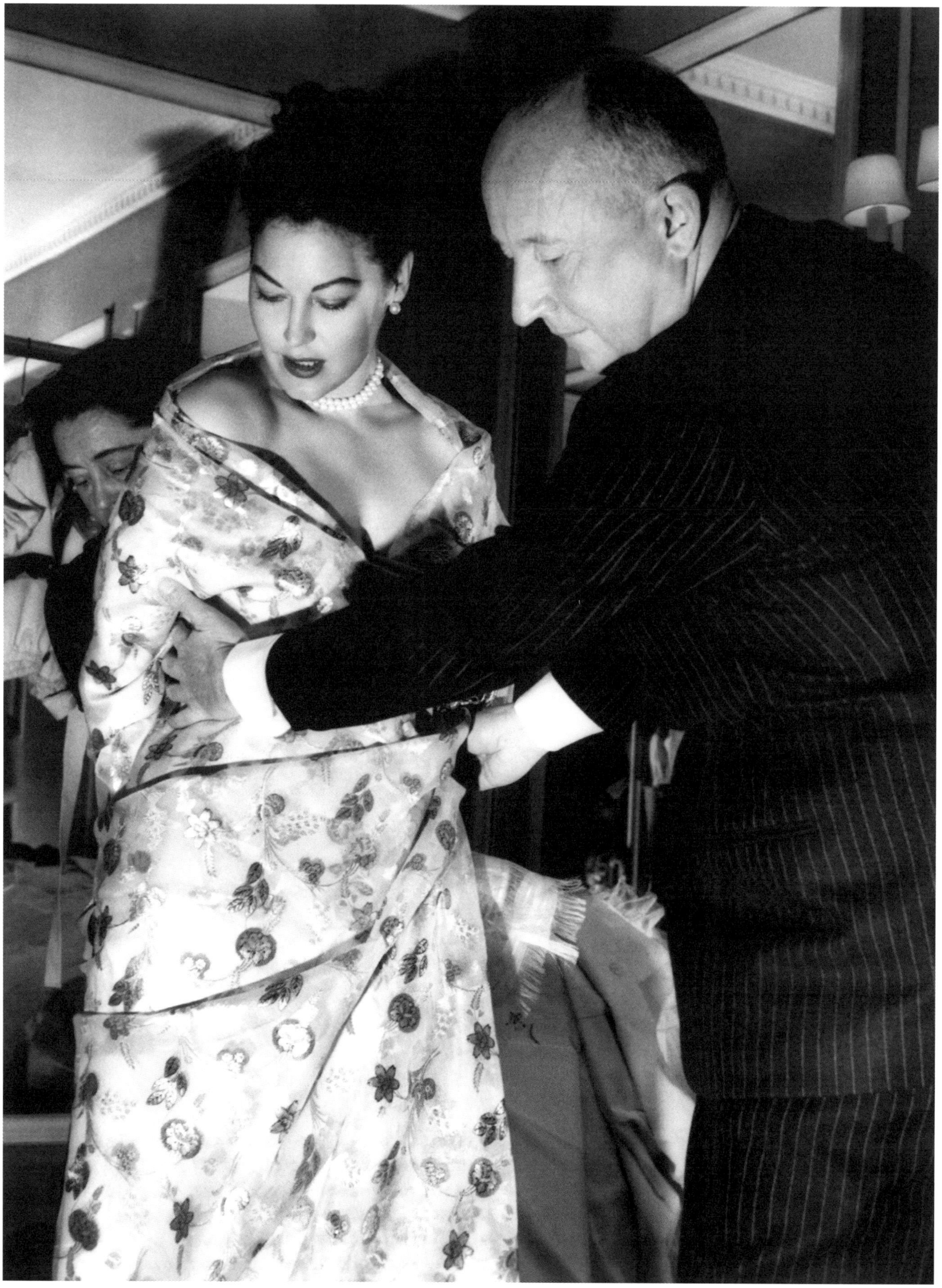

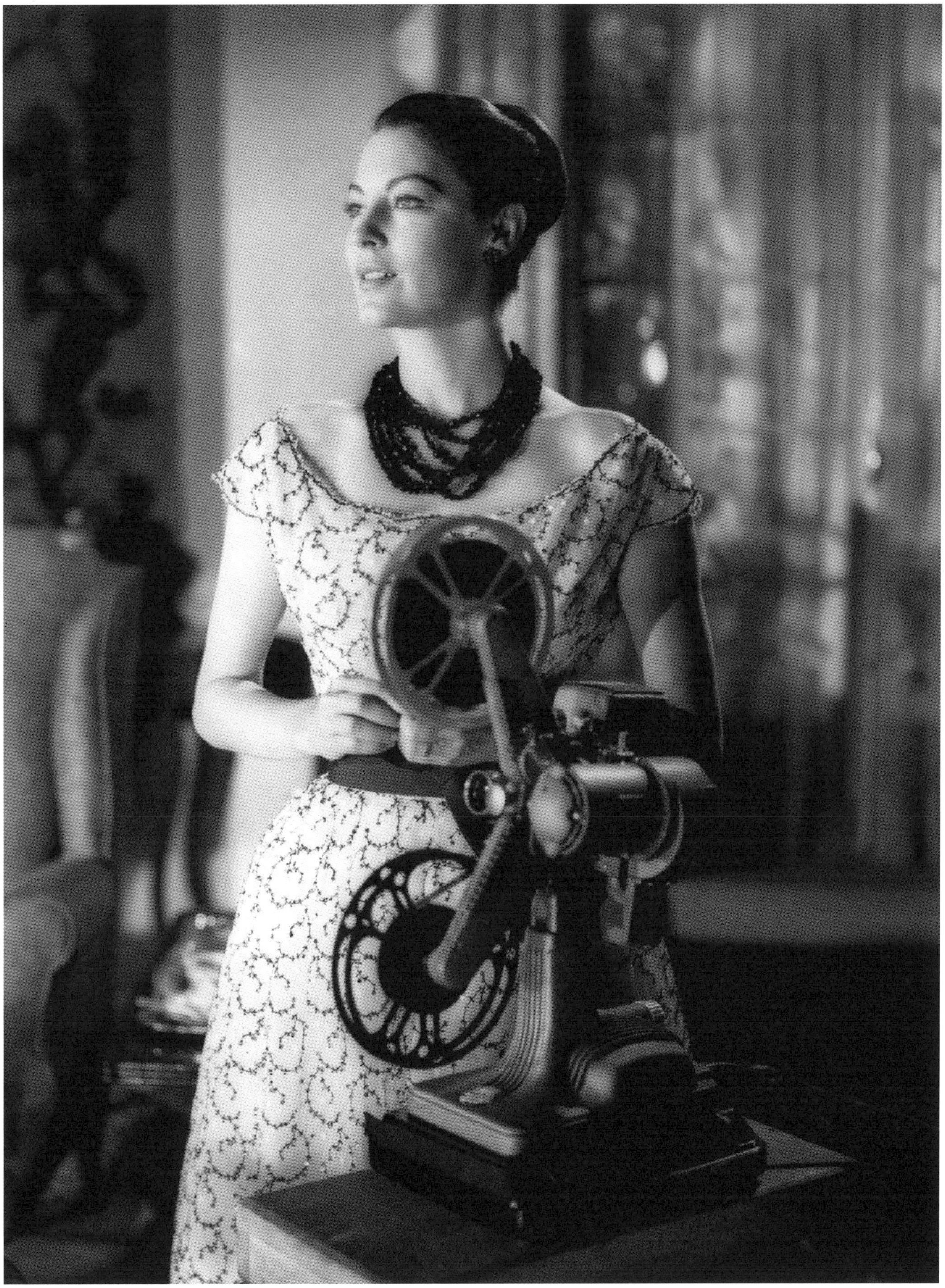

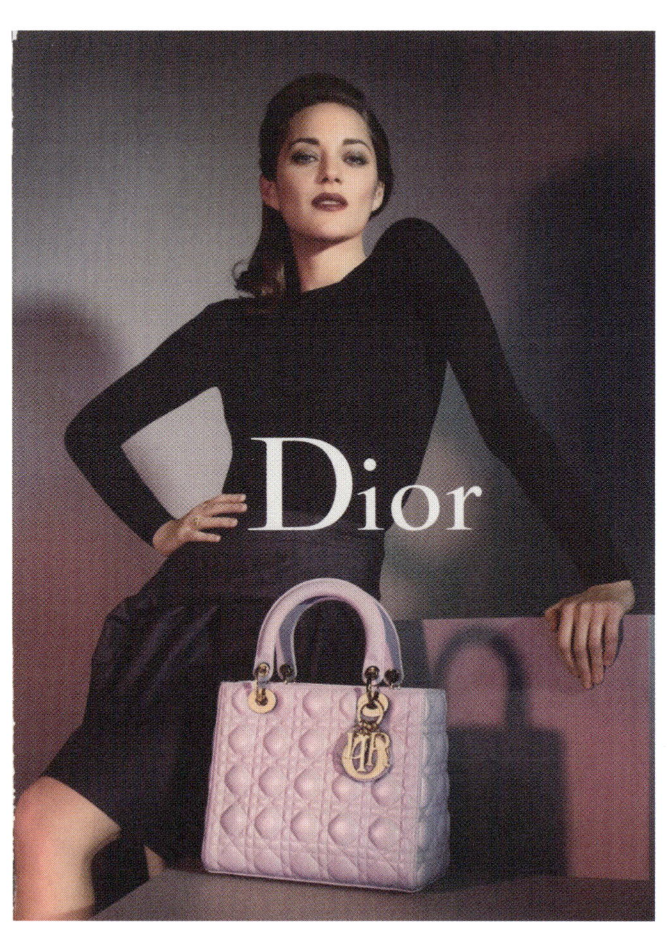
Dior

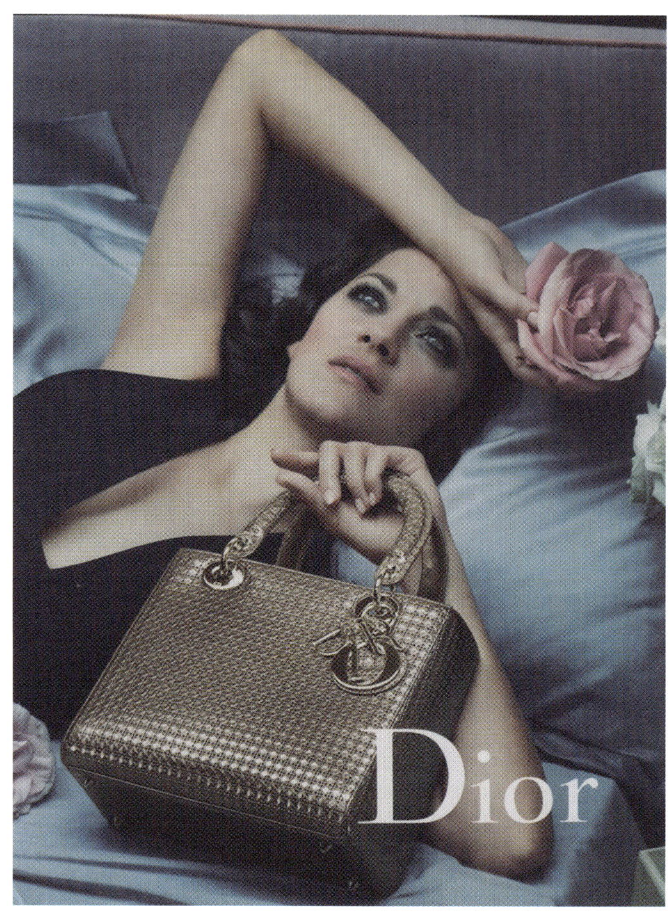
Dior

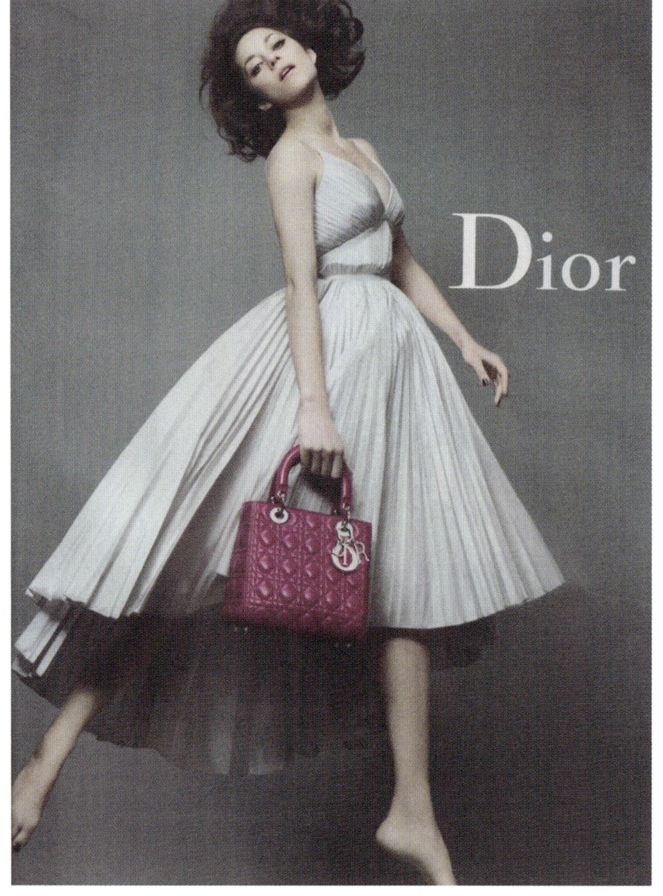
Dior

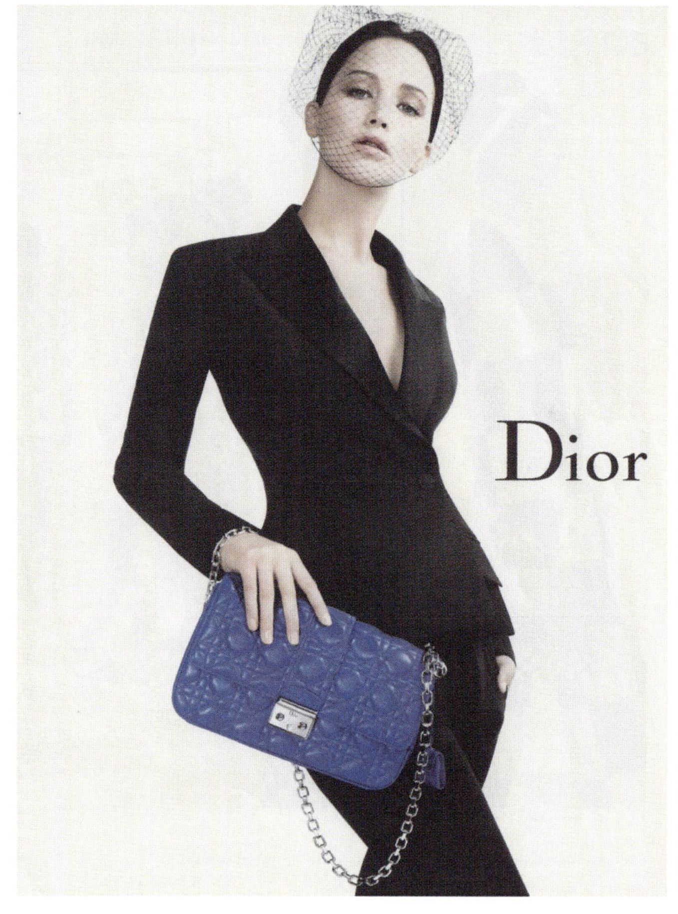
Dior

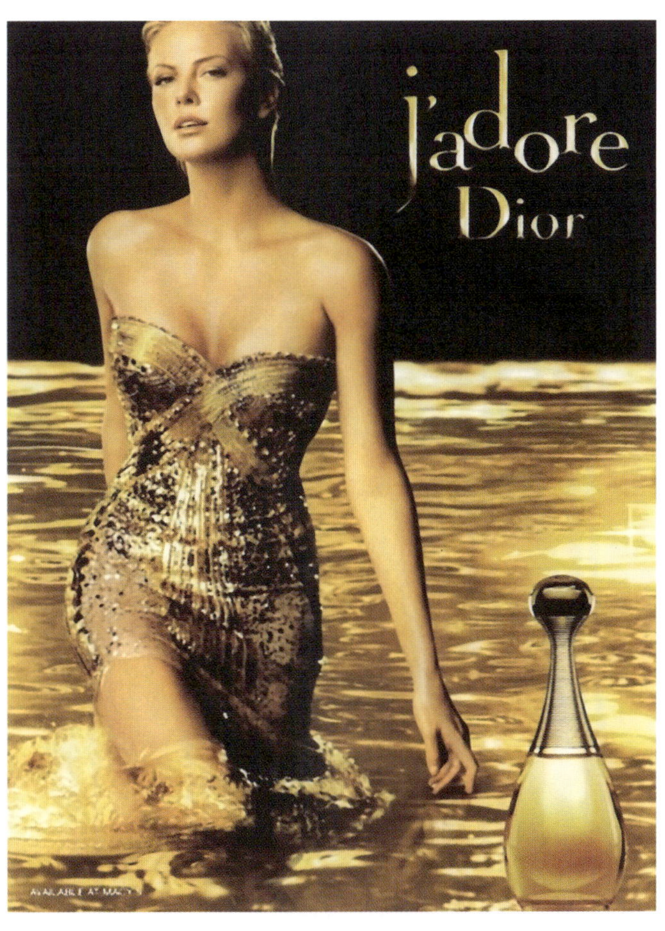

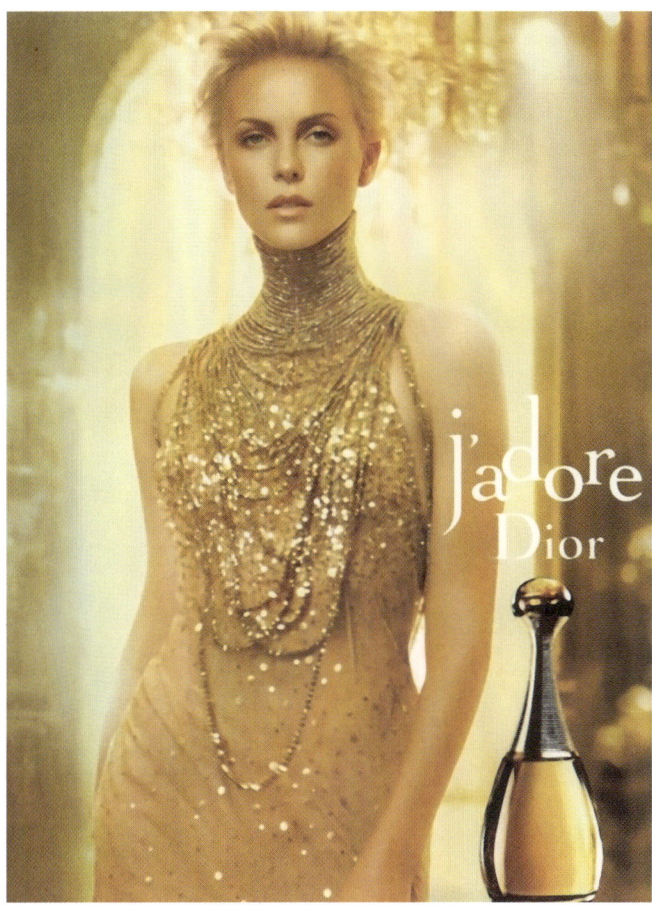

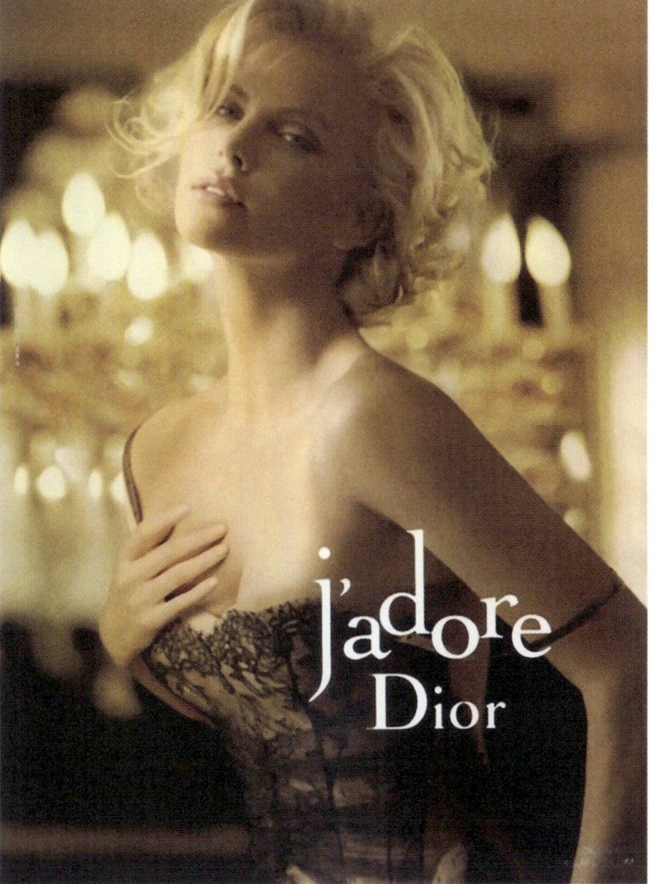

Page 140: Ava Gardner and Christian Dior are photographed during a costume fitting on the set of the movie *The Little Hut* in 1957

Page 141: Ava Gardner wears Christian Dior in *The Little Hut*, 1957

Previous page: Magazine advertisements for Dior bags feature Jennifer Lawrence (2013, bottom right) and Marion Cotillard (2013–2015)

This page: The J'Adore Perfume advertising campaign stars Charlize Theron, 2010

Page 145: Dior exhibit at La Galerie Dior in Paris, 2023

Pages 146/147: Todd Philips (left), Joaquin Phoenix (right), and Lady Gaga (in Dior Couture) attend the Venice Film Festival, 2024

Pages 148/149: Paris and Nicky Hilton are spotted with their Lady Dior bags in New York City in 2019 (left page) and Portofino in 2010 (right page)

Page 150: A sporty cross-body bag features in the Spring/Summer 2025 collection in Paris, 2024

Page 151: A model showcases a bowling bag with an oblique design on the runway during the Spring/Summer 2025 Womenswear show in Paris, 2024

144

DIOR BLENDS BEAUTI-FULLY WITH ELEMENTS OF POPULAR CULTURE

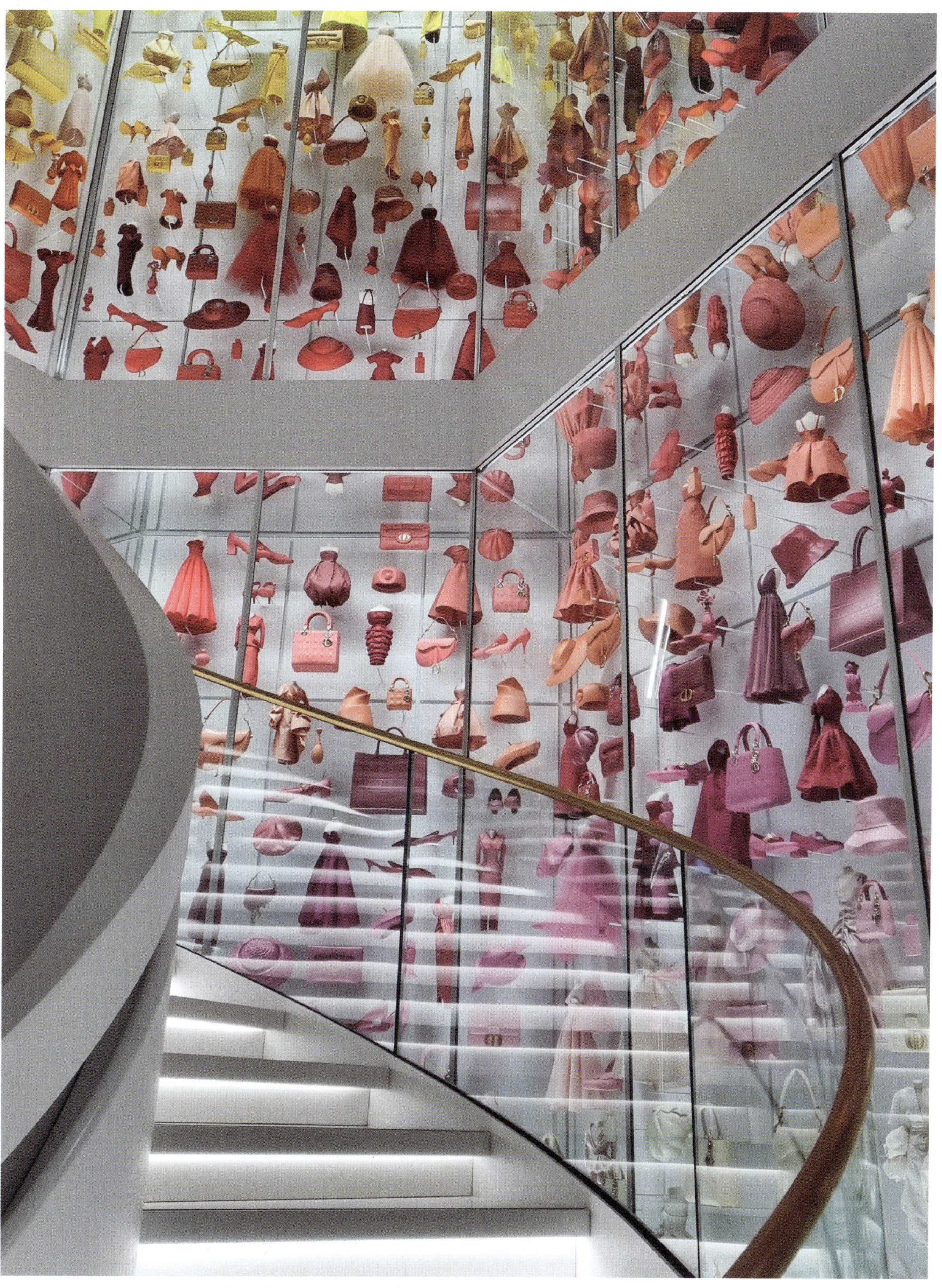

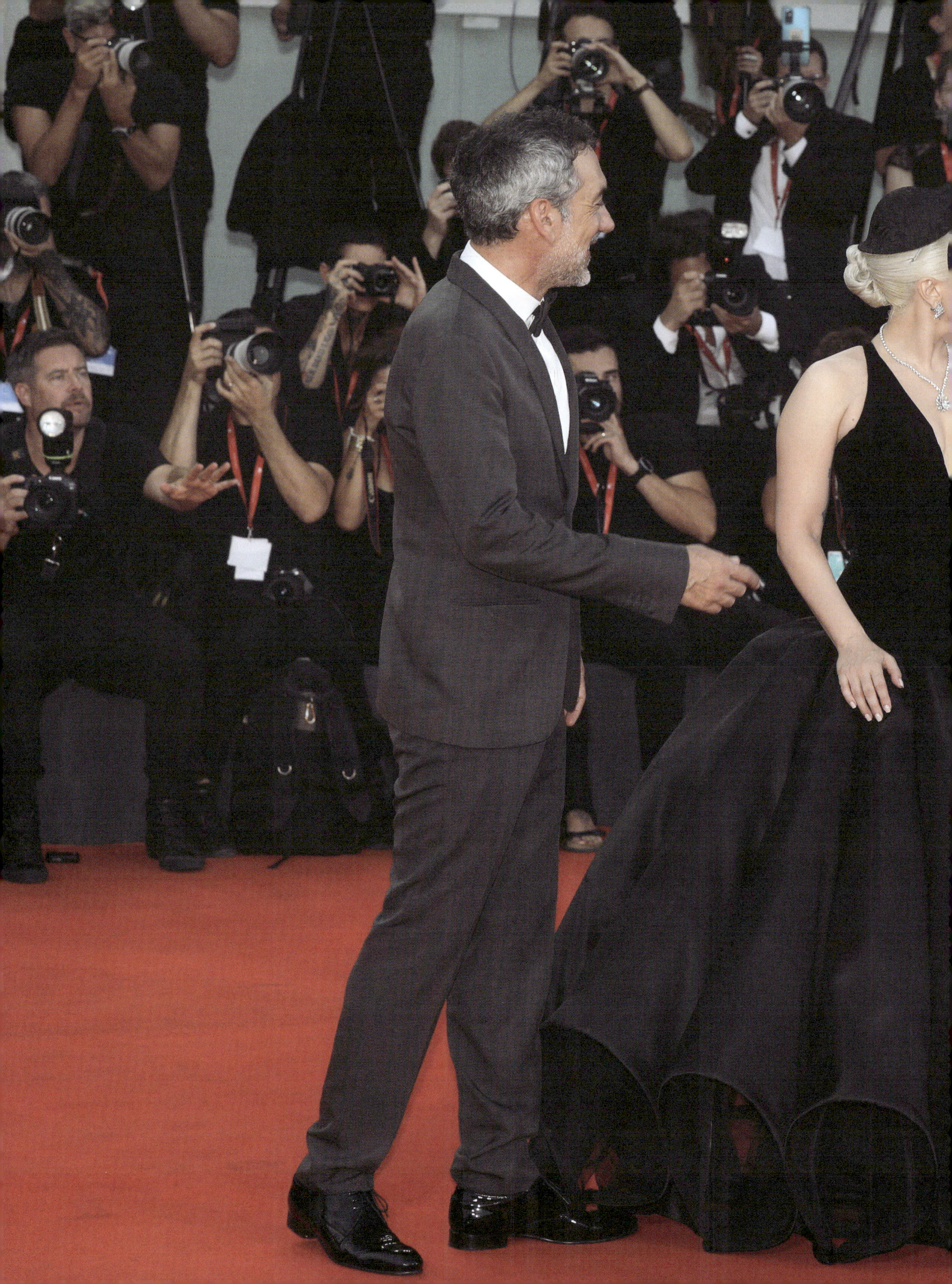

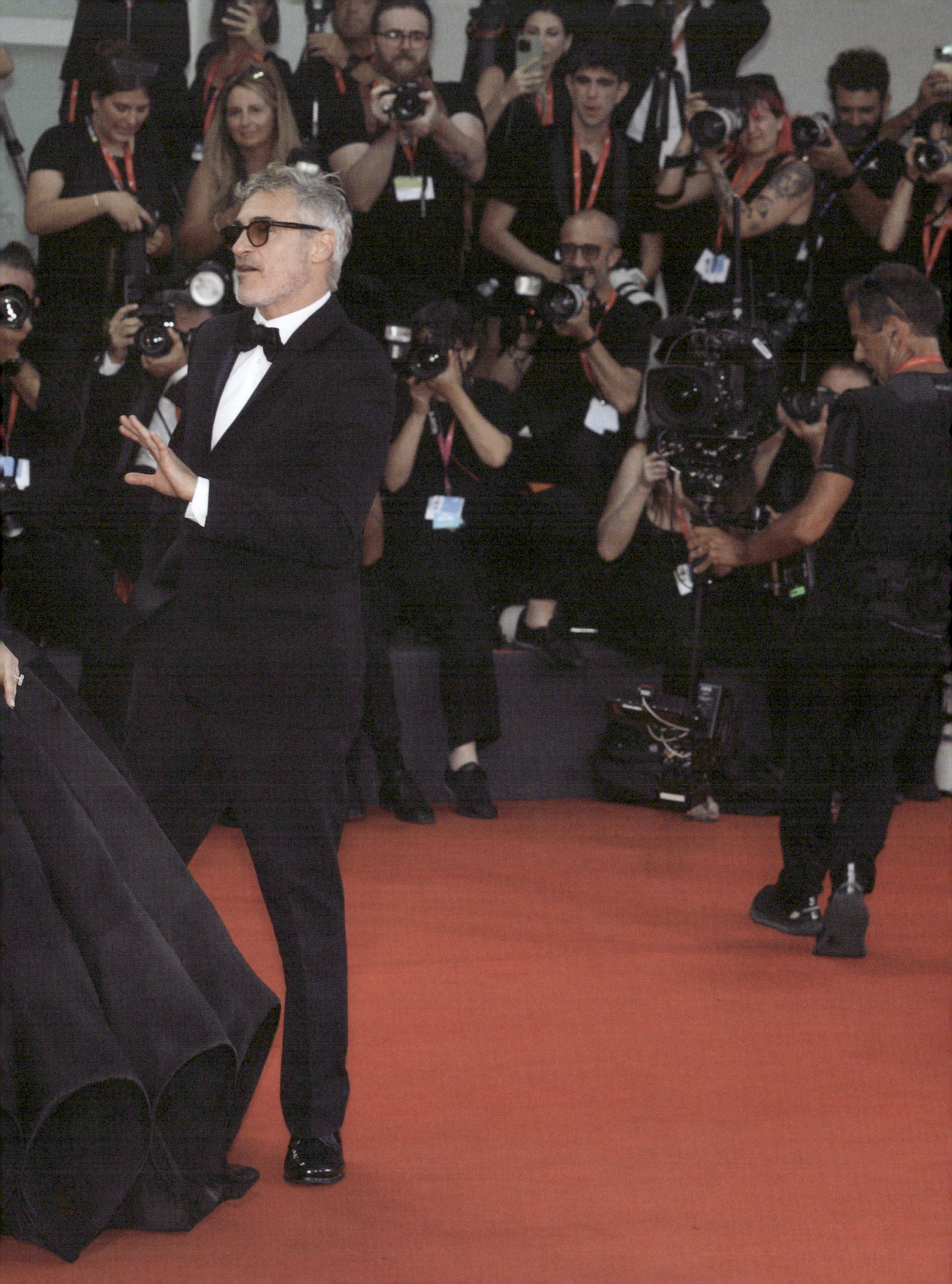

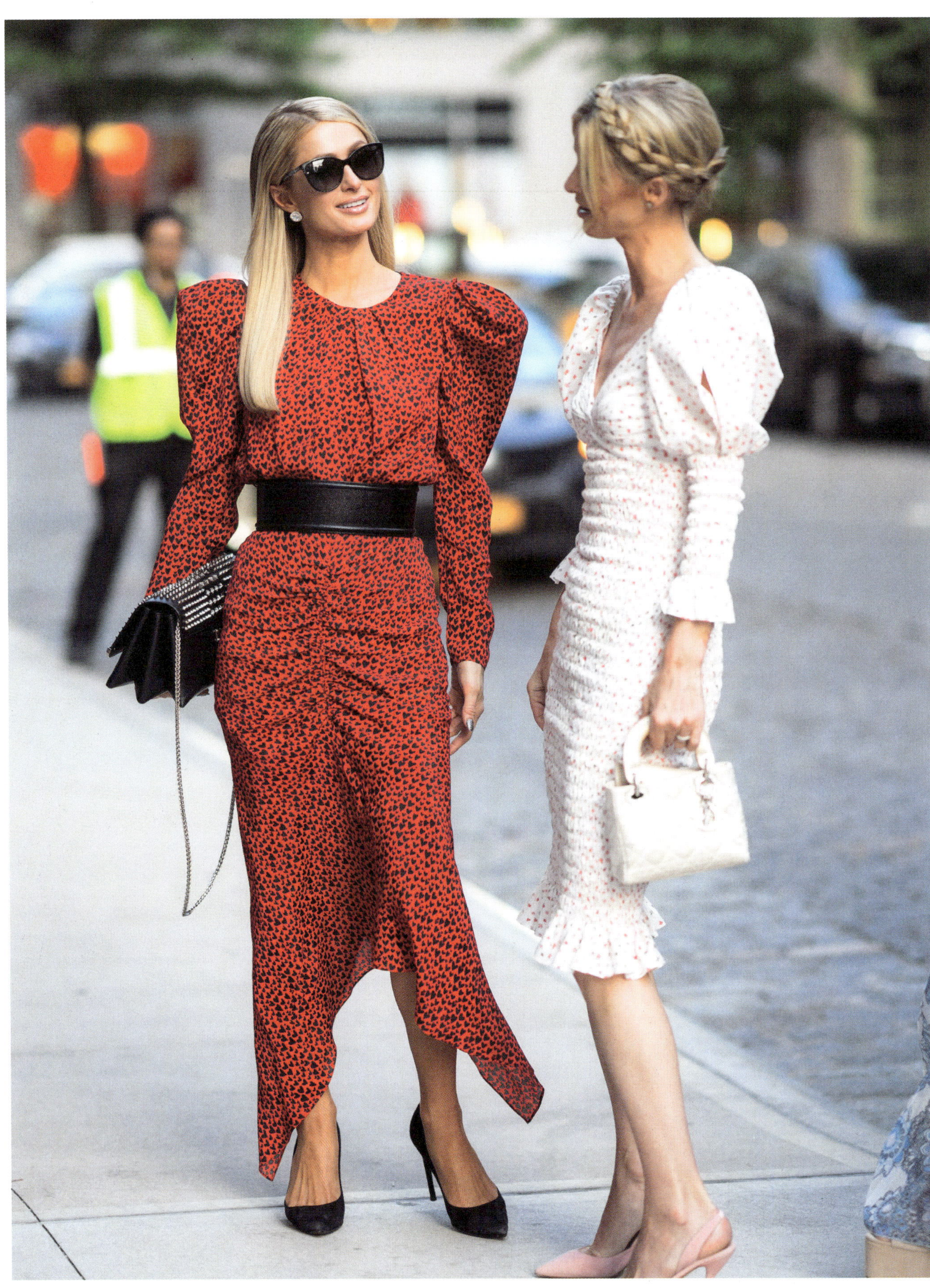

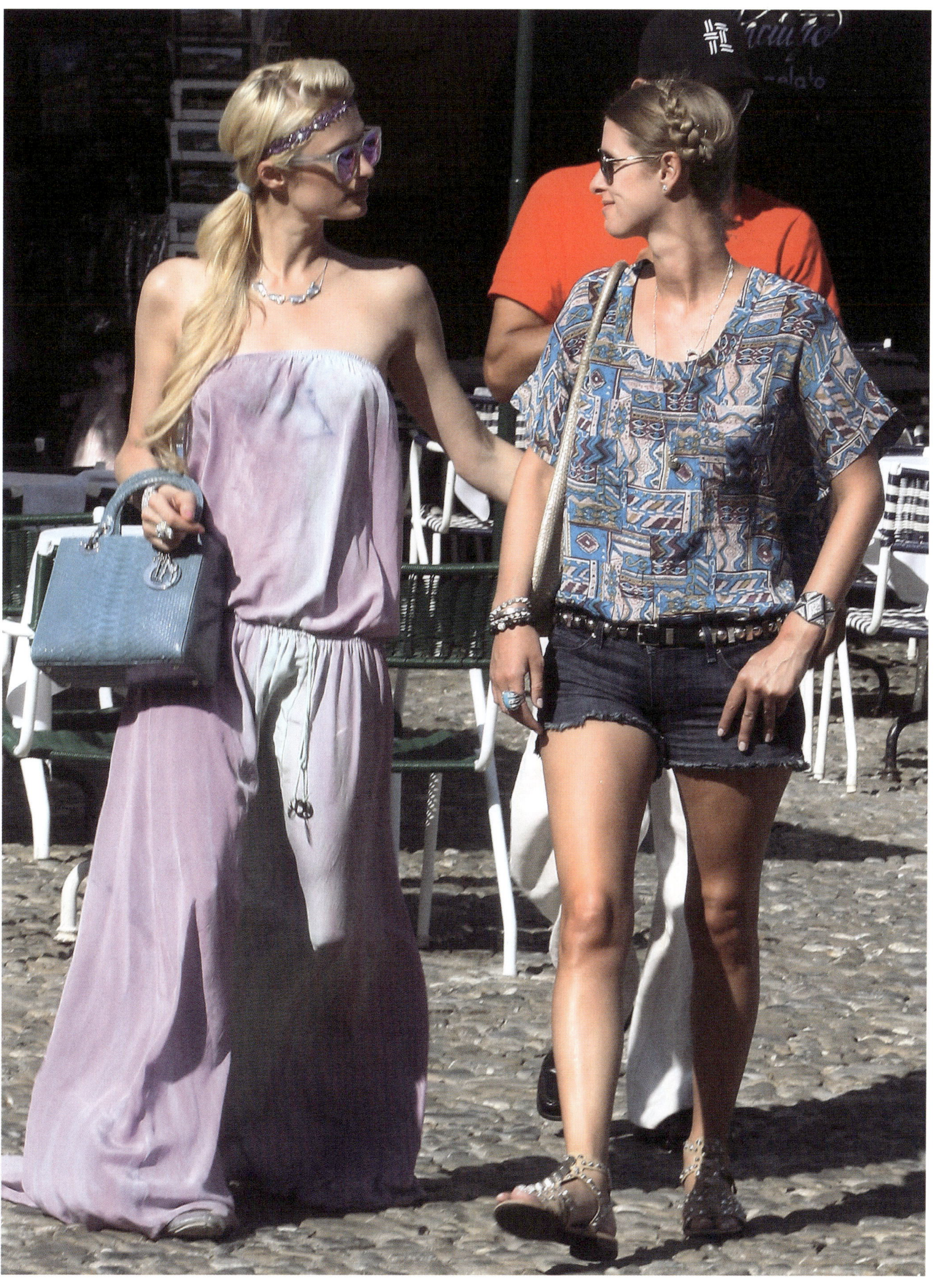

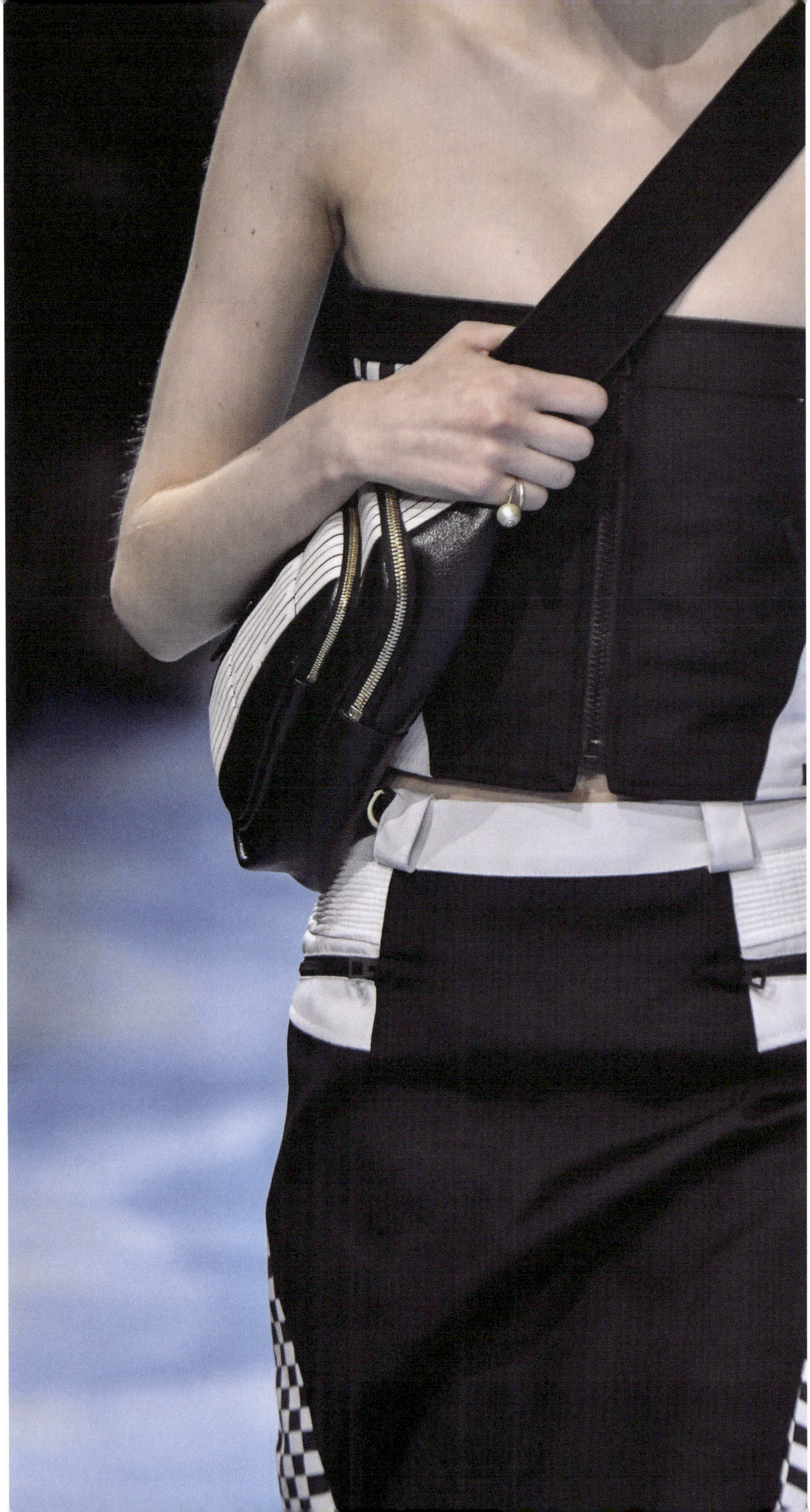

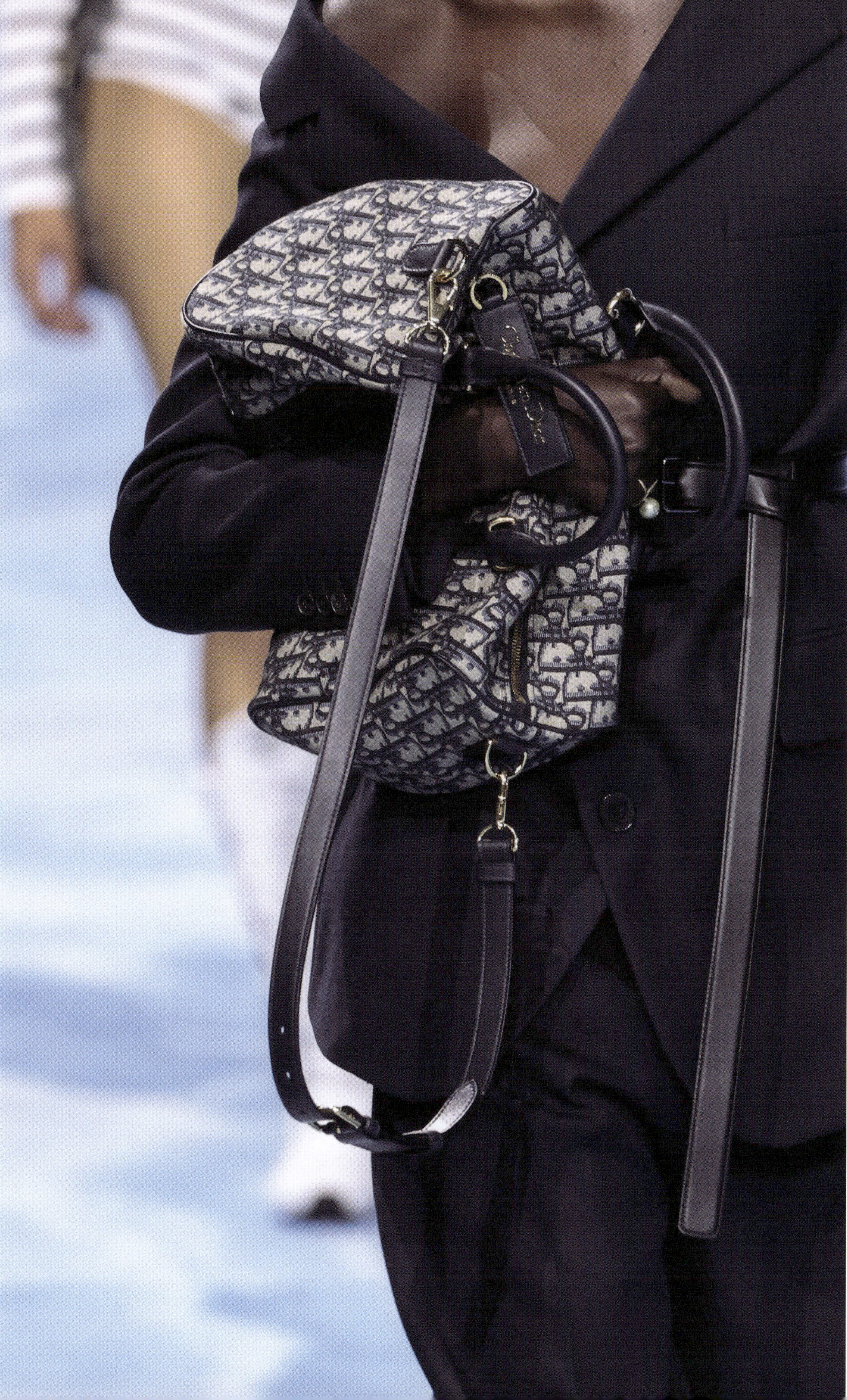

This page: Foxy Brown attends the opening of a Christian Dior boutique in New York City, 1999

Next page: Rihanna carries a Saddle bag in Los Angeles, 2024

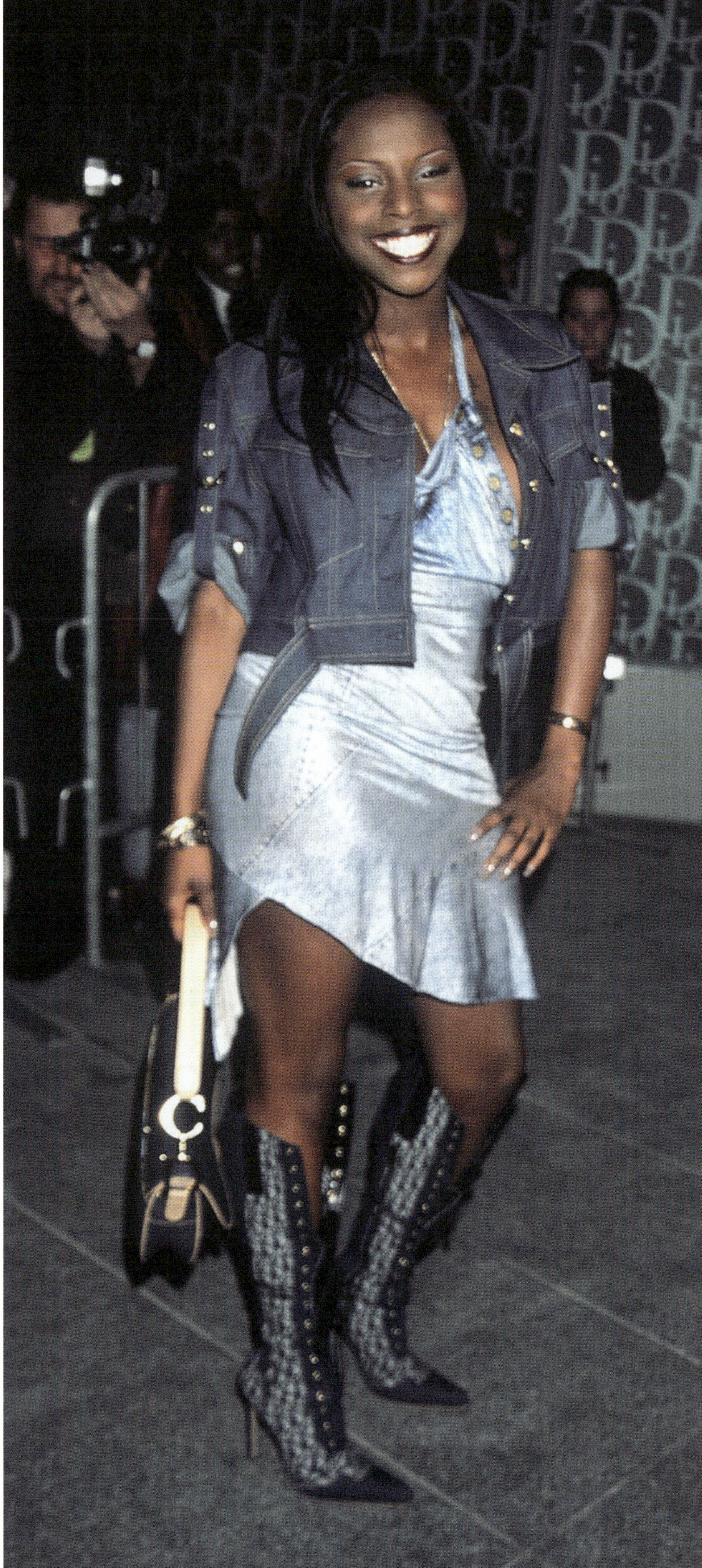

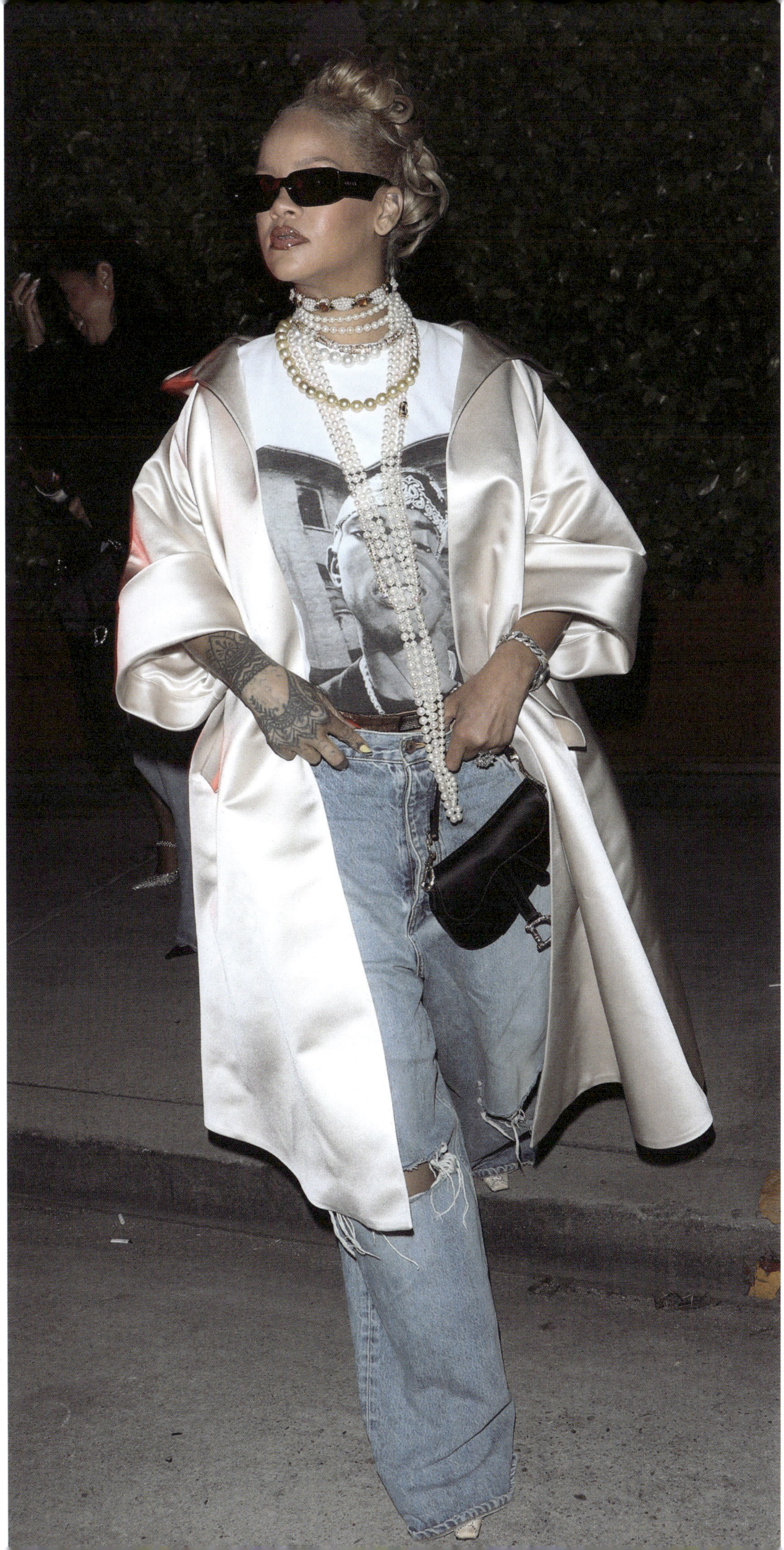

Romee Strijd arrives at Dior's Womenswear Spring/Summer 2020 show in Paris with a Caro bag in September 2019

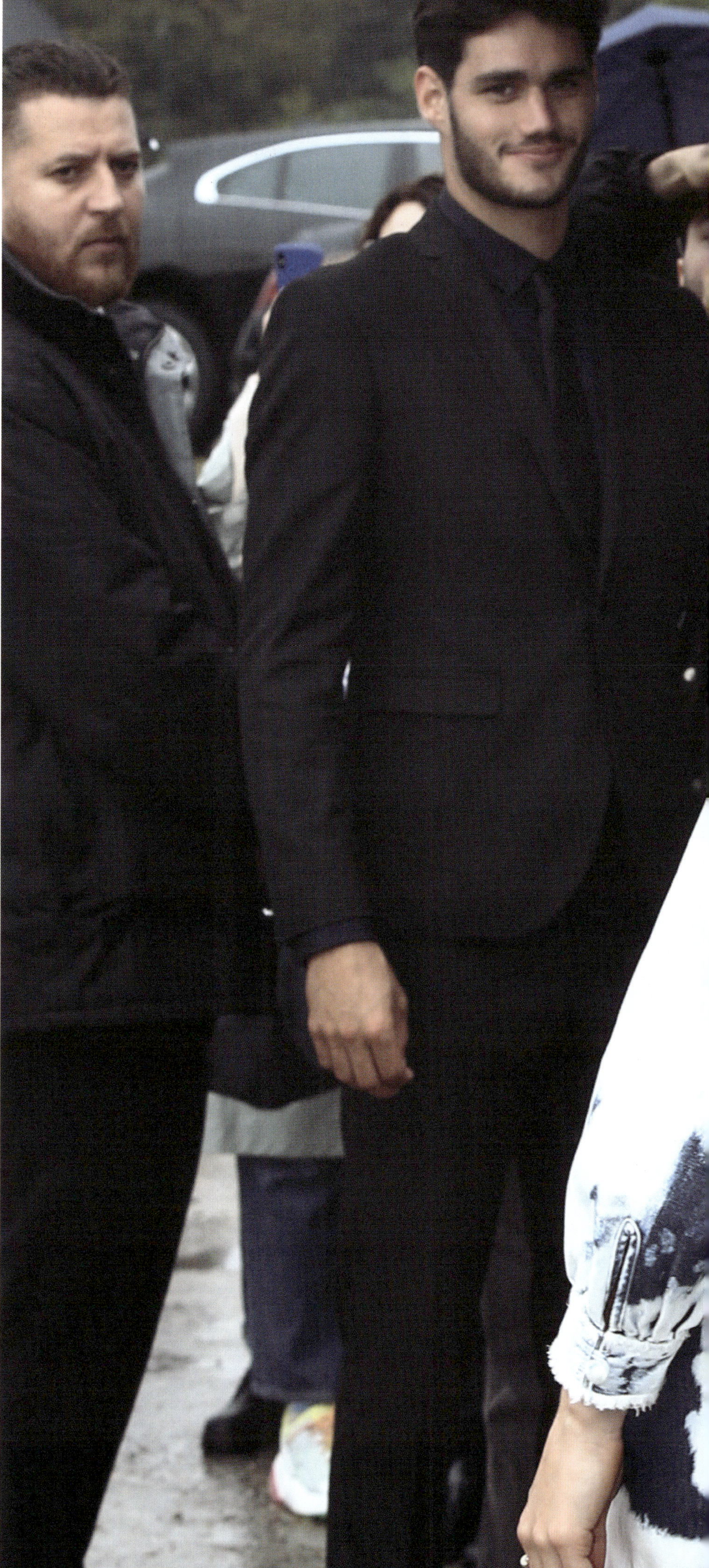

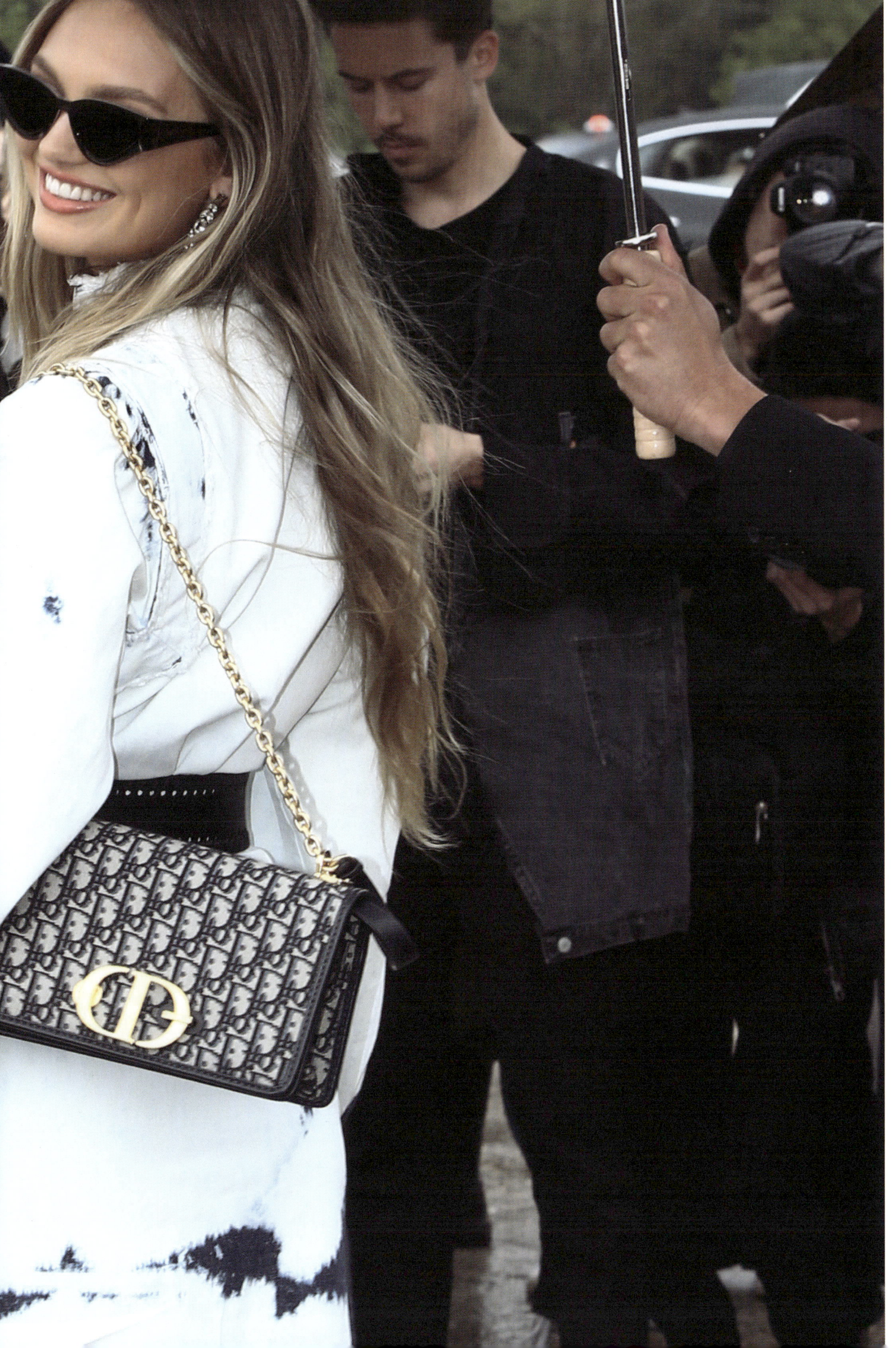

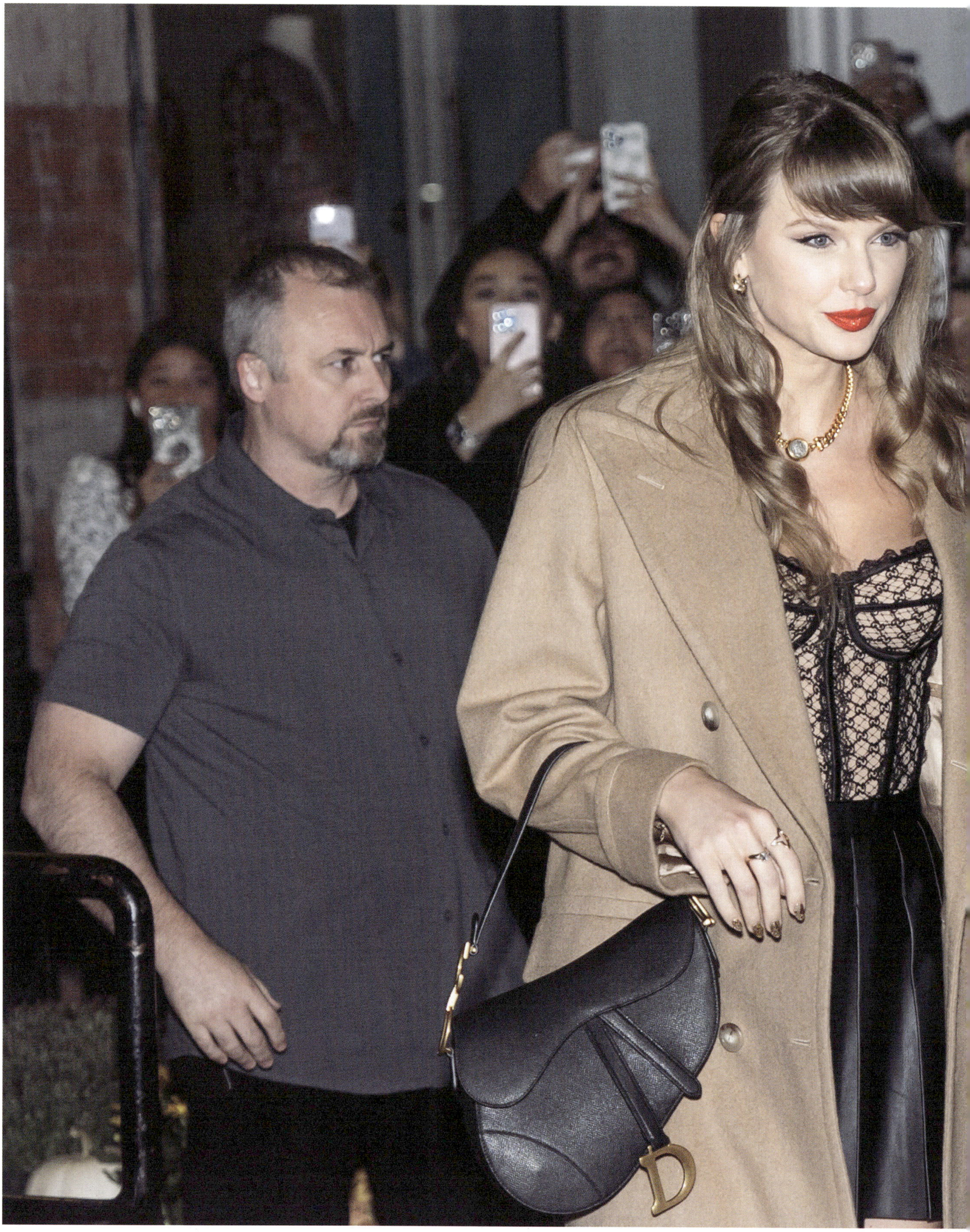

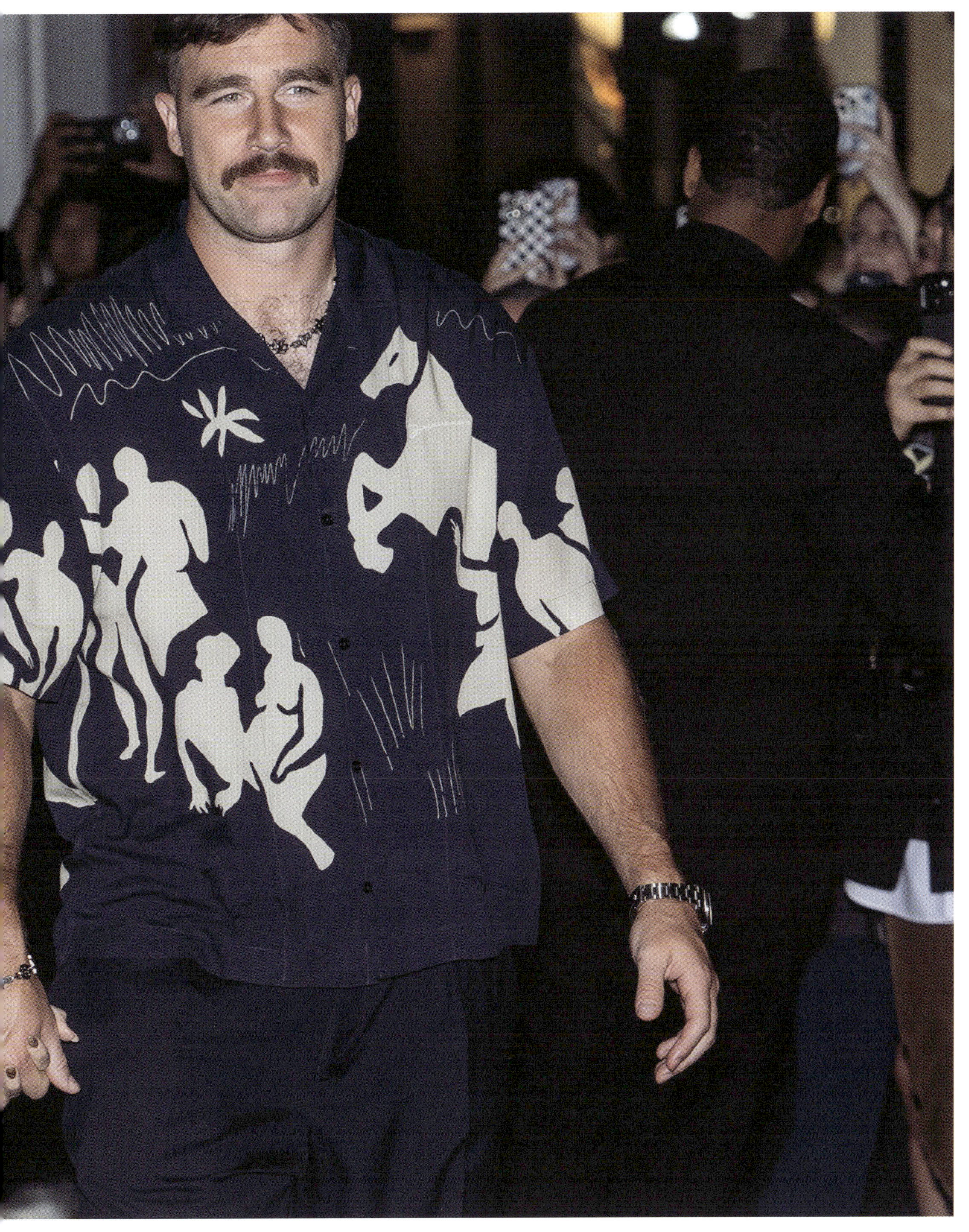

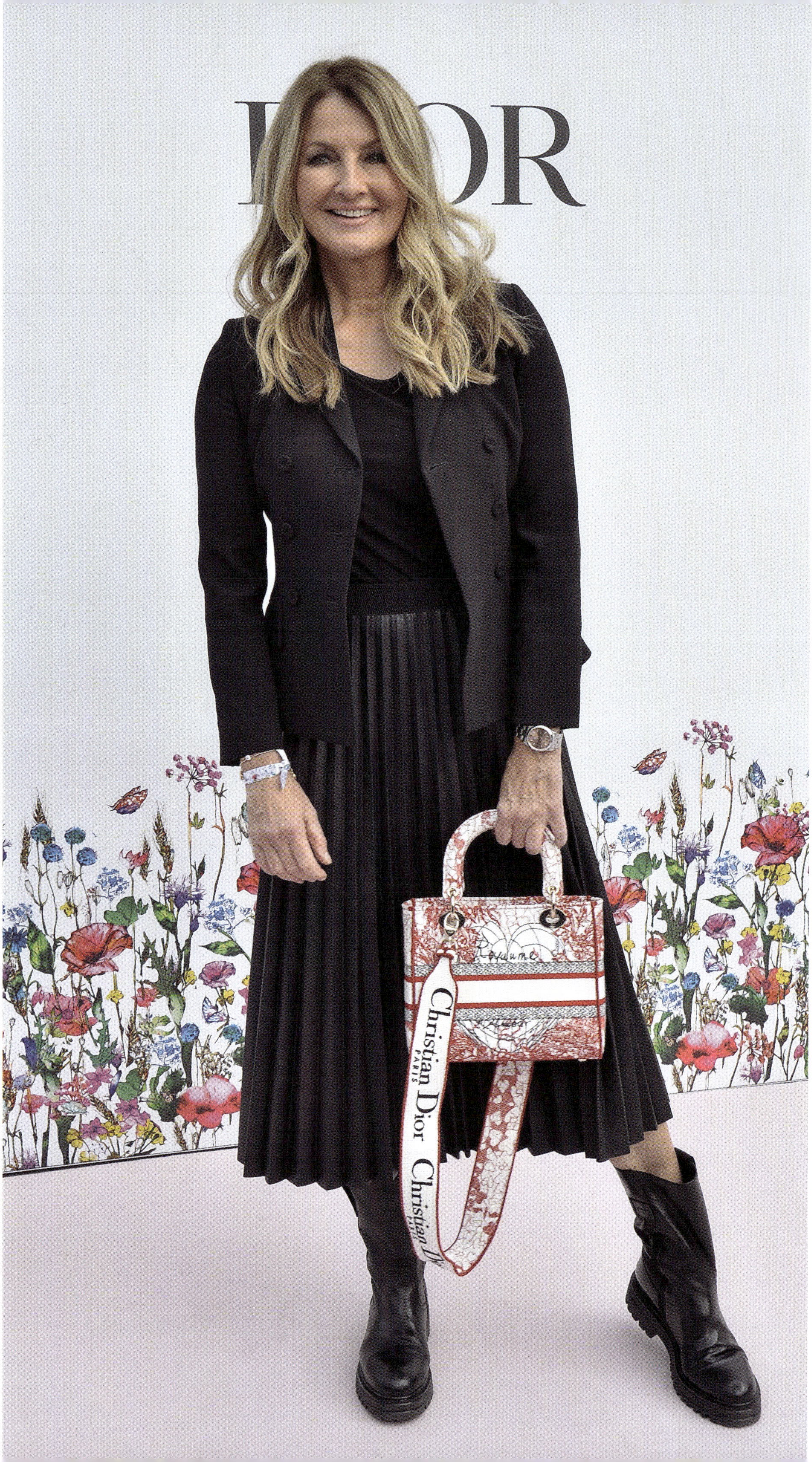

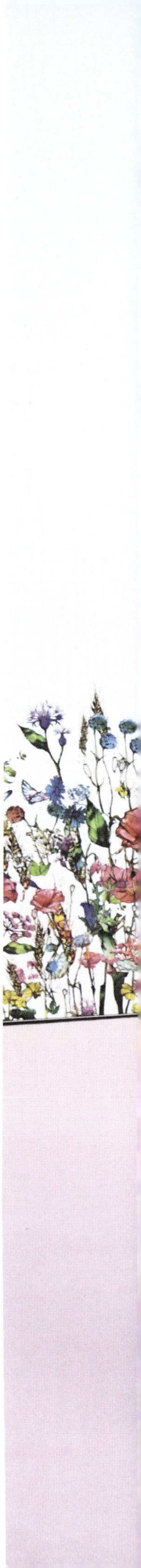

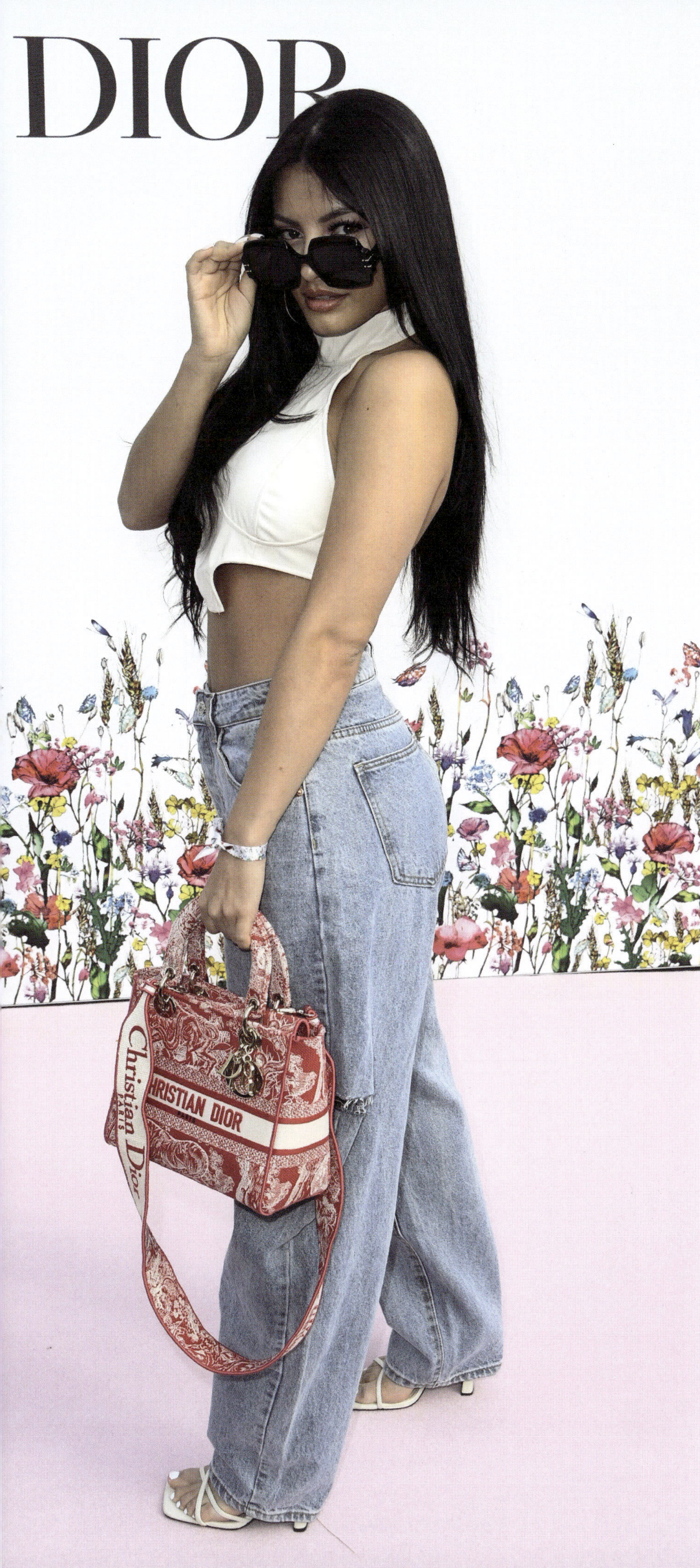

Pages 156/157: Taylor Swift (with a Saddle bag) and Travis Kelce are seen in New York City, October 2024

This page: Frauke Ludowig (left) and Ivana Santacruz (right) showcase floral Book Totes at the presentation of the new Miss Dior Eau de Parfum by Christian Dior in Düsseldorf, September 2021

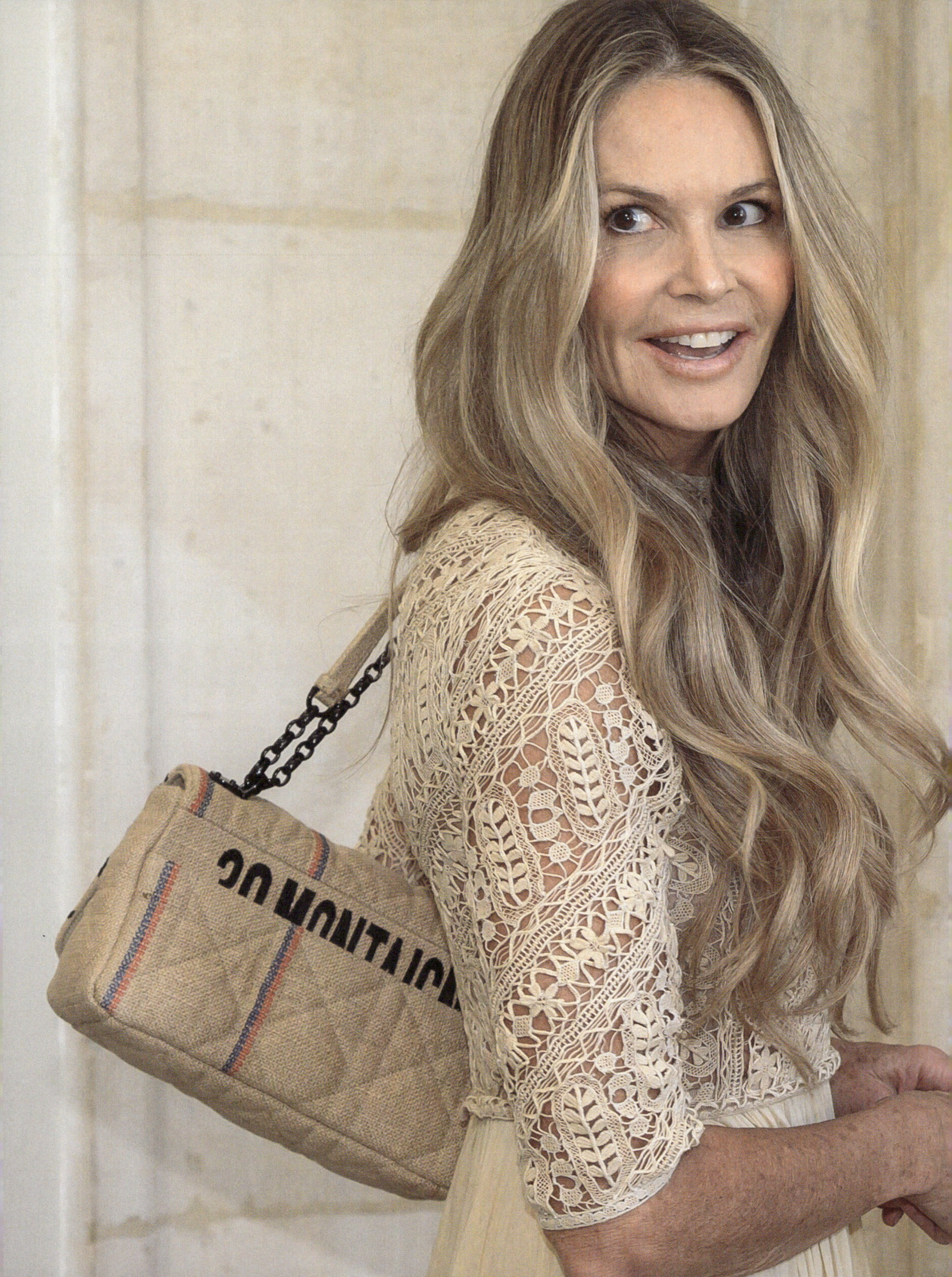

Elle Macpherson attends the Christian Dior Haute Couture Fall/Winter 2022 show with a Caro bag in Paris, 2022

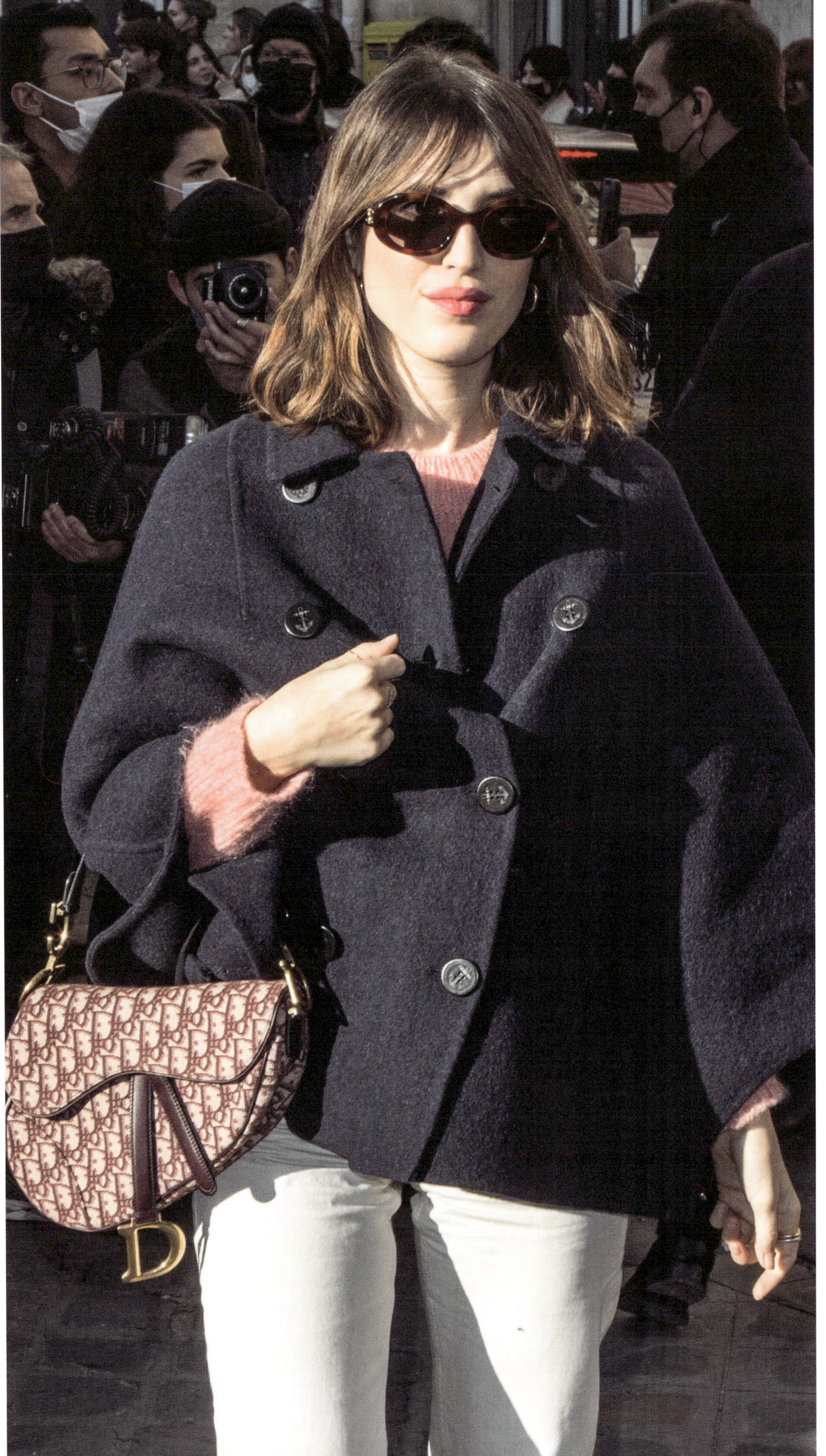

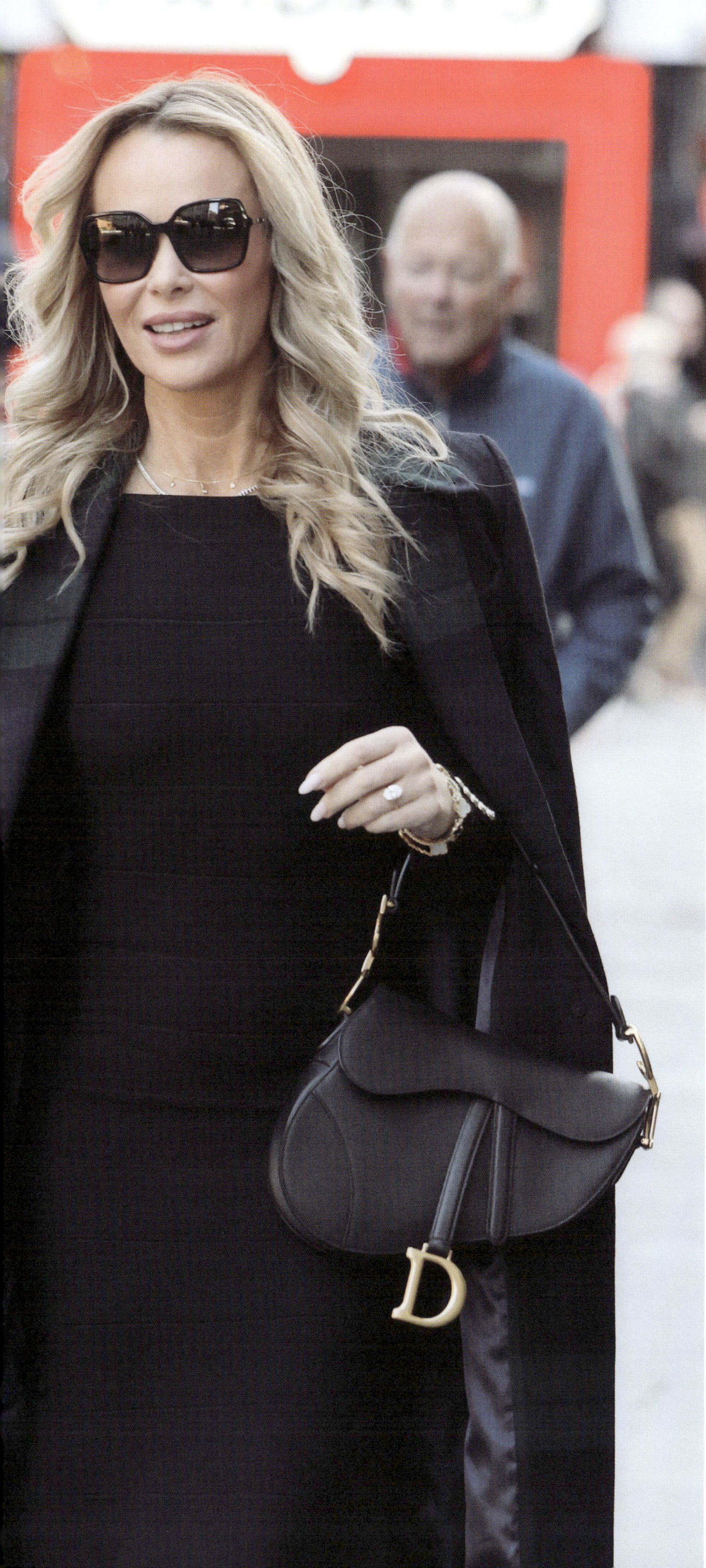

Previous page: Jeanne Damas carries a Saddle bag with a red *oblique* motif at Dior's Haute Couture Spring/Summer 2022 show in Paris, 2022

This page: Amanda Holden departs Heart Breakfast Radio Studios on November 25, 2024, in London, with a black Saddle bag

Pages 164/165: Tong Chenjie (left) and Lin Yun (right) attend the opening ceremony of the Dior Lady Art Exhibition on November 7, 2024, in Shanghai, both carrying Lady Dior bags

Pages 166/167: At the Dior Cruise 2025 show, Rosamund Pike carries a Lady Dior while Jennifer Lawrence presents a Lady D-Joy at Drummond Castle, Perthshire, 2024

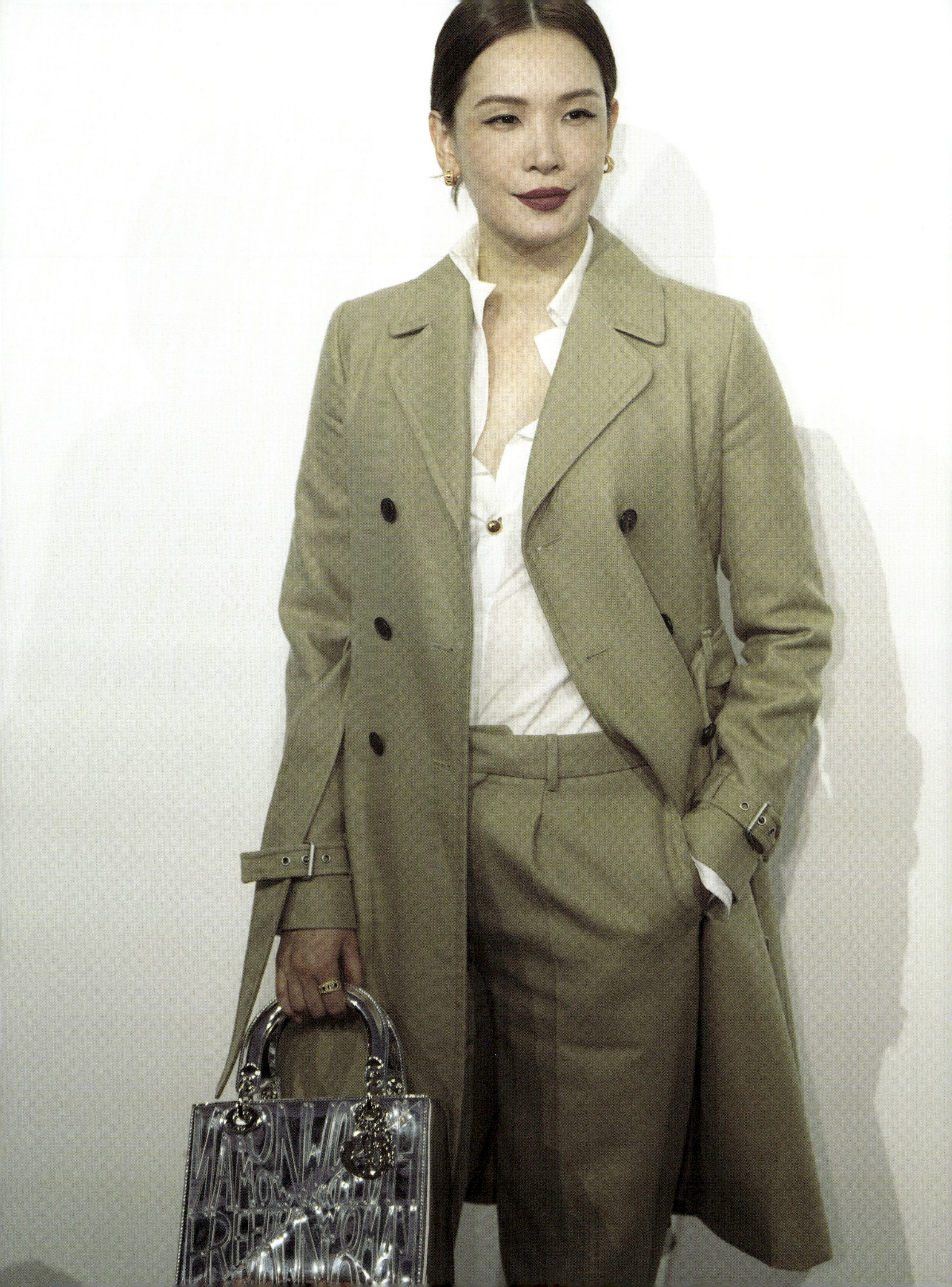

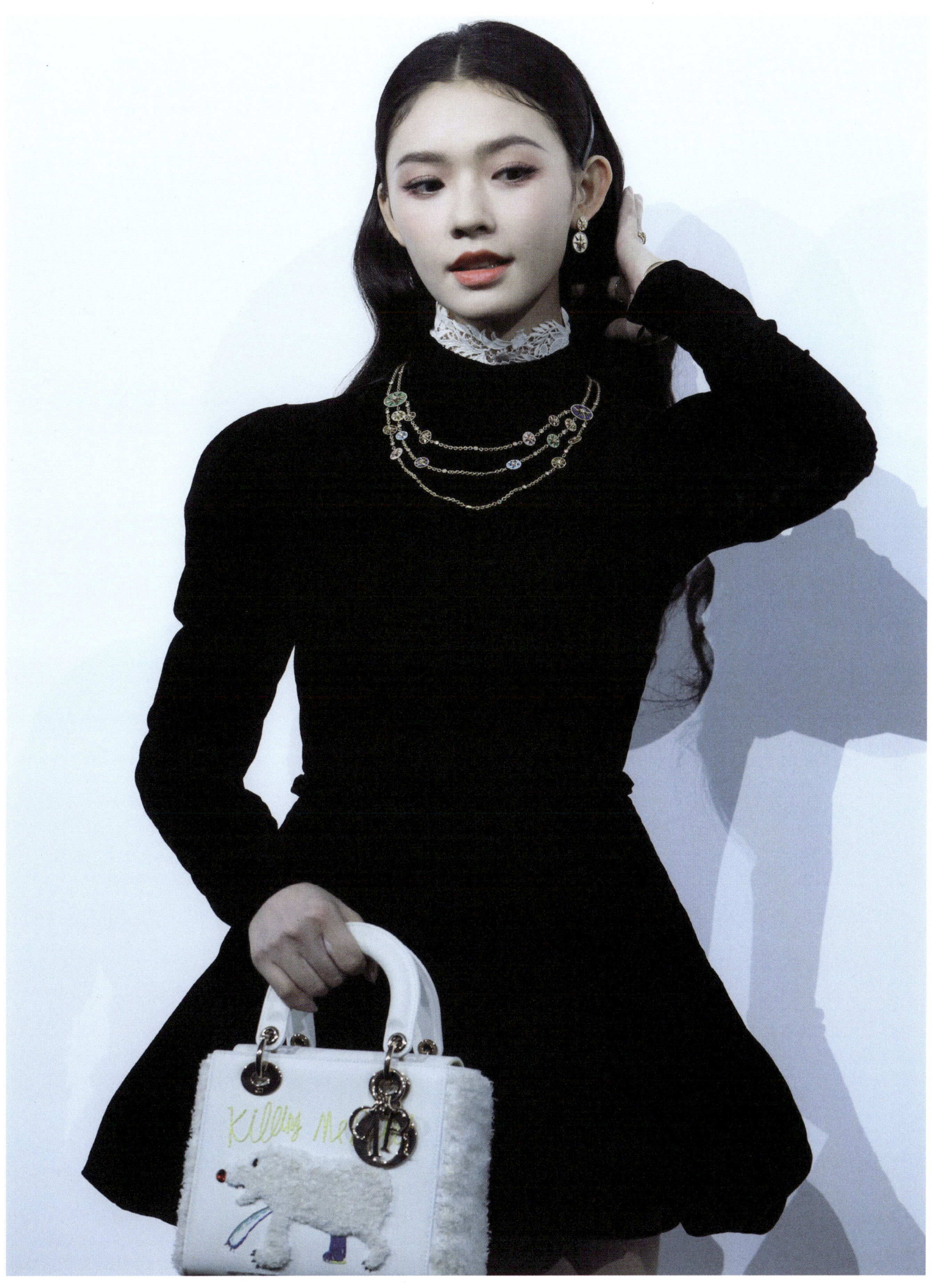

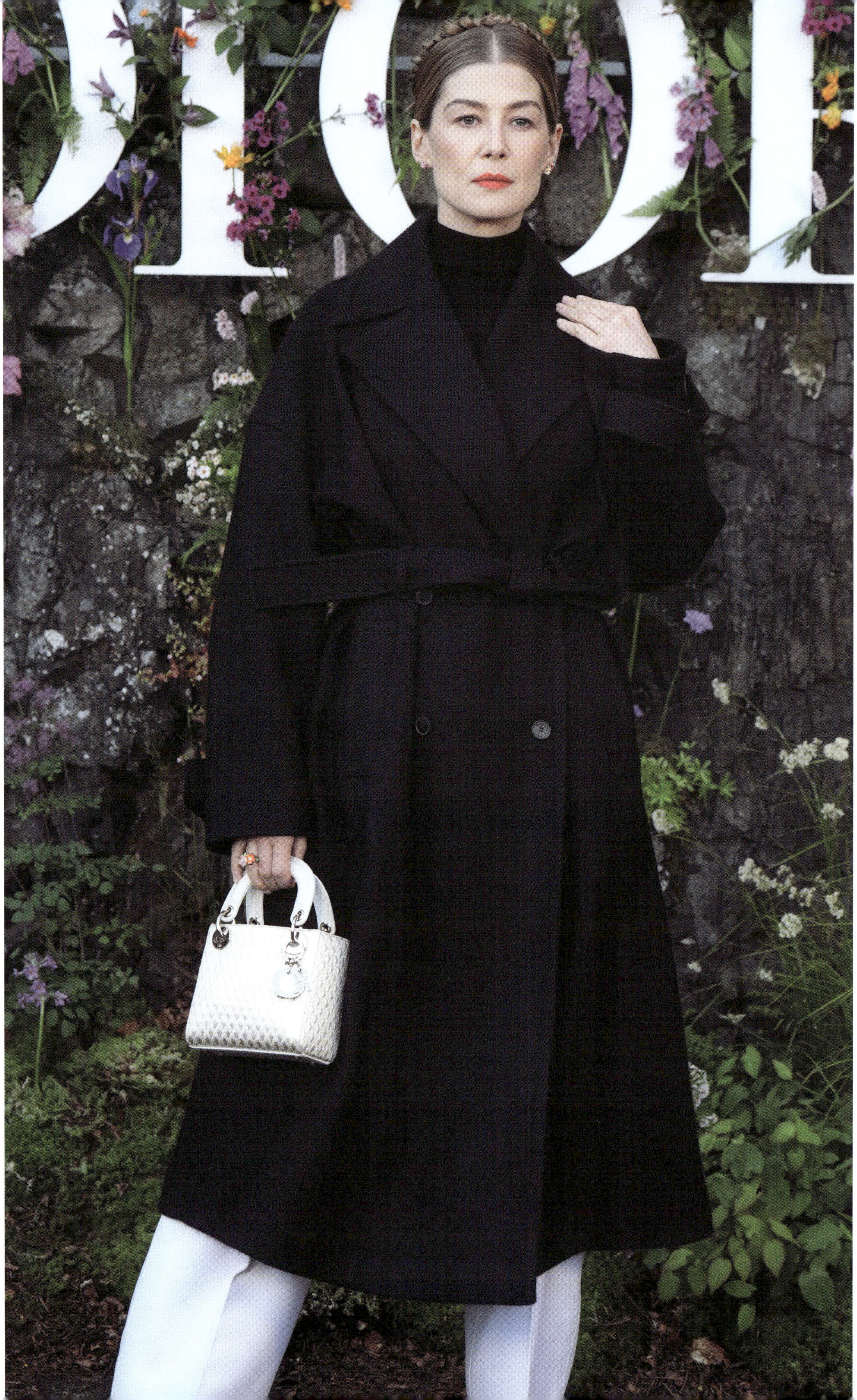

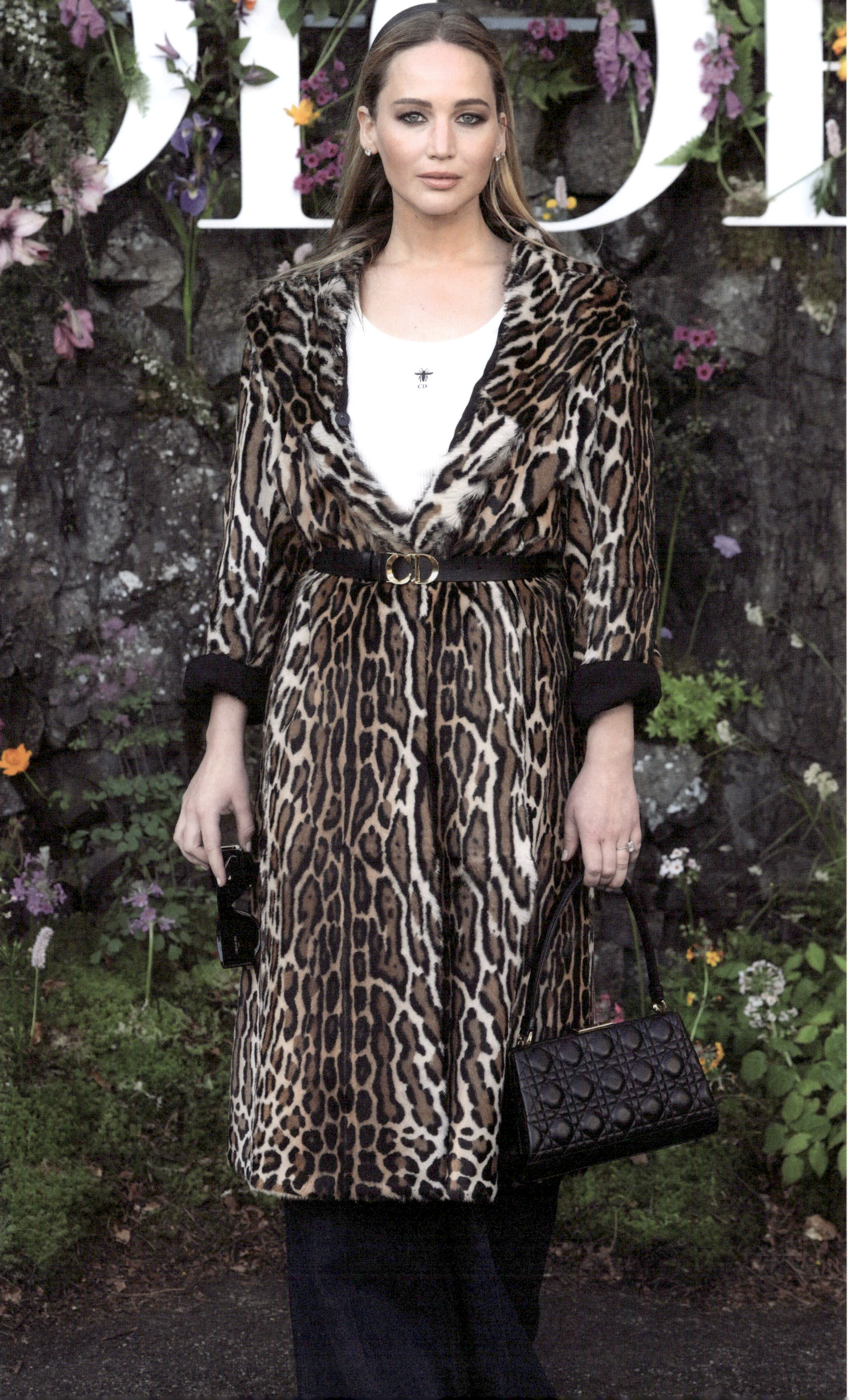

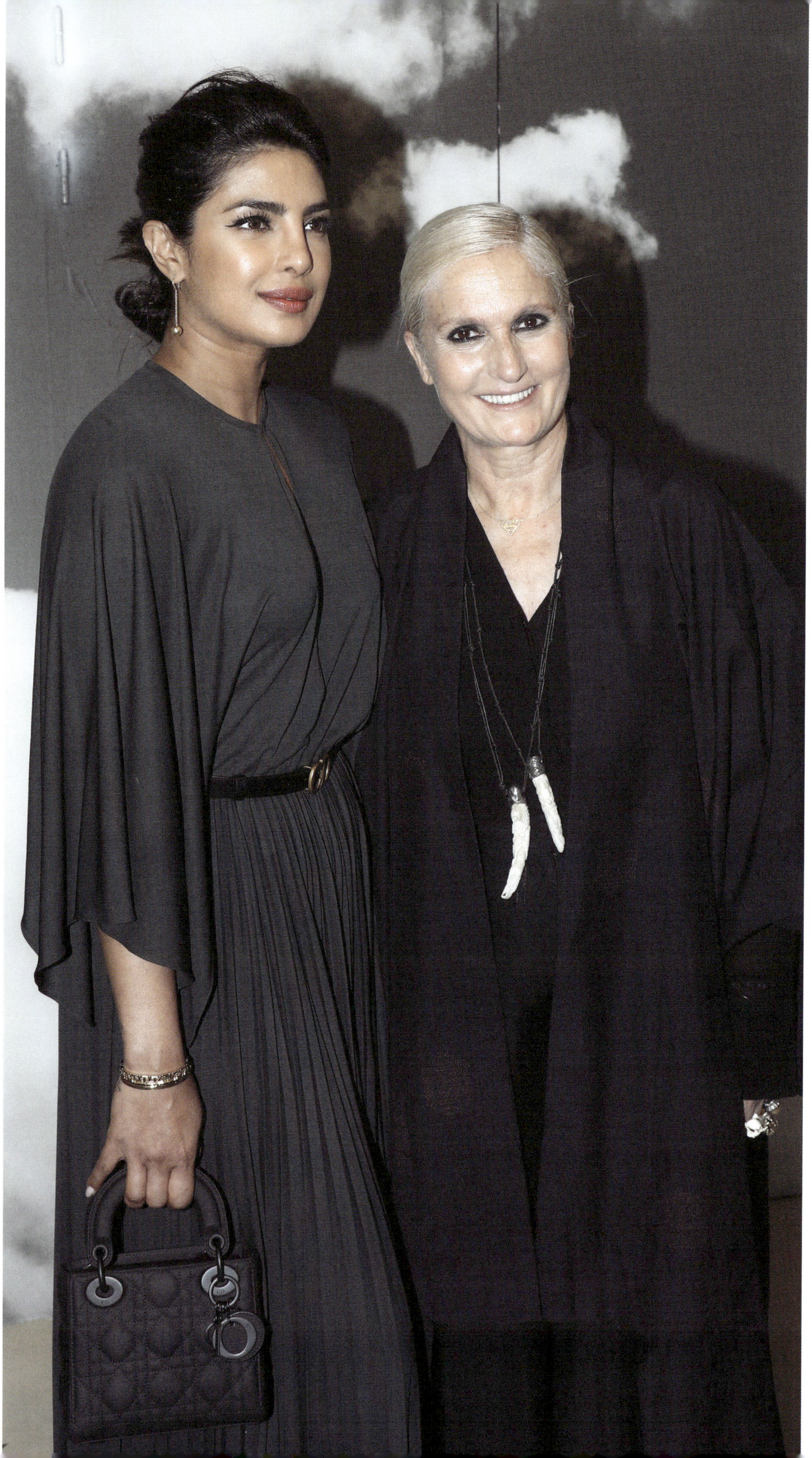

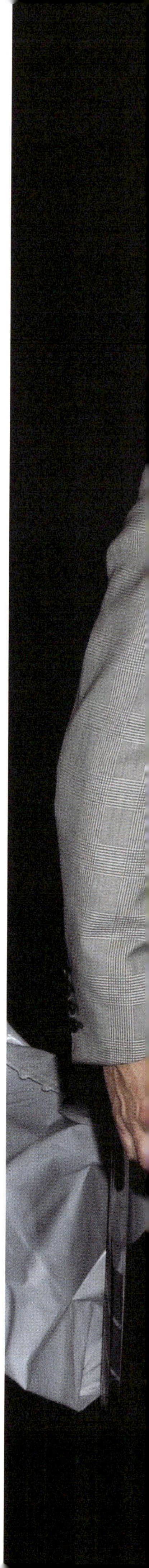

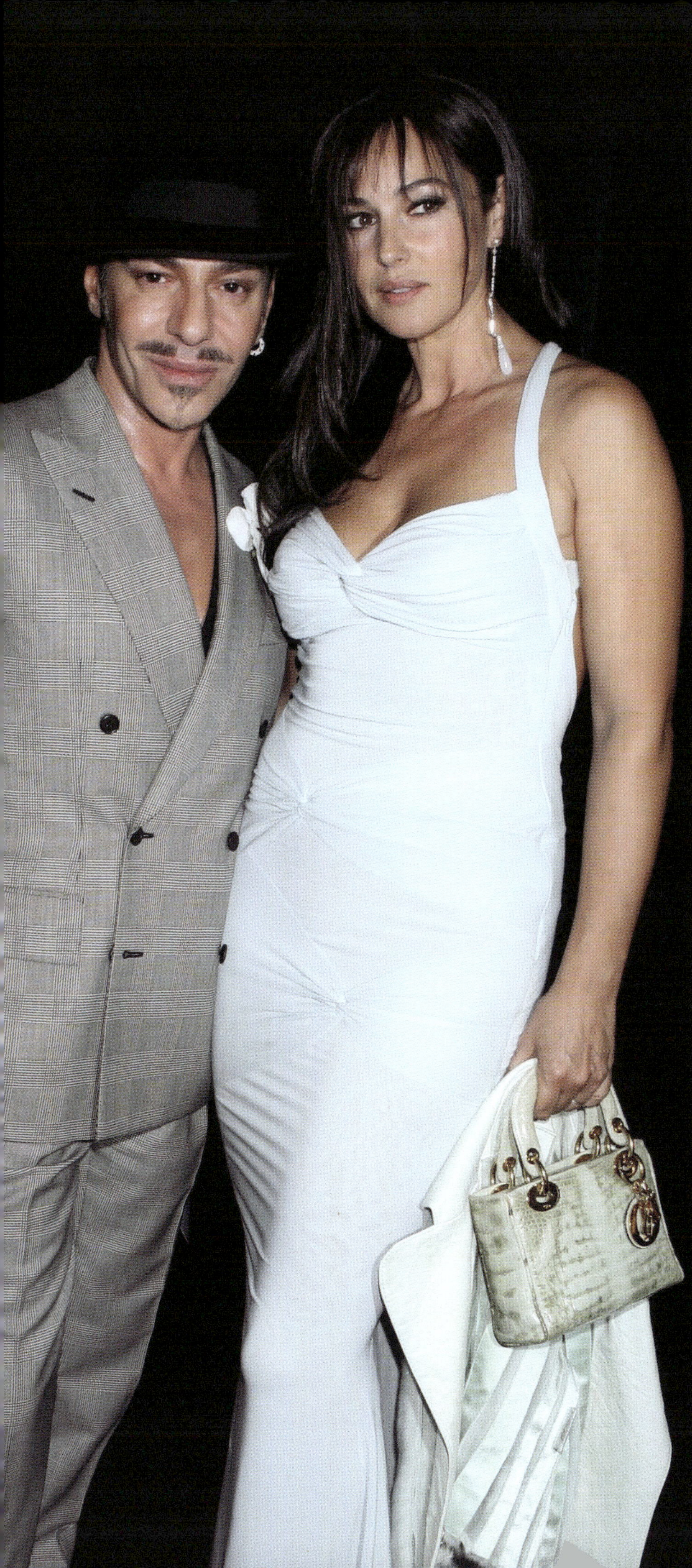

Previous page: Priyanka Chopra (with a Lady Dior) and Maria Grazia Chiuri pose after the Christian Dior Haute Couture Fall/Winter 2019 show in Paris, 2019

This page: John Galliano and Monica Bellucci (with a Lady Dior bag) appear at Dior's ready-to-wear Spring/Summer 2007 fashion show in Paris, 2006

Page 172: Monica Bellucci is photographed at a Dior party in Madrid, 2006

Page 173: Jisoo of BLACKPINK attends the photo call for the "Lady Dior Celebration" event at DIOR Seongsu on September 1, 2023, in Seoul

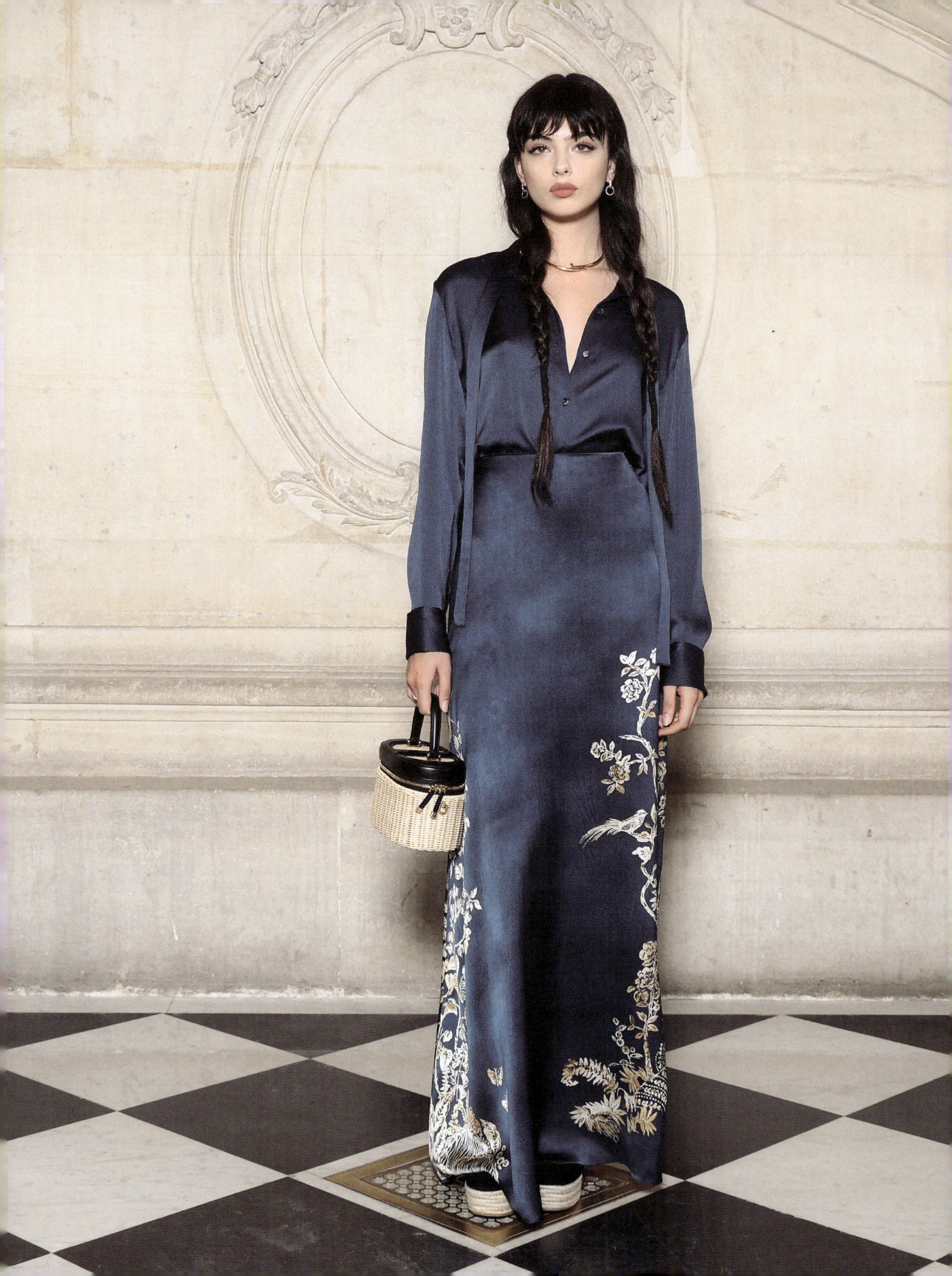

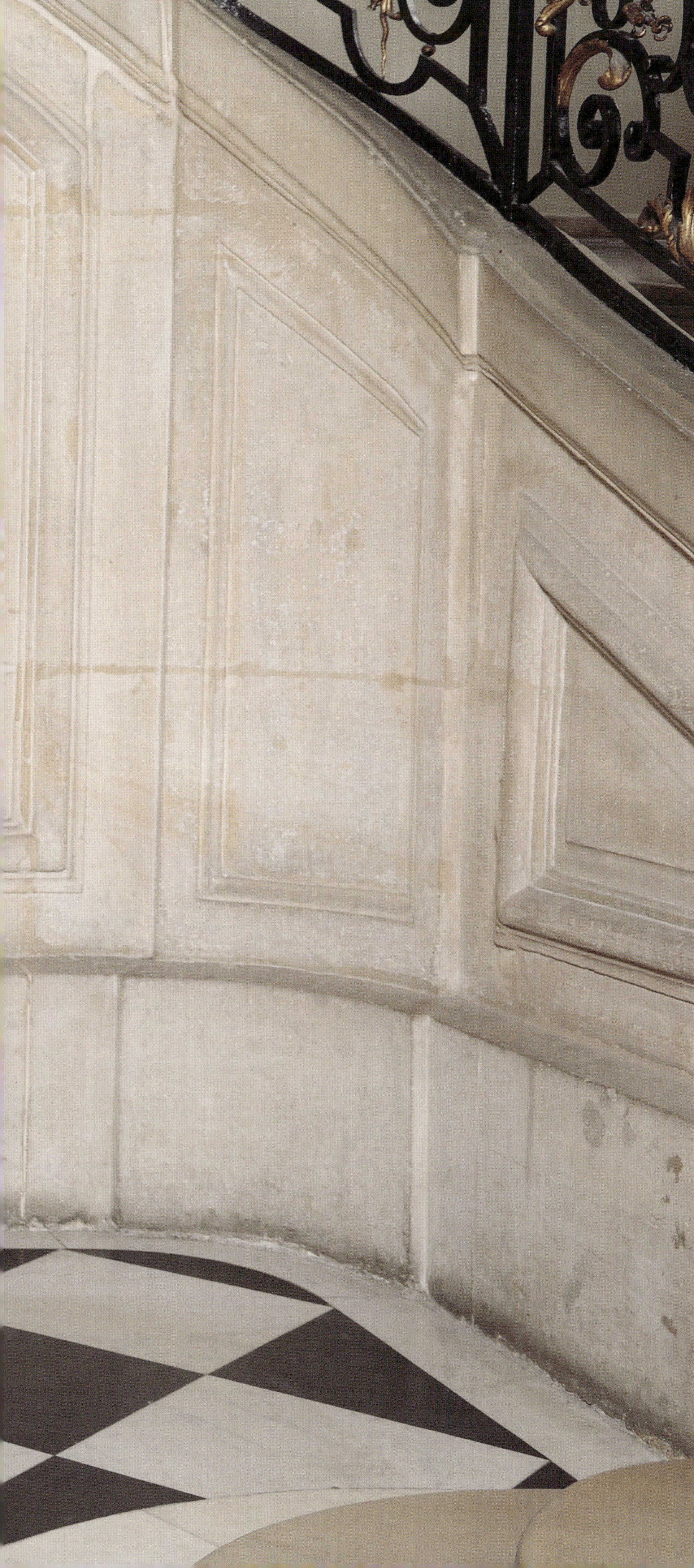

Deva Cassel (daughter of Monica Bellucci and Vincent Cassel) attends the Christian Dior Haute Couture Fall/Winter 2024 show, showcasing a Wicker Vanity Case with a top handle in Paris, 2024

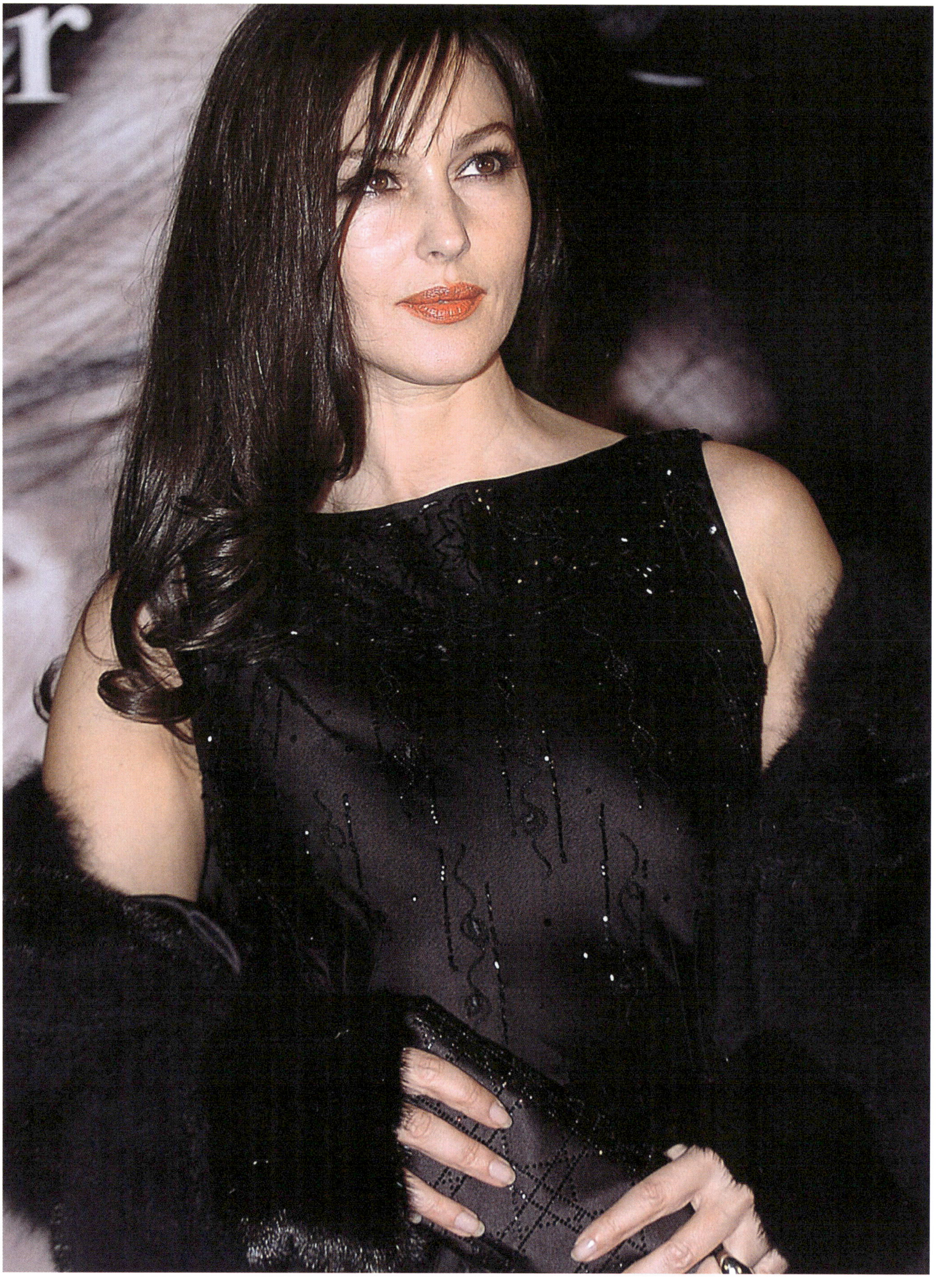

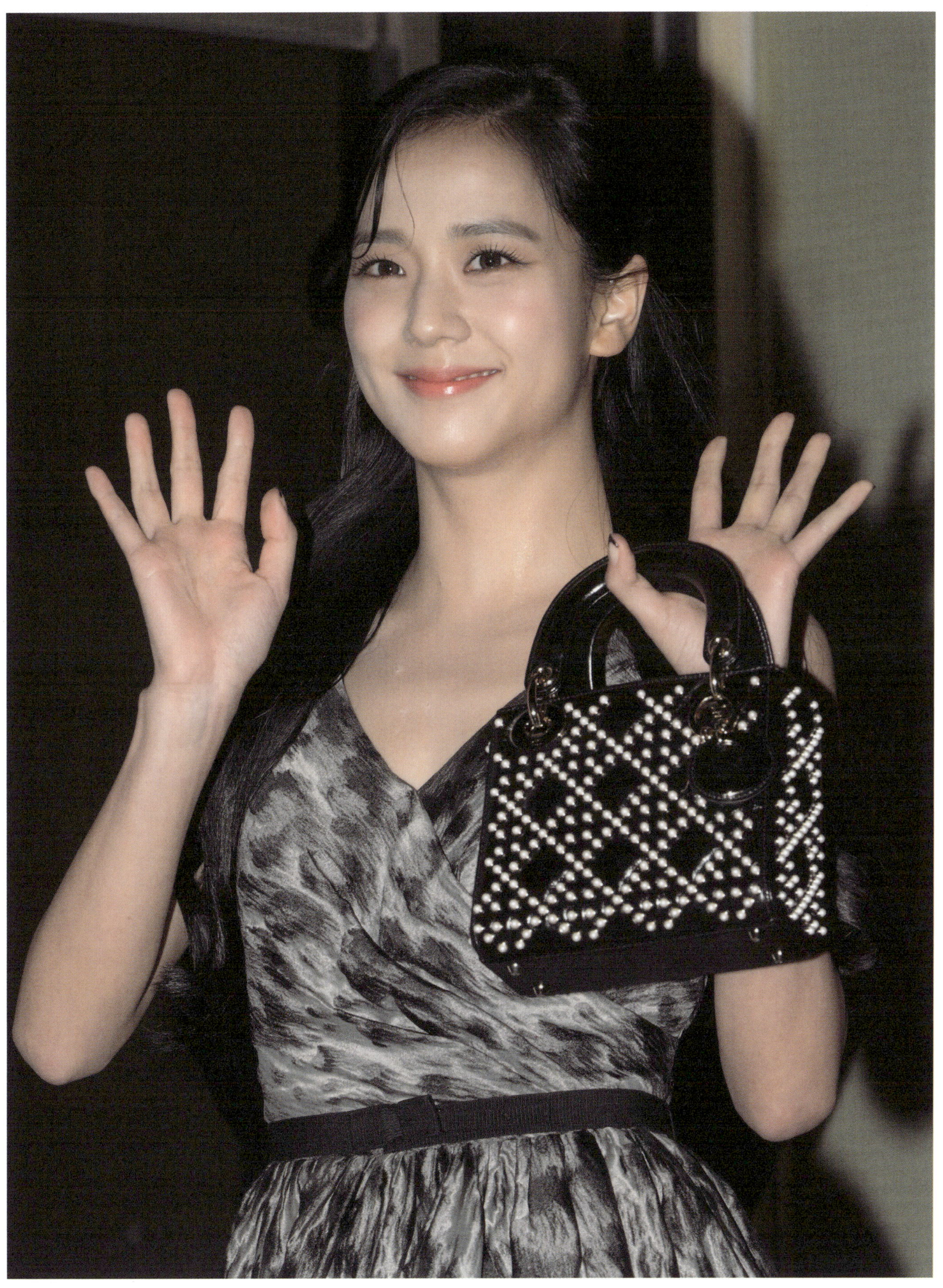

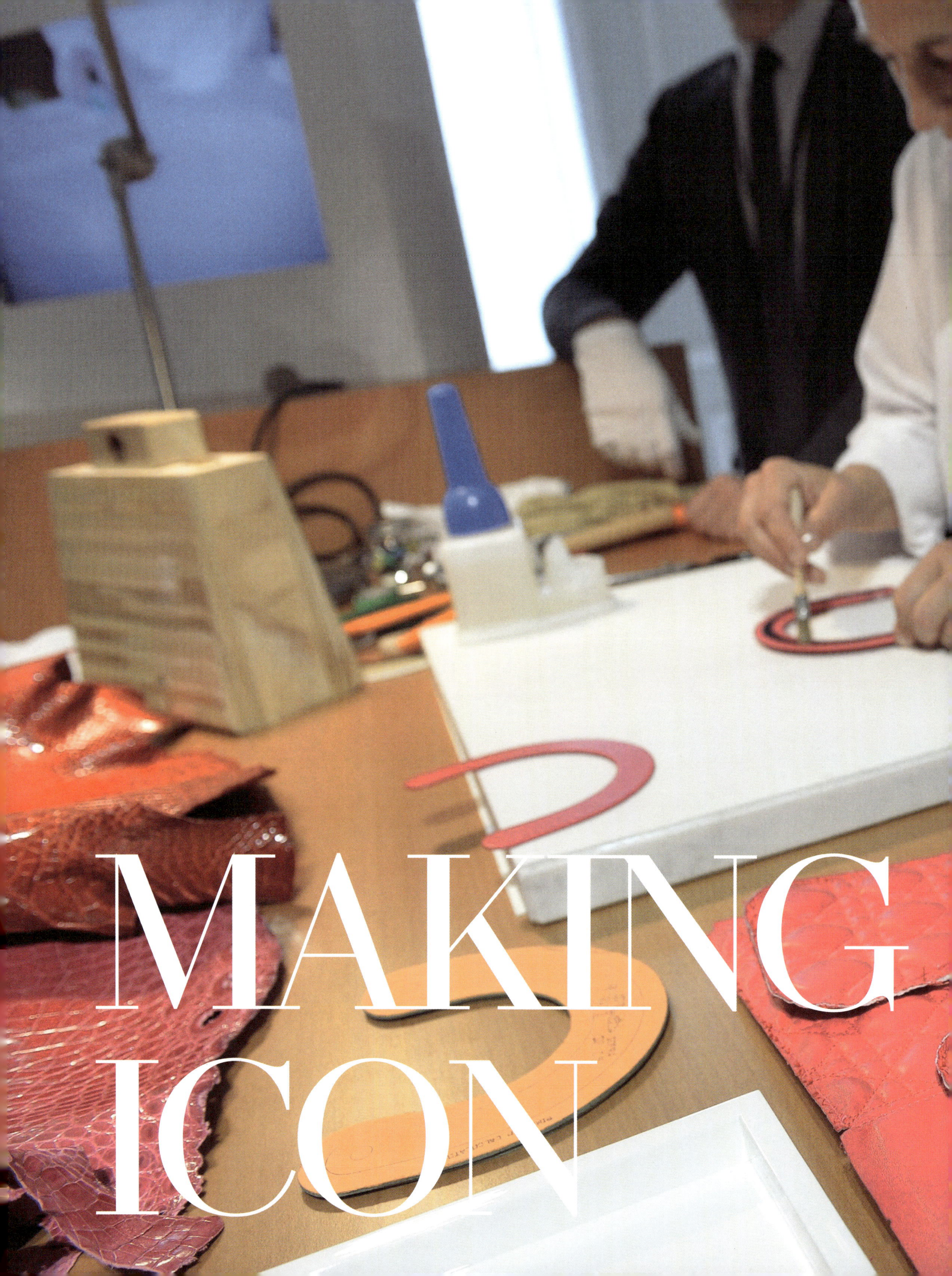

MAKING ICON

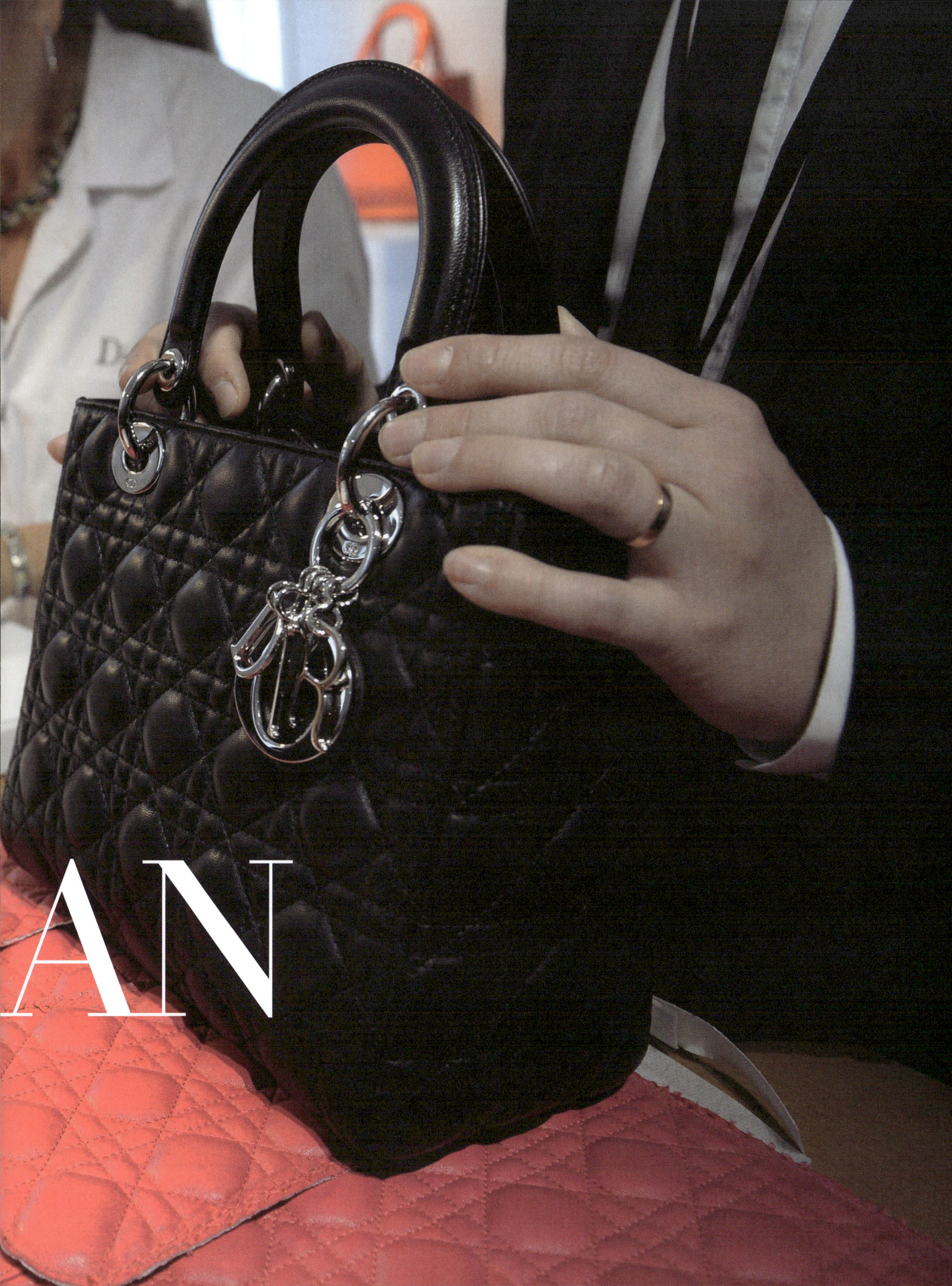

AN

BEHIND THE SCENES

LVMH (which stands for Louis Vuitton Moët Hennessy) is one of the biggest luxury corporations in the world. The group owns 75 elite brands across the categories of fashion, beauty, jewelry and alcohol including Tiffany & Co, Givenchy, Celine, Bulgari—and Dom Pérignon champagne. LVMH's biggest rival is the Kering group. While they own far fewer brands—only 13—Kering's focus is more fashion-led with Gucci, Saint Laurent, Balenciaga and Bottega Veneta all part of the Pinault-family owned group.

Since 2017 LVMH has been the majority shareholder of Dior, after a buy-out of an alleged $13.1 billion of Dior shares led by Bernard Arnault, France's richest man (Arnault's net worth is $181.3 billion). Dior's CEO is Arnault's daughter Delphine. She has held this role since February 2023, although she has worked at Dior since 2001, first as commercial director and subsequently as deputy managing director, before joining Louis Vuitton for a short period. While at Dior, Delphine has helped to steer one of the *maison's* most successful periods, helping the leather goods category achieve unprecedented growth and overseeing the house after Galliano's departure and subsequent creative director vacancies.

With big business backing, Dior has managed to navigate the corporate needs of a conglomerate with ever-exciting design and creativity balanced with fervent customer demand and celebrity collaborations. One reason for this is the continued high standards of excellence, expertise and materials used in the creation of all Dior goods, particularly handbags. While Dior doesn't reach the levels of obsession or commitment some other luxury brands inspire, or have as high a price tag in store (or at resale), their bags are still artisan-created works of art that command attention and carry a significant history behind each style.

All leather goods, including handbags, are made in Europe, and Dior has purchased several workshops across the continent to ensure the preservation of specific skills. Each item is made in the region with the most specialized talent required for that particular item. Dior watches are produced in Switzerland, and Japanese *ateliers* make Dior's denim pieces and jeans.

But before creation comes ideation. One might say that anyone could draw a handbag, but Dior's design team will sketch their vision, consider all the elements that may challenge the production, and contemplate any market forces, trends and patterns before any potential bag is brought to life.

The physical creation of each bag begins with materials carefully chosen for their superior quality, whether it's calfskin, lambskin or embroidered textiles used for the iconic *oblique* monogram. Every material is chosen for a specific reason that complements the style and intended use.

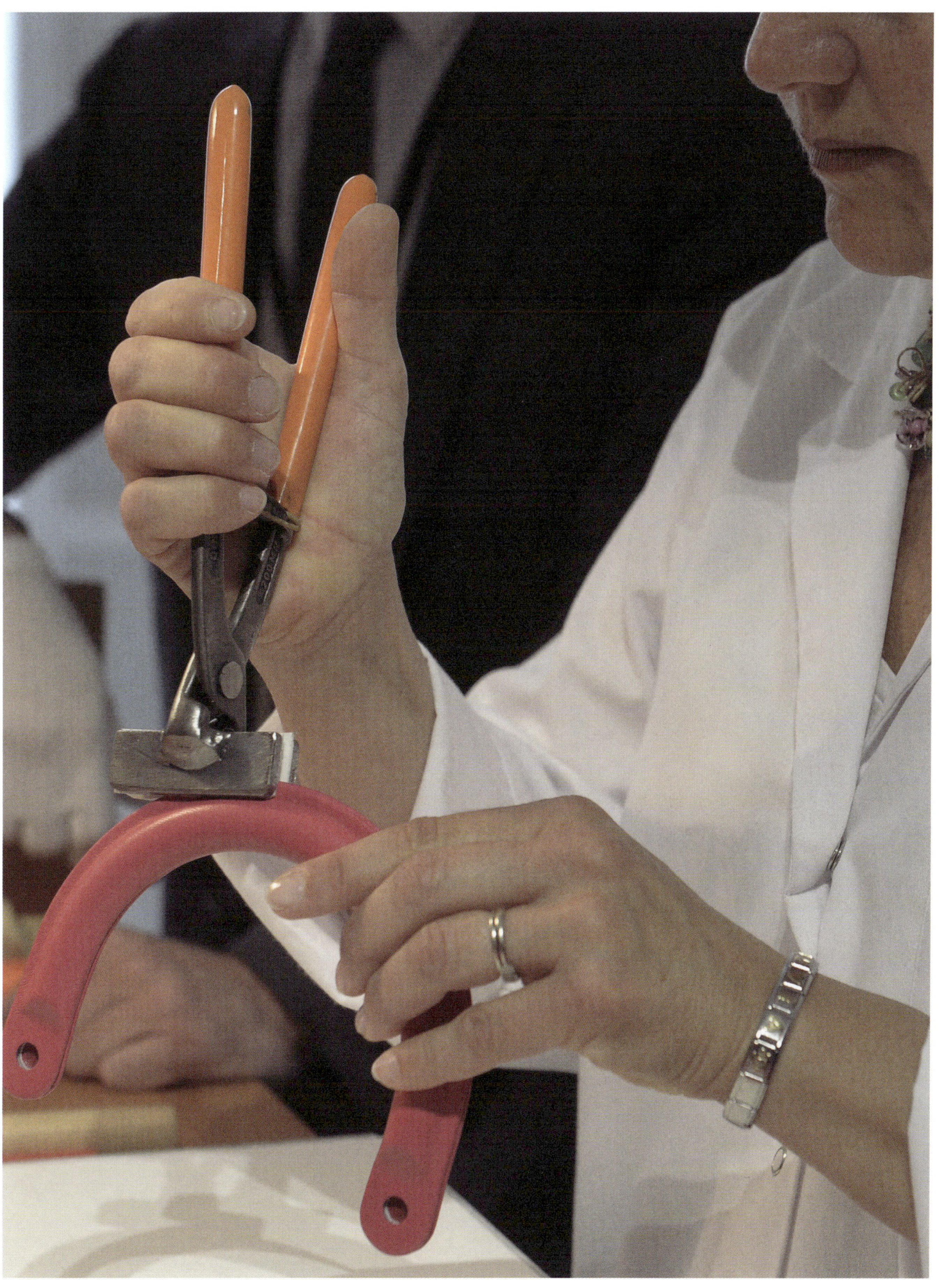

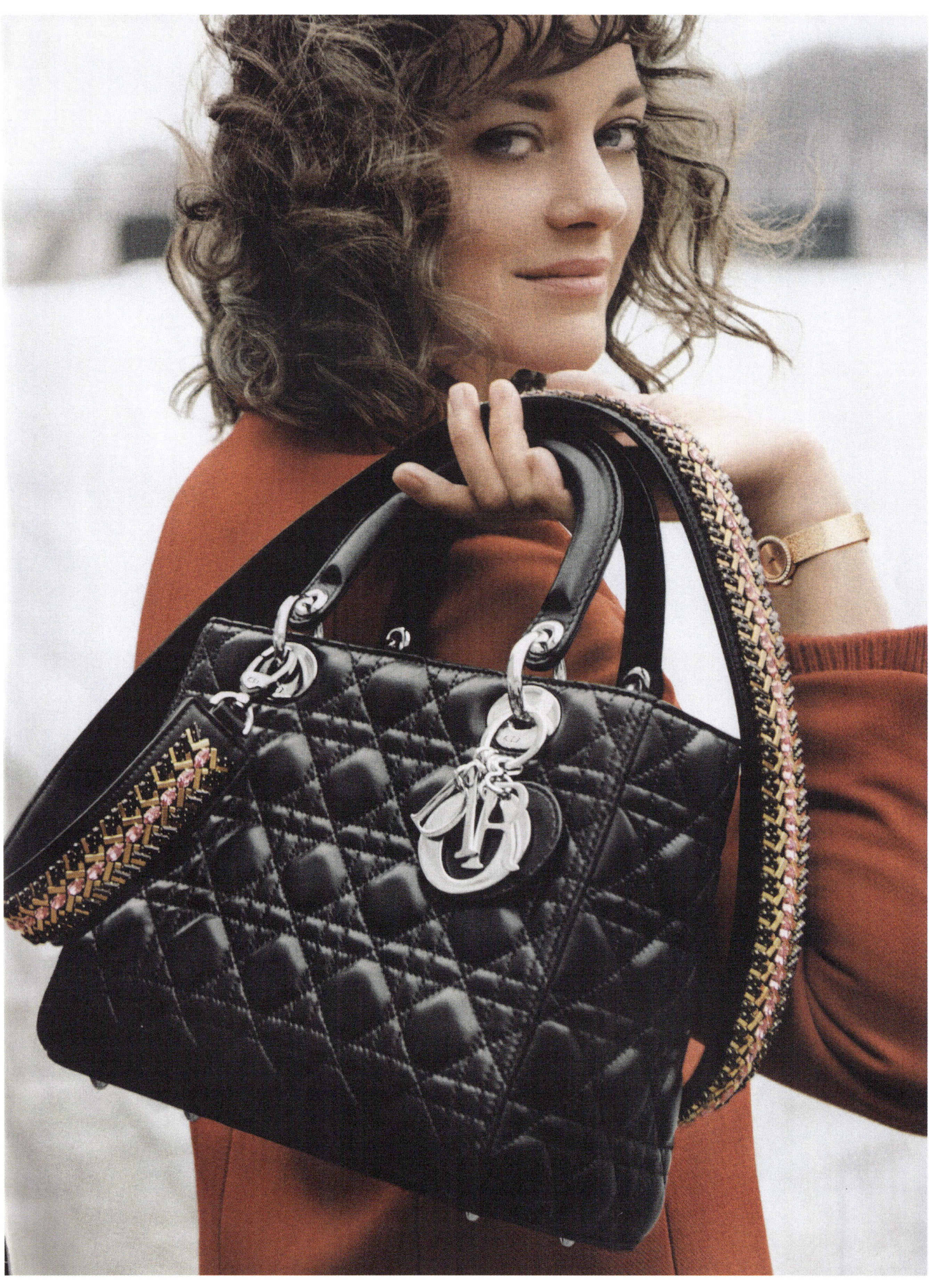

Some of the most popular bags are created from the following materials:

Lambskin can scuff easily and is hard to keep clean if you choose a light-colored bag. However, lambskin is noted for its durability and ability to hold its shape.

Patent leather is tantalizingly glossy with a mirror shine finish. It looks bold in all colors, but its flawless finish means that scuffs are particularly noticeable, and any scratches will likely be permanent.

Grained leather, as is often used on the Saddle Bag, has a scratch-resistant finish and a pleasing texture that elevates the look of the bag, also making the bag ideal for daily wear. It makes sense that when choosing such a timelessly designed bag, it needs to be made from an equally durable material to ensure longevity. Grained calfskin leather is a tough material and one of the most popular and durable choices at Dior.

Deerskin leather is a rarer finish, which is smooth with a light texture. It holds its structure so your bag won't sag. This leather has a great mix of softness and strength if cared for correctly.

Canvas is often used as the base for the *oblique* monogram and has a distinct advantage over traditional leathers, as it's lighter. It's perfect for large bags like the Book Tote, which can fit many items without becoming too heavy to use. However, canvas can be more prone to slouching compared to leather bags, so canvas bags should always be stored with the correct stuffing to maintain their shape.

Dior continues to use exotic skins in production, mainly on custom orders or limited edition pieces. Alligator, crocodile, lizard, python, ostrich and Ayers leather (a type of snakeskin) are rare finishes that carry high price tags, particularly on the resale market, and also require extra care from any potential owner.

Once the material for a bag is selected, hours of handcrafted labor will follow. Dior uses a mix of traditional handmade techniques and cutting-edge technology to ensure the best possible quality. Some elements can only be made by hand, while precision machine cutting is done to provide high-tech accuracy. The Caro bag requires 18,000 machine stitches to create the unique *cannage* design, and its pattern-cutting is mainly done by machine. Threads are often cut with a laser instead of scissors for an immaculate finish.

Some bag styles can take weeks to make, depending on the materials and complexity of the design. The Book Tote requires around 37 hours of work to bring to life. Then, once a bag is completed, every seam and stitch is scrutinized to make sure the bag is perfect before it is shipped to stores for sale.

French-made luxury has a legendary status and an image of integrity, the product of centuries of artisan-made craftwork and good PR. However, in 2024 Dior came under investigation for allegations that were the antithesis of this image. It was revealed that some subcontracted factories used by Dior were employing illegal workers. The investigation conducted by AGCM, the Italian Competition Authority, found that employees in factories on the outskirts of Milan were forced to sleep in the factory so they would always be on hand to fulfill orders, were subjected to unsafe working conditions, and were victims of huge price discrepancies between their wages and the bag's retail price. Reuters revealed that one specific bag cost €53 to

FRENCH-MADE LUXURY HAS A LEGENDARY STATUS AND AN IMAGE OF INTEGRITY, THE PRODUCT OF CENTURIES OF ARTISAN-MADE CRAFTWORK

make and was sold for €2600, leaving many consumers incredulous at the mark-up and questioning whether the price of luxury is really justified, especially during recessions or economic downturns.

The Business of Fashion reported that Jean-Jacques Guiony, chief financial officer at LVMH, claimed, "We had no idea about this situation." Dior has disputed some elements of the case: the specific factory under investigation was working on one element of one style of men's bag. Dior has since cut ties with the factories in question and taken steps to shore up their suppliers' code of conduct.

The revelation led Instagram account Diet Prada to question whether a fake bag would be a better choice than an authentic bag that had been made under less than auspicious circumstances. In a post dated July 2024, they mused, "Another facet of the ever-shifting prism of luxury is the rise of fake bags in both prevalence and quality. Shoppers can more easily get a high-quality copy of desired goods, for less than the real thing, and when the real thing can't even guarantee to have been made with favorable working conditions or of prestigious material, it's no wonder so many are questioning their choices."

Despite the scandal, which was soon replaced in the public consciousness by Dior's role in the Paris Olympics, it's clear that fake bags are never in fashion. Counterfeit bags infringe on intellectual property rights and are often directly linked to human trafficking, drug and weapons smuggling, and sex trafficking. It's a murky and illegal world, and the European Union Intellectual Property Office (EUIPO) says it costs the luxury industry €1.7 billion each year, along with the loss of 19,000 jobs due to foregone sales.

If you are making a purchase in a Dior boutique, then you can rest assured that your new piece is authentic. Dior will also repair items bought in their stores or from their online boutique, if they need to be restored due to excessive wear or damage. However, if you are shopping elsewhere, how can you ensure that your potential purchase is a genuine Dior? It's very important to note that specifics can't be revealed, since counterfeiters use this information to update their fakes, but there are always a few dead giveaways on a counterfeit bag.

Make sure that your retailer offers online and IRL authentication services as part of their sales package. As the popularity of preloved pieces swells, particularly with shoppers eager to score an authentic Y2K gem like a Galliano-era Saddle Bag, resale sites and stores should have robust anti-fake procedures in place. If they don't, you're leaving yourself open to potentially purchasing an illegal counterfeit. If you can look at the bag in person, study the details. Is the stitching uniform and neat? Where does the logo sit, compared to authentic versions? Is it centered or slightly wonky? Does the font match the original? Often fakes skip the nuances of an individual typeface for generic text. If the bag has a zipper, is it Dior branded? Feel the bag and consider its construction. Real bags have a solid feel, whereas you might be able to feel a cardboard frame under flimsy fabric on a fake. Is the hardware lustrous or merely shiny and tinny? Does the lining align with the real version? If fabric lined, is it a rich silk material or insubstantial polyester? If the bag is leather or suede, is it real leather or suede, or a glue-scented pleather version? In fact, what does the whole bag smell like? However convincing a fake *looks*, if it smells of chemicals and synthetics, don't be duped.

Some fakes go so far as to present invalid authenticity tags or dustbags, so check these too. Inside each valid Dior bag, there is a neatly stitched leather tag known as the date tag or date stamp, so make sure it is present and check it carefully. The corners of the tag will have rounded edges and the tag will be heat stamped in gold or silver, or with a colorless stamp, with 'Christian Dior PARIS' followed by MADE IN ITALY (or Spain). On the back of the tag, you'll find a unique code of letters and numbers that designate the year the bag was made and where it was produced. If there is a number on an authenticity card, this will be the style number, which is not to be confused with the date code. Inside your bag, the date tag is usually found on the lining, or in the interior pocket, although on some styles, the date code is on a second tag. The order of the letters and numbers on the tag may seem random, but each element means something specific. Bag codes follow a pattern of numbers, letters and numbers divided by hyphens, such as 02-AB-0185.

The letters note the country the bag was made in and the last four numbers are the month and year it was made. If your bag code states MA or BO that means it's made in Italy, while MC denotes a Spanish-made bag.

The first and third numbers of the code represent the month of manufacture and the second and final number relate to the year the bag was produced.. With the example code above, it would mean the bag was made in August (08) of 2015 (15.)

This information applies to the manufacturing details of new bags. Older bags separate the letters and numbers with just a space rather than the hyphen used for newer models. Older bags use a shortened pattern of two letters followed by four numbers to determine place and date of manufacture. Before 1990, Dior bags were all made in France, so these vintage styles don't have serial numbers. To determine the country of manufacture, there will often be a metal plaque inside the bag, which is sometimes accompanied by a 'Made in France' stamp. After 1990, Dior moved all bag production to Italy and Spain, and their bags have never been produced outside these three European countries.

Whether you are scrutinizing the interior of a lucky vintage find in a provincial charity shop or about to tap your card on the reader in a Dior boutique, fortified by a glass of complimentary champagne, rest assured that any Dior bag will continue to represent the legacy of *Monsieur* Dior. The unique mix of elegance and classicism will always make these bags the epitome of perfect taste. To quote the sage advice given by the designer himself, "Don't buy much, but make sure that what you buy is good." At Dior, it's *all* good.

Pages 174-177: A craftswoman works on the handle of a Lady Dior bag at the accessories workshop of the French luxury brand Dior in Paris on June 15, 2013

Page 178: Magazine advertisement for the Lady Dior featuring Marion Cotillard in 2016

Next page: Close-up of a sequin Lady Dior captured in street style at Paris Fashion Week, July 2015

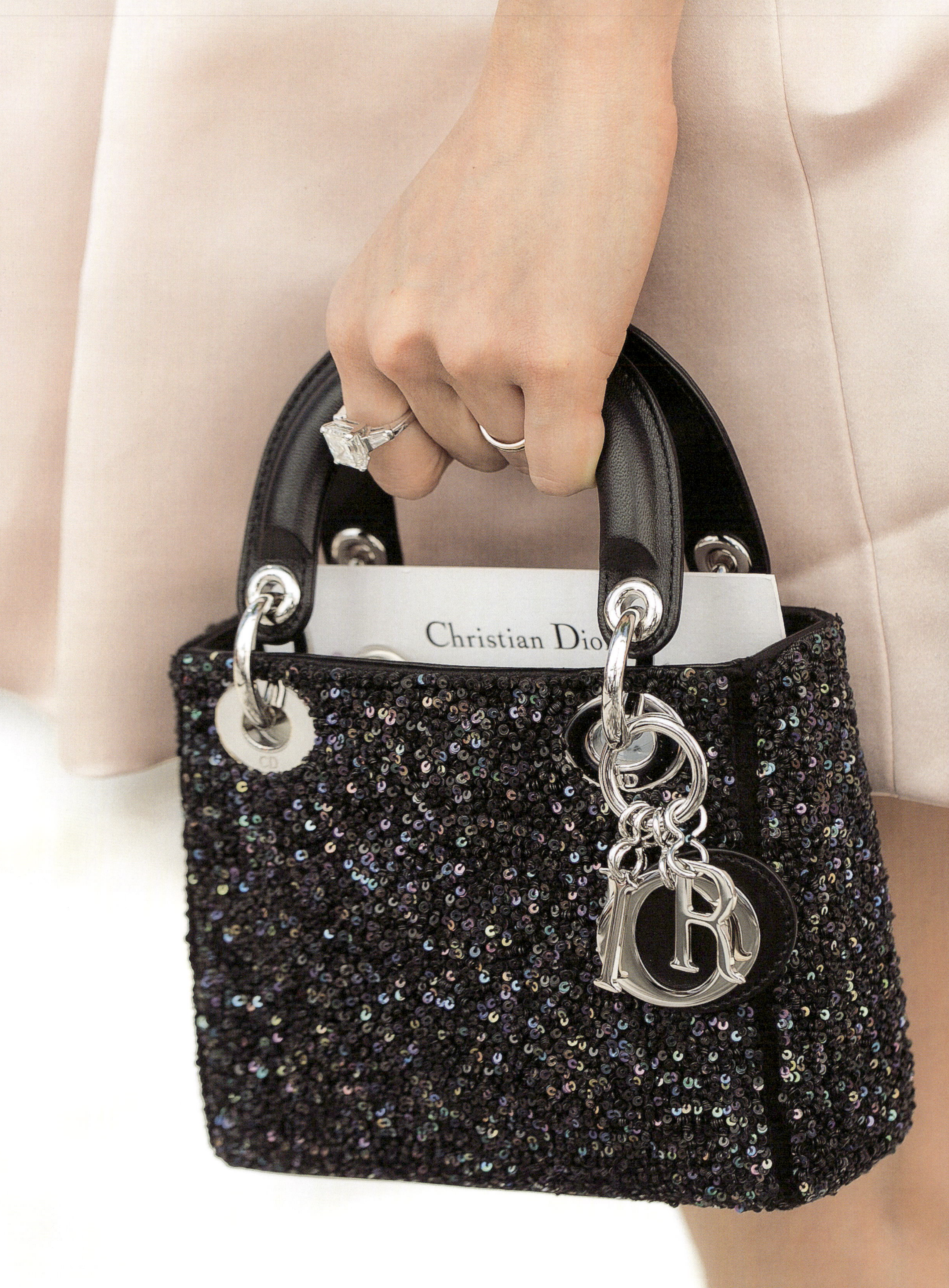
Christian Dio

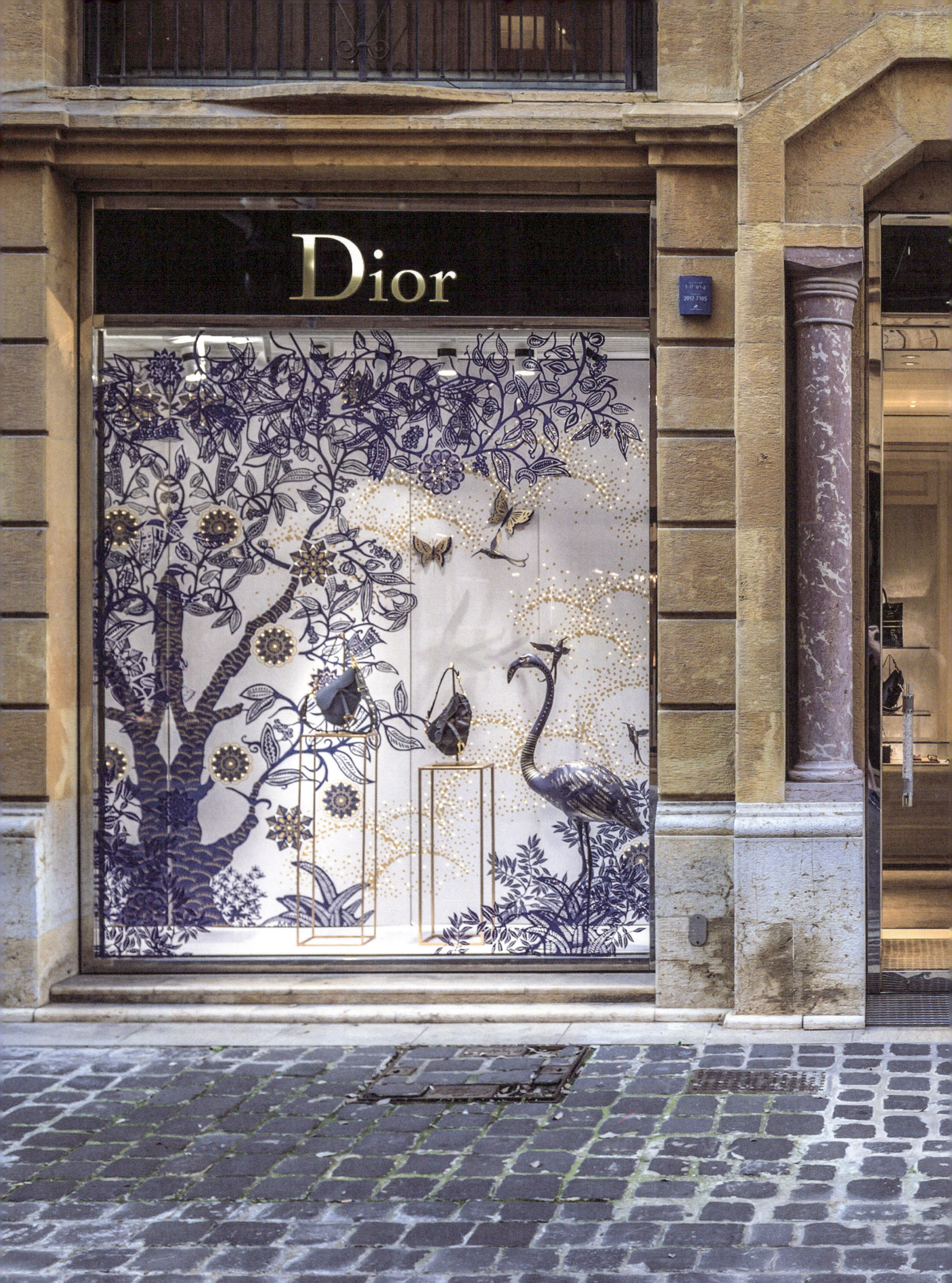
Dior

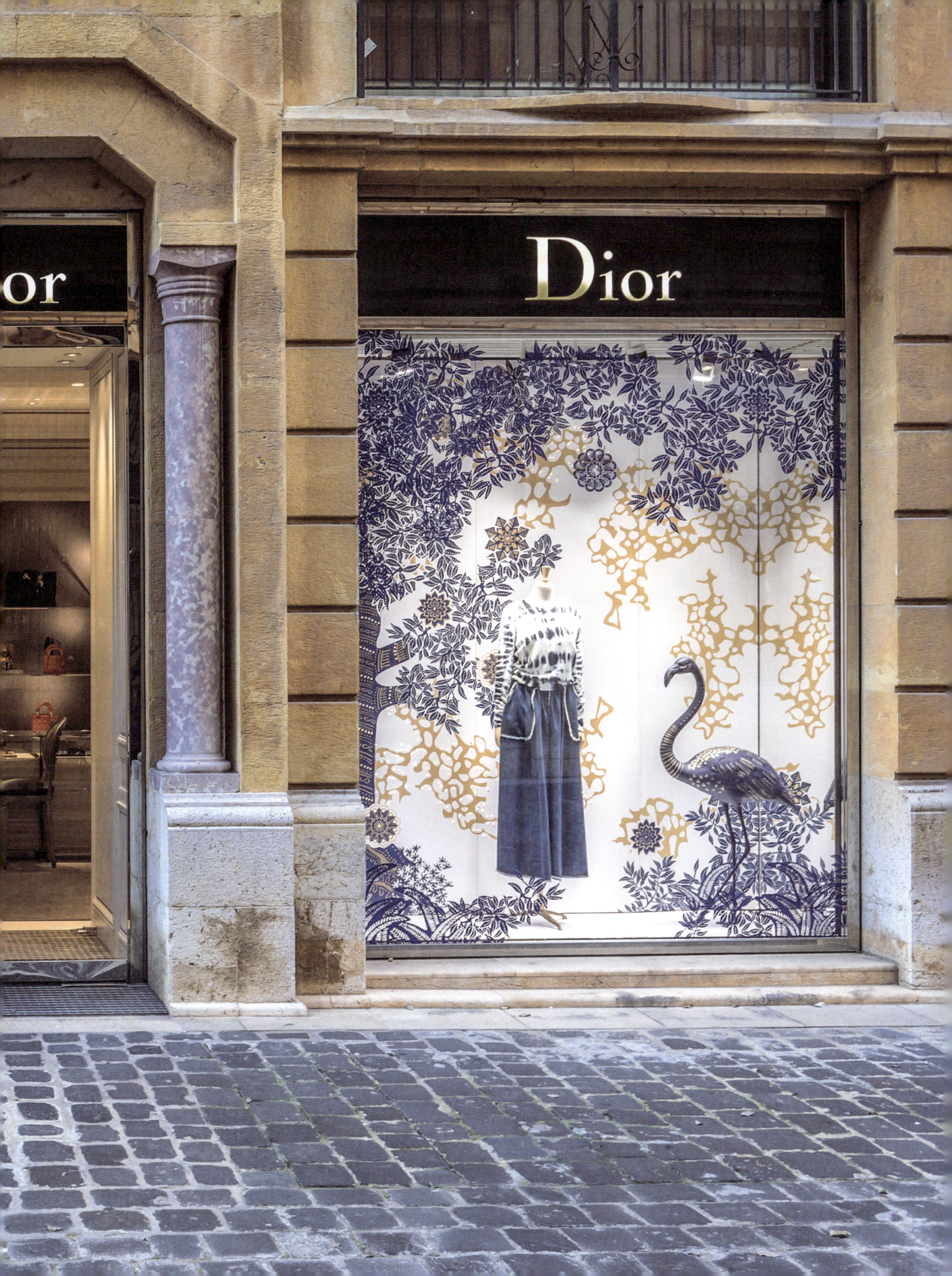
Dior

BIBLIOGRAPHY

- The Thames and Hudson Dictionary of Fashion and Fashion Designers, by Georgina O'Hara Callan
- The Little Book of Dior, by Karen Homer
- The Beautiful Fall, by Alicia Drake

RETAILERS

- https://www.dior.com/en_gb/fashion
- https://www.harrods.com/en-gb
- https://hardlyeverwornit.com/
- https://signofthetimeslondon.com/
- https://uk.designerexchange.com/
- https://www.bagreligion.com/

RESOURCES

- https://en.wikipedia.org/wiki/Christian_Dior
- https://en.wikipedia.org/wiki/Marc_Bohan
- https://10magazine.com/christian-dior-the-man-who-ruled-the-world/
- https://wwd.com/feature/raf-simons-exit-dior-10267081/#
- https://www.theguardian.com/film/2024/mar/04/john-galliano-high-and-low-kevin-macdonald-documentary
- https://www.purseblog.com/dior/the-history-of-the-lady-dior-bag/
- https://www.vogue.co.uk/article/princess-diana-met-gala
- https://collectorscage.com/
- https://thevintagebar.com/the-archive/back-in-the-dior-saddle
- https://www.vogue.co.uk/fashion/article/dior-bobby-bag
- https://www.nssmag.com/
- https://www.bagreligion.com/
- https://www.bragmybag.com/dior-leather-guide/

Pages 184/185: Dior store in Beirut, 2020

Next page: Grunge fashion designed by John Galliano for Christian Dior, Spring 2000 Haute Couture collection

Pages 188/189: The "Christian Dior: Designer of Dreams" exhibition at the V&A takes place in London, February 2019

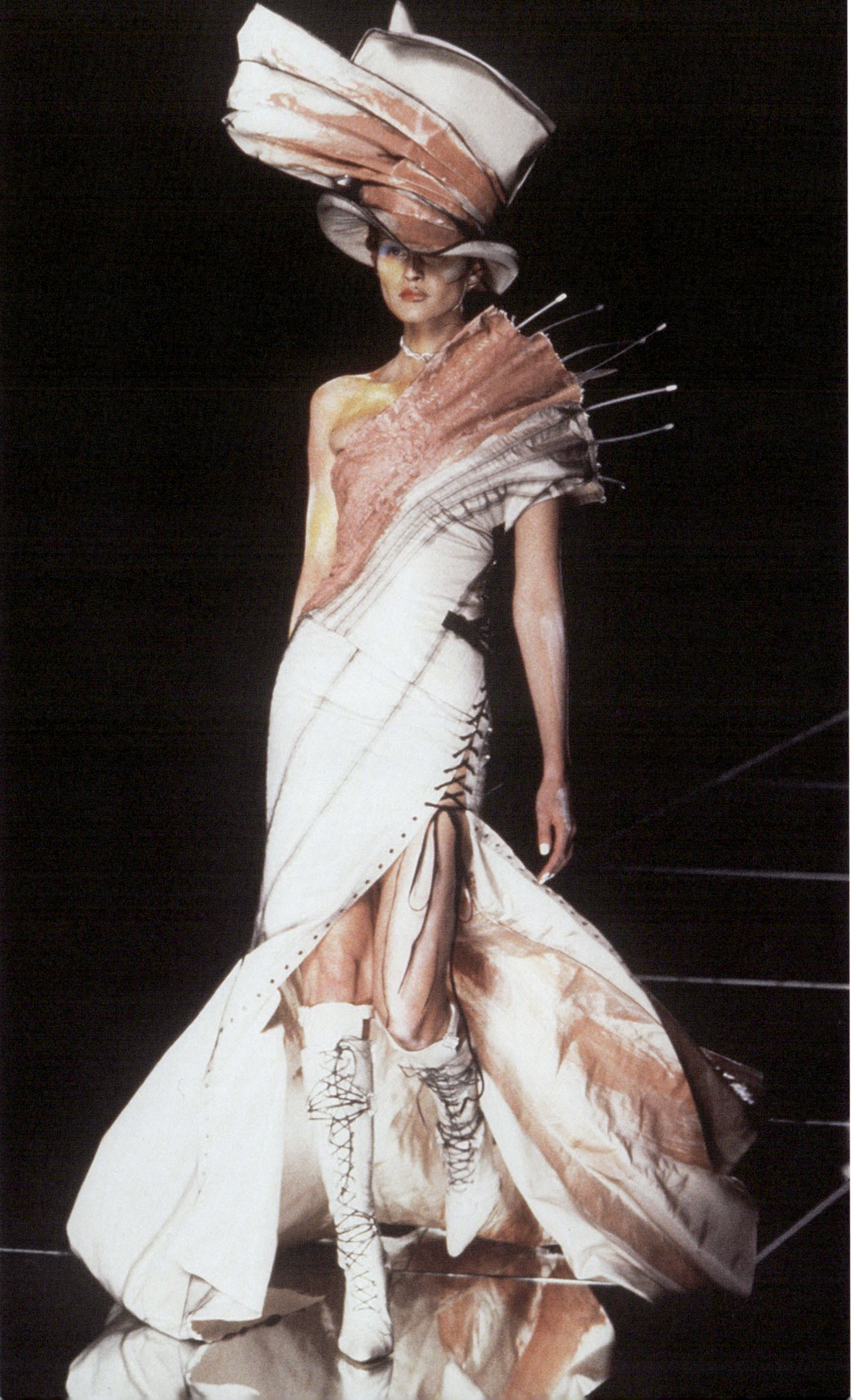

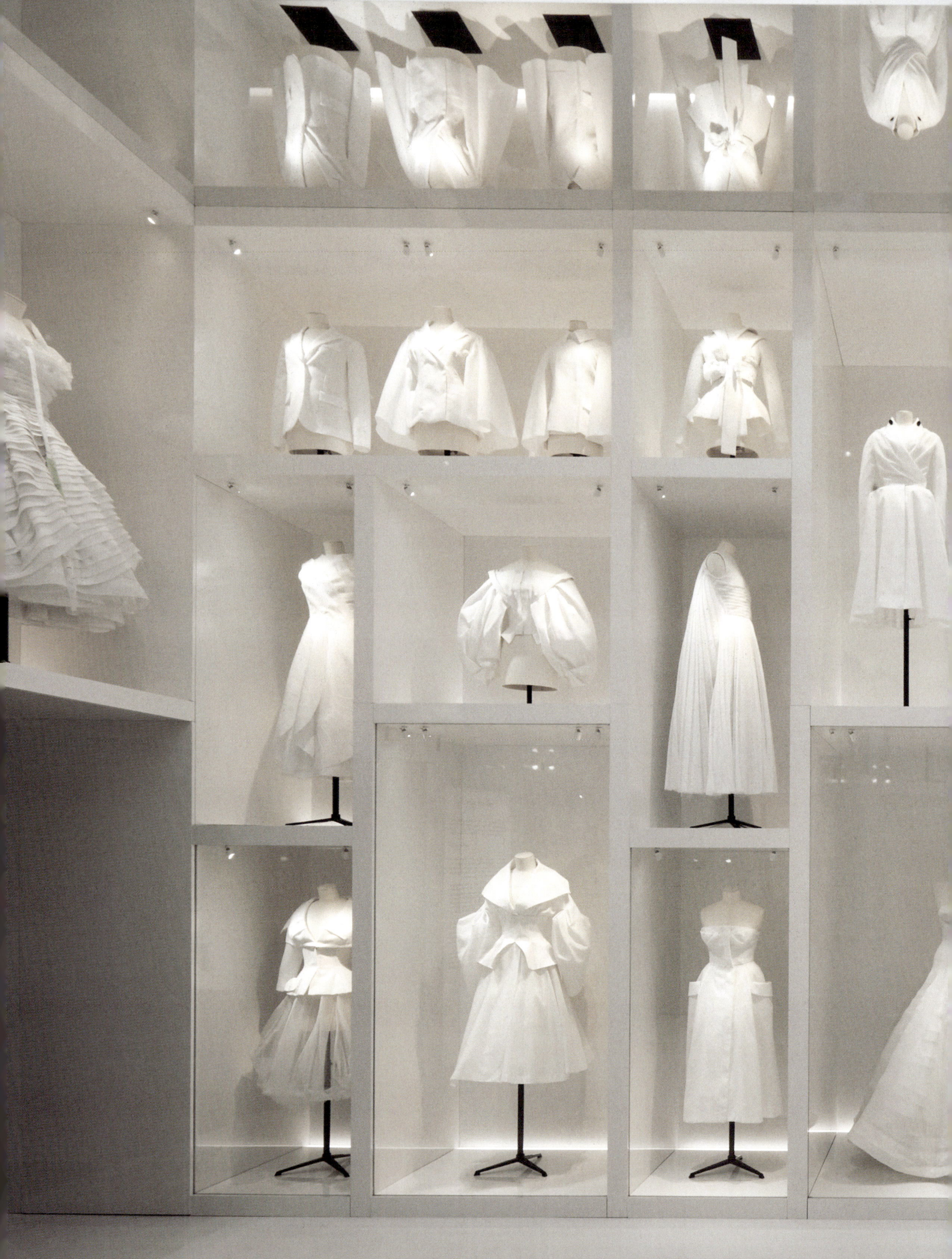

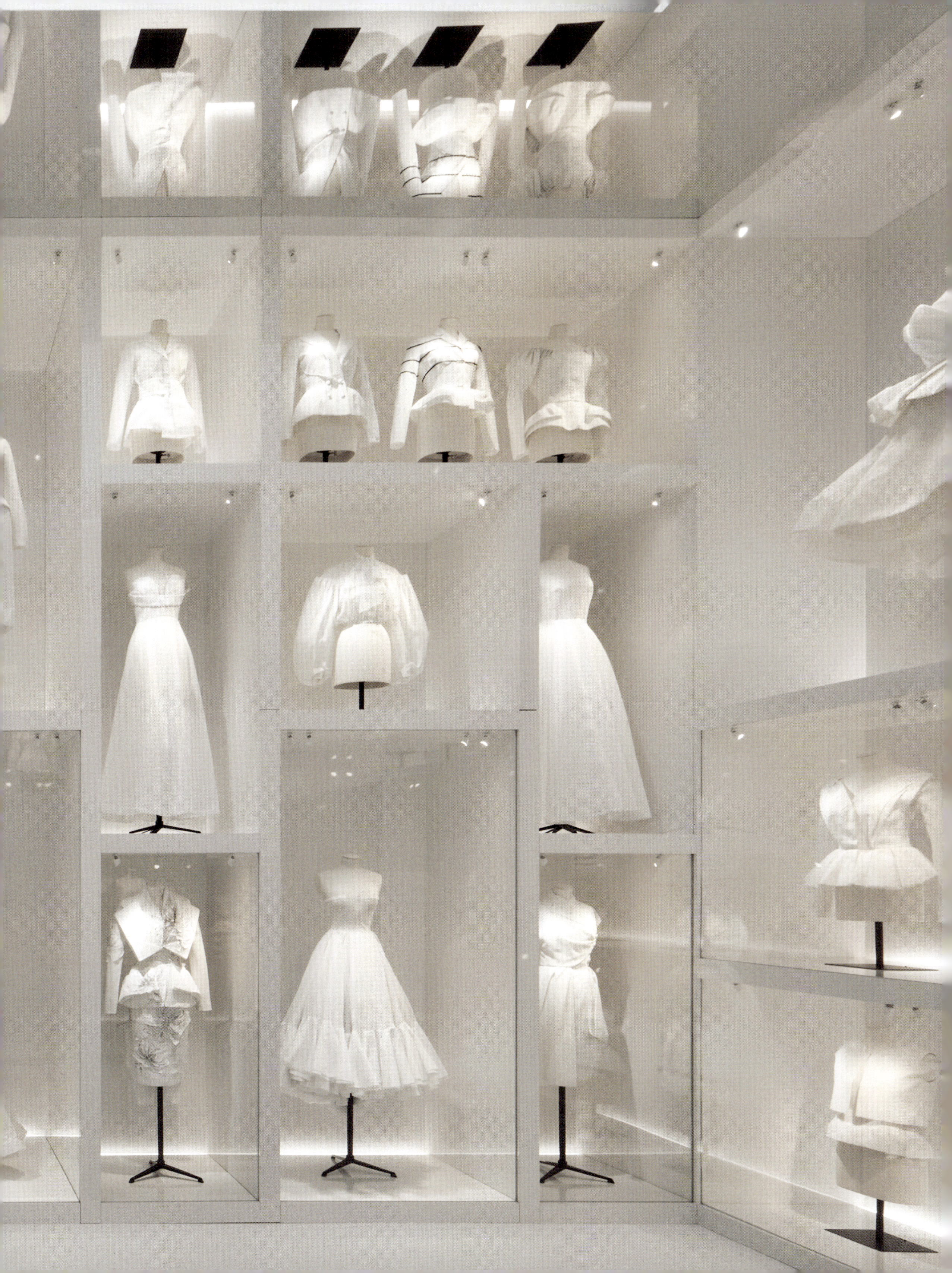

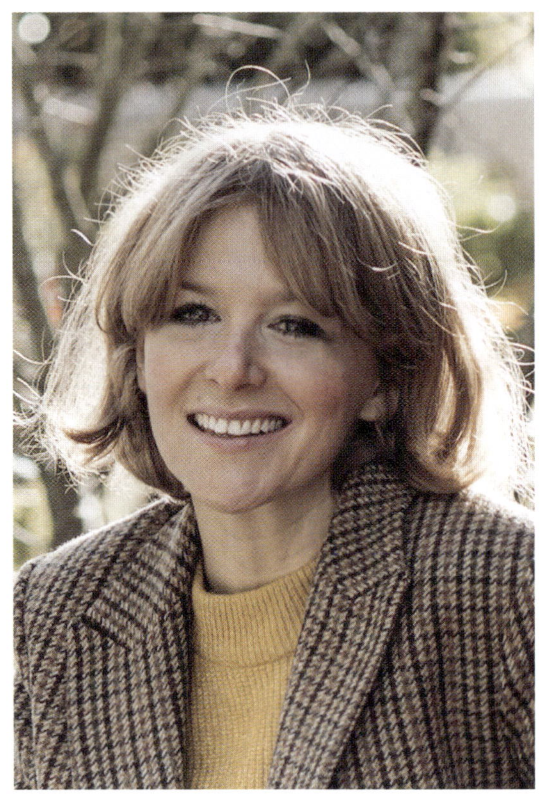

ALEXANDRA FULLERTON

Alexandra Fullerton is an Essex Girl by birth and former Londoner, however she now resides in Norfolk, having done a pandemic pivot towards a more rural life. She lives in a small village with her husband, daughter, long-haired chihuahua Ozzie and Nibbles the rabbit. The majority of Alex's career has been spent on magazines as a fashion director (7.5 years as Fashion director at Stylist magazine, 5 years as fashion director at large of Glamour UK) which meant styling A list actors, musical icons and celebrities (including Kylie Minogue, Rosie Huntington-Whiteley, Sophie Turner, Florence Welch and Kelly Rowland), travelling the world to shoot fashion stories and sitting front row at fashion shows. Now Alex is self-employed and has a portfolio career that combines fashion writing for The Telegraph and Bazaar Arabia, commercial styling (brands she has worked with include Stella McCartney and Marks & Spencer), personal styling, ghostwriting, writing her own books and running a shopping platform My3Words.co. When not working, Alex loves to explore provincial charity shops and dreams of unearthing a stash of Hermès Birkin bags. alexandrafullerton.com / @alexandrafullerton

IMAGE CREDITS

Cover Illustration: Jasmin Taeschner

p. 3 Victor Virgile/Gamma-Rapho/Getty Images, p. 5 Aris Messinis/AFP/Getty Images, p. 7 Max Cisotti/Dave Benett/Getty Images for Parfums Christian Dior, p. 8 Claire Doherty/Sipa USA/ddp images, pp. 11, 12 Granger/Bridgeman Images, pp. 16,18 AGIP/Bridgeman Images, p. 19 ASSOCIATED PRESS/Michel Laurent/dpa picture-alliance, p. 20 brandstaetter images/Votava/dpa picture-alliance, p. 21 ASSOCIATED PRESS/Anonymous/dpa picture-alliance, p. 22 REPORTERS ASSOCIES/Gamma-Rapho/Getty Images, p. 25 Philip Berryman/Alamy/mauritius images, p. 27 Scott A Garfitt/Invision/AP/dpa picture-alliance, p. 28 ZUMAPRESS.com/Ray Tang/dpa picture-alliance, p. 30 Victor Virgile/Gamma-Rapho/Getty Images, p. 33 Edward Berthelot/Getty Images, p. 34 Arnold Jerocki/GC Images/Getty Images, p. 35 Edward Berthelot/Getty Images, p. 37 AdsR/Alamy/mauritius images, pp. 38, 39 Grzegorz Czapski/Alamy Stock Photos/mauritius images, p. 41 Tim Graham Photo Library/Getty Images, p. 42 PG/Bauer-Griffin/GC Images/Getty Images, pp. 43, 44 Edward Berthelot/Getty Images, pp. 46,47 Ik Aldama/dpa picture alliance, p. 48 Dave Tacon/WWD/Penske Media/Getty Images, p. 49 Stephane Cardinale/Corbis/Getty Images, p. 50 Nina Westervelt/WWD/Getty Images, p. 52 Photolime/Alamy Stock Photos/mauritius images, p. 53 Victor Virgile/Gamma-Rapho/Getty Images, pp. 54, 55 Claudio Lavenia/Getty Images, p. 56 andersphoto/Shutterstock.com, p. 57 Creative Lab/Shutterstock.com, p. 58 Edward Berthelot/Getty Images, p. 59 Kirstin Sinclair/Getty Images, p. 60 Edward Berthelot/Getty Images, p. 63 Runway Manhattan/Zach Chase/dpa picture alliance, p. 65 Edward Berthelot/Getty Images, pp. 66, 67 Frazer Harrison/Getty Images, p. 69 Victor Virgile/Gamma-Rapho/Getty Images, pp. 70, 71 Jeremy Moeller/Getty Images, p. 72 Wendell Teodoro/Getty Images, p. 73 Wendell Teodoro/Getty Images, p. 74 Getty Raimonda Kulikauskiene/Getty Images, p. 75 Edward Berthelot/Getty Images, p. 77 Nina Westervelt/WWD/Getty Images, p. 79 Peter White/Getty Images, p. 80 Claudio Lavenia/Getty Images, p. 83, 84 Edward Berthelot/Getty Images, p. 87 Grzegorz Czapski/Alamy Stock Photos/mauritius images, p. 88 Frédéric Vielcanet/Alamy Stock Photos/mauritius images, p. 89 Papin Lab / Shutterstock.com, p.89 andersphoto/Shutterstock.com, p. 91 Edward Berthelot/Getty Images, p. 93 a.l., a.r. Peter White/Getty Images, b.l. Victor Virgile/Gamma-Rapho/Getty Images, b.r. Kuba Dabrowski/WWD/Getty Images, p. 94 Victor Virgile/Gamma-Rapho/Getty Images, p. 96 Christian Vierig/Getty Images, p. 97 Photo by Jason Jean/WWD/Getty Images, p. 99 Two eyes/Shutterstock.com, p. 100 Photo by Dave Tacon/WWD/Penske Media/Getty Images, p. 101 Dave Tacon/WWD/Penske Media/Getty Images, pp. 102, 103 Christian Vierig/Getty Images, p. 104 Berthelot/Getty Images, pp. 105, 106, 107, 109 Jeremy Moeller/Getty Images, pp. 110, 111 BG009/Bauer-Griffin/GC Images, p. 113 Stephane Cardinale/Corbis/Getty Images, p. 115 Edward Berthelot/Getty Images, p. 116 Dominique Charriau/WireImage, p. 117 Peter White/Getty Images, p.119 Edward Berthelot/Getty Images, p. 120 above: andersphoto/Shutterstock.com, below: Photo-lime/AdobeStock, p. 121 Franco Origlia/WireImage, pp. 122,123 Victor Virgile/Gamma-Rapho/Getty Images, p. 124 Nataliya Petrova/NurPhoto/Getty Images, p. 126 Peter White/Getty Images, pp. 127,128 Victor Virgile/Gamma-Rapho/Getty Images, p.129 Peter White/Getty Images, p. 130 eversummerphoto/Shutterstock.com, p. 133 Everett Collection/imago images, p. 134 Tim Graham Photo Library/Getty Images, p. 136 PictureLux/The Hollywood Archive/The Legacy Collection/dpa picture alliance, p. 138 Everett Collection/imago images, p. 140 Courtesy Everett Collection/ddp, p. 141 Everett Collection/Courtesy Everett Collection/dpa picture alliance, p. 142 Grzegorz Czapski/Alamy Stock Photos/mauritius images, p. 143 AdsR/Alamy Stock Photos/mauritius images, p.145 Kukharchuk Pasha/Shutterstock.com, p. 146 ZUMA Press Inc/Alamy Stock Photos/mauritius images, p. 148 Gotham/GC Images/Getty Images, p. 149 Jacopo Raule/FilmMagic/Getty Images, p. 150 SAVIKO/Gamma-Rapho/Getty Images, p. 151 Peter White/Getty Images, p. 152 ZUMA Press Inc/Alamy Stock Photos/mauritius images, p. 153 The Hollywood Curtain/Bauer-Griffin/GC Images/Getty Images, p. 154 Pierre Teyssot/Shutterstock.com, p.156 TheStewartofNY/GC Images/Getty Images, p. 158 AAPimages/Timm/AAPimages/dpa picture alliance, p. 159 Geisler-Fotopress/Frederic Kern/Geisler-Fotopress/dap picture alliance, p. 160 abaca/Zabulon Laurent/ABACA/dpa picture alliance, p. 162 Berzane Nasser/abaca/Getty Images, p. 163 Neil Mockford/GC Images/Getty Images, pp. 164,165 VCG/VCG/Getty Images, p. 166 Andrew Milligan/dpa picture alliance, p. 167 empics/Andrew Milligan/dpa picture alliance, p. 168 Rindoff/Charriau/Getty Images, p. 169 Serge Benhamou/Gamma-Rapho/Getty Images, p.170 Pascal Le Segretain/Getty Images for Christian Dior, p. 172 Eduardo Parra/FilmMagic/Getty Images, p. 173 The Chosunilbo JNS/Imazins/Getty Images, pp. 174, 177 Miguel Medina/AFP/Getty Images, p. 178 Grzegorz Czapski/Alamy Stock Photos/mauritius images, p.183 DKSStyle/Shutterstock.com, p.184 Fotokon/Adobe Stock, p. 187 ZUMA Press Inc/Alamy Stock Photos/mauritius images, p.188 V&A/Cover Images/Cover Images/dpa picture alliance, p. 190 Rekha Damhar

IMPRINT

The Ultimate Guide to Dior Bags
This book was conceived, edited, and designed by teNeues.

Text by Alexandra Fullerton
Proofreading by Amanda Ennis, Nadine Weinhold, Benine Mayer
Editorial Management by Nadine Weinhold
Design by Marcus Taeschner
Layout by Marcus Taeschner
Picture Editing by Heide Christiansen
Production by Sandra Jansen-Dorn, Nele Jansen
Color Separation and Prepress by Jens Grundei

Printed in the Czech Republic by Finidr
Produced in Europe

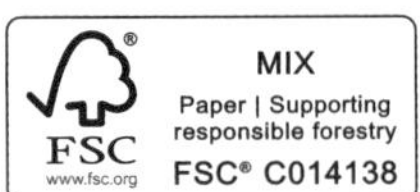

Published by gestalten, Berlin 2025
ISBN 978-3-96171-713-2

1st printing, 2025

The German edition is available under ISBN 978-3-96171-731-6.

For more information, and to order books, please visit www.teneues.com and www.gestalten.com

Die Gestalten Verlag GmbH & Co. KG
Mariannenstrasse 9–10, 10999 Berlin, Germany
hello@gestalten.com

Düsseldorf Office
Waldenburger Straße 13, 41564 Kaarst, Germany
verlag@teneues.com

teNeues Press Department
press@gestalten.com

Bibliographic information published by the Deutsche Nationalbibliothek. The Deutsche Nationalbibliothek lists this publication in the Deutsche Nationalbibliografie; detailed bibliographic data is available online at www.dnb.de

https://instagram.com/teneuespublishing

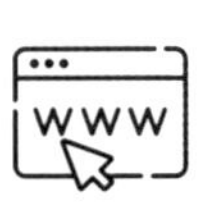

www.teneues.com